GREAT ASHES BATTLES

Bernard Whimpress and Nigel Hart have written two other books together: *Adelaide Oval Test Cricket 1884–1984* (1984) and *Australian Eleven* (1997), and Bernard edited and assisted publication of Nigel's *J.N. Crawford: His record innings by innings* (2003). Independently Bernard has written several other books, including *Passport to Nowhere: Aborigines in Australian Cricket 1850–1939* (1999) and *Chuckers: A history of throwing in Australian Cricket* (2004). In 2003 Bernard updated the 1993 edition of Chris Harte's *A History of Australian Cricket* which was released in Australia as *The Penguin History of Australian Cricket*. Their wider writing include chapters in various books and contributions to historical journals and sports magazines in Australia and overseas.

Both authors have worked in a number of professional areas: Bernard as a sports journalist, photographer, magazine editor, university tutor, historian and curator of the Adelaide Oval Museum; Nigel as a university administrator and lecturer in classical studies, communications and romantic and detective fiction. Married with three daughters, Nigel died, aged 48, in 1997.

GREAT ASHES BATTLES

FROM MELBOURNE 1877 TO TRENT BRIDGE 2005

BERNARD WHIMPRESS
NIGEL HART

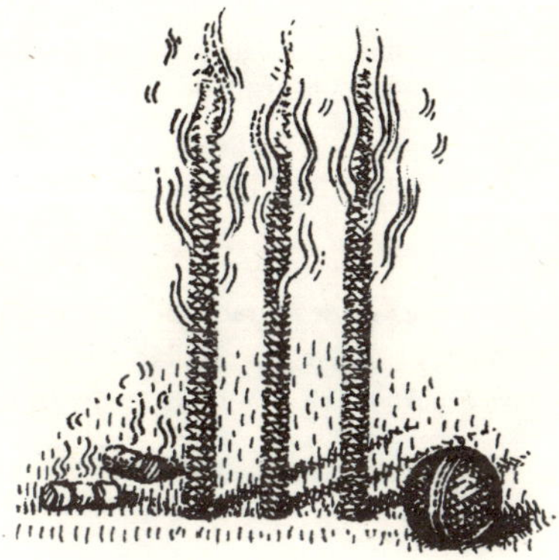

SEVENOAKS

First published in Australia under the title, *Test Eleven: Great Ashes Battles*, in 1994
by Wakefield Press
First published in Great Britain in 1995, by André Deutsch
an imprint of Carlton Books, 20 Mortimer Street, London W1T 3JW

Reprinted and updated in 2005

This edition published 2006.

ISBN-10: 1-86200-337-8
ISBN-13: 978-1-86200-337-8

Cataloguing-in-Publication data available for this title
from the British Library.

Printed and bound in Great Britain

CONTENTS

PREFACE

Selecting eleven great Anglo–Australian test matches was not easy. We have called them 'Ashes' battles even though the 1877 match preceded the creation of The Ashes in 1882, and the 1977 Centenary Test was a commemorative event, and not part of the Ashes contests.

Why eleven? Well, it seemed like a good cricketing number at the time. It also allowed us to develop greater depth of description and analysis than would have been possible in trying to cover fifty matches, as Patrick Murphy attempted in his *Fifty Incredible Cricket Matches*. Eleven tests also allowed us to concentrate more closely on that level of play than was possible for Handasyde Buchanan, who edited *Great Cricket Matches* in 1962. We acknowledge that there is some overlap with Buchanan's excellent anthology but, since we discovered the coincidences after settling on our own eleven choices, that merely reinforces our selections.

Buchanan's book, long out of print, drew upon single first-hand accounts which he edited minimally. Our approach has been to compile and critique as many contemporary match and tour reports for each chapter as possible. We have also drawn upon reminiscences from participants on both sides. Finally, we have added our own interpretative comment, and tried to provide a 'theme' or 'themes' for each match account rather than follow the more traditional approach of homing-in on a hero and his exploits.

We wanted to keep in mind that, for most of its history, Anglo–Australian test cricket has been a long and even struggle. We have therefore described five England wins, five Australian wins, and one draw. We have chosen three matches before the first world war, two in the inter-war period, three in the period from the end of the second world war to 1970–71, and three in the years since then.

Six of our matches were played in Australia and five in England. We have tried to include a spread of grounds. Sydney, however, has scored three matches (1894, 1954 and 1971); Melbourne, two (1877 and 1977); and Adelaide, one (1929). In England there are two Leeds matches (1938 and 1981); and one each in Manchester (1902), Lord's (1961), and Nottingham (1993). Of current grounds that have witnessed Ashes battles, The Oval, Birmingham, Brisbane and Perth have missed out.

Most of the games in our selection see England or Australia triumphing away from home. The First Test in 1877 and the Centenary Test in 1977 are Australia's only home wins, while England's only win at home is the Leeds match of 1981. The drawn game of 1993 exemplifies an interesting match in which an outright result was not achieved, and perhaps indicates that balance between Australian and English cricket may be restored after Australian dominance in the last three series.

In making our eleven choices we tried for balance in period, place and outcome. We did not always succeed, of course. Of our ten result matches, for instance, only two are by a wickets margin, and eight by runs. Perhaps when you have finished this book you might like to spend a few hours devising your own combination of matches, trying to keep balance in mind.

We have also looked for 'greatness' and this poses the key question: *What makes a great cricket match?* In the eleven chapters we answer this question implicitly. But perhaps we should be explicit here.

Great cricket matches fluctuate: they contain 'turn-around' factors. Our match reports include recovery from disaster, the battle against adversity and, in two cases, the snatching of defeat from the jaws of victory. These were games where something, or someone, came along to change the pattern of play against expectations.

Great matches are shaped by epic performances, and sometimes by cameos. While we were not tempted to name 'player of the match' awards, cricket as a team sport has its champions and its bit players. Both get their due in this account, and some of the best individual performers end up on the losing side. We have shown in several places that gritty thirties and forties at the right times win test matches as effectively as big hundreds, and that big hundreds are often less significant than they are made to seem.

Great matches are close matches. In the eight games decided by runs the average winning margin is less than thirty, and ranges from three runs by Australia to sixty-two runs in England's favour.

Finally, great matches are absorbing matches. We give primary emphasis to the drama of the play and the manoeuvres, on-field and off, that affect it.

The structure of *Test Eleven* is chronological, and the matches are set within the context of Anglo–Australian test cricket history, but we have used this framework for some further explorations and some revision of that history. For instance, a number of issues emerge: national versus regional loyalties in both countries, professionalism and amateurism, player dissent, cronyism, selection and captaincy debates, uncovered pitches, slow over rates, intimidatory bowling, as well as linkages provided by the heroes of the game.

We enjoyed writing this book, and hope readers will enjoy re-visiting matches they have seen and read about, as well as discovering more about games with which they are less familiar. Whatever familiarity may breed, we have only admiration for those whose exploits we present.

Bernard Whimpress
Nigel Hart
October 1994

PREFACE TO SECOND EDITION

I am very pleased that Andre Deutsch both reprinted *Great Ashes Battles* in June, a little over ten years after its original edition, and then commissioned me to add two additional chapters from the recent Ashes series, perhaps the greatest of all time.

When Nigel Hart and I wrote the original book as *Test Eleven*, we concentrated on the historical value of the contest. Even though Australia had dominated England from 1989, it was worth reminding ourselves that Anglo–Australian cricket rivalry went back 128 years.

Over the past decade the Mark Taylor, Steve Waugh and Ricky Ponting-led Australian sides have produced superb positive cricket and the 2005 team – though ageing – looked to be a high-quality side, with Adam Gilchrist in full flight the most destructive cricketer in the game. Before the series began, a big question would be whether Andrew Flintoff would be able to match his skills against the best side in the world. The answer was, yes. Flintoff bowled and batted superbly, especially against Shane Warne who, himself, produced the most marvellous all-round form of his spectacular career..

As I look back on the wonderful matches just past, I regret I was unable to share them with my writing partner who died tragically early in 1997. Nigel would have been barracking strongly for England and, as a long-time member of Yorkshire, would have been pleased that a White Rose man was leading the side. I'm sure he would have pointed out to me that, when England has experienced other long Ashes droughts (1934–53) and (1959–71), they regained the urn only because Yorkshiremen Len Hutton and Ray Illingworth were at the helm.

Bernard Whimpress
Adelaide, October 2005

·MELBOURNE 1877·

A COMBINATION MATCH

Cricket historians and statisticians have long agreed on this match as the first of all test matches, but debate on its place in a developing Australian sense of nationhood must remain open. The game was significant for being staged, and it was a 'test' match in the sense of testing player performances on even terms. Problems of the representative nature of the teams are acknowledged. While there was a good deal of breast-beating following the colonial team's win, it is difficult to see this as more than a sign of an emerging Australia. The 'Combination' suggests some temporary coming-together of separate elements rather than an ongoing amalgamation. Although there is an attempt to proclaim an Australian national hero in Charles Bannerman, regional factors demonstrated in matters of selection and team captaincy are a powerful force. Together with feelings of pro-imperial sentiment, they will remain important for a long time to come.

AUSTRALIA v ENGLAND 1877 (1st Test)

Played at Melbourne Cricket Ground on 15, 16, 17, 19 March.
Toss: Australia. Result: AUSTRALIA won by 45 runs.

AUSTRALIA

C Bannerman	retired hurt	165	b Ulyett	4
NFD Thomson	b Hill	1	c Emmett b Shaw	7
TP Horan	c Hill b Shaw	12	c Selby b Hill	20
DW Gregory*	run out	1	(9) b Shaw	3
BB Ccooper	b Southerton	15	b Shaw	3
WE Midwinter	c Ulyett b Southerton	5	c Southerton b Ulyett	17
EJ Gregory	c Greenwood b Lillywhite	0	c Emmett b Ulyett	11
JM Blackham†	b Southerton b Shaw	17	lbw b Shaw	6
TW Garrett	not out	18	(4) c Emmett b Shaw	0
T Kendall	c Southerton b Shaw	3	not out	17
JR Hodges	b Shaw	0	b Lillywhite	8
Extras	(B 4, LB 2, W 2)	8	(B 5, LB 3)	8
Total		**245**		**104**

ENGLAND

H Jupp	lbw b Garrett	63	(3) lbw b Midwinter	4
J Selby†	c Cooper b Hodges	7	(5) c Horan b Hodges	38
HRJ Charlwood	c Blackham b Midwinter	36	(4) b Kendall	13
G Ulyett	lbw b Thomson	10	(6) b Kendall	24
A Greenwood	c EJ Gregory b Midwinter	1	(2) c Midwinter b Kendall	5
T Armitage	c Blackham b Midwinter	9	(8) c Blackham b Kendall	3
A Shaw	b Midwinter	10	st Blackham b Kendall	2
T Emmett	b Midwinter	8	(9) b Kendall	9
A Hill	not out	35	(1) c Thomson b Kendall	0
J Lillywhite*	c and b Kendall	10	b Hodges	4
J Southerton	c Cooper b Garrett	6	not out	1
Extras	(LB 1)	1	(B 4, LB 1)	5
Total		**196**		**108**

ENGLAND	O	M	R	W	O	M	R	W
Shaw	55.3	34	51	3	34	16	38	5
Hill	23	10	42	1	14	6	18	1
Ulyett	25	12	36	0	19	7	39	3
Southerton	37	17	61	3				
Armitage	3	0	15	0				
Lillywhite	14	5	19	1	1	0	1	1
Emmett	12	7	13	0				
AUSTRALIA								
Hodges	9	0	27	1	7	5	7	2
Garrett	18.1	10	22	2	2	0	9	0
Kendall	38	16	54	1	33.1	12	55	7
Midwinter	54	23	78	5	19	7	23	1
Thomson	17	10	14	1				
DW Gregory					5	1	9	0

FALL OF WICKETS

	A	E	A	E
Wkt	**1st**	**1st**	**2nd**	**2nd**
1st	2	23	7	0
2nd	40	79	27	7
3rd	41	98	31	20
4th	118	109	31	22
5th	142	121	35	62
6th	143	135	58	68
7th	197	145	71	92
8th	243	145	75	93
9th	245	168	75	100
10th	–	196	104	108

Umpires: CA Reid and RB Terry.

Melbourne Cricket Ground, 15 March 1877. Test cricket would begin that day.

(Courtesy Melbourne Cricket Club)

'Bar WG we're as good as they are and some day we'll lick 'em with eleven.' These immortal words of transplanted Surrey-born professional cricketer Sam Cosstick summed up the spirit of nationalism emerging in Australian cricket during the 1870s. Cosstick made his prediction toward the end of WG Grace's All England Eleven 1873–74 tour of Australia, after he had helped Eighteen of Victoria to inflict an innings defeat on Grace's team. Victories in New South Wales, as well as Victoria, had clearly instilled confidence in local cricketers.

Three years later, there were no Graces – EM, WG, or GF – in the team organised by James Lillywhite and Alfred Shaw. The occasion of the fulfilment of Cosstick's boast was the first match organised on even terms between 'representative' sides from Australia and England.

Several factors might rule against its inclusion in a book of Ashes battles. First, it was only recognised as the first 'test' match considerably later. Second, the final winning margin, forty-five runs, was not close by contemporary standards. Third, the concept of The Ashes originated in England in 1882, and their physical embodiment occurred later still.

The game qualifies for inclusion in this book for several positive reasons which outweigh those already noted. First, the pendulum swung from one side to the other throughout to make it an absorbing contest. Second, the game represents a starting point for serious international cricket. Third, as a link to Australian nationalism and corrective to colonial regionalism, it saw the emergence of a genuine Australian hero in Charles Bannerman and a tradition of sporting opposition to England.

The English season of 1876 ended on Saturday, 9 September, with a drawn North versus South encounter played at Rochdale, Lancashire, for the benefit of the Cricketers' Fund. A fortnight later, nine of the players in the Rochdale match joined three other cricketers on the SS *Poonah*, which sailed for Australia from Southampton. The twelve, described by Arthur Haygarth as 'by no means the best in England, but the best that could be tempted to go' by the £200 per head guarantee of the promoters, was the fourth England team to visit Australia. James Lillywhite junior (Sussex) was promoter, manager and player. Alfred Shaw (Nottingham) and James Southerton, variously Hampshire and Sussex but currently Surrey, and Henry Jupp, Surrey's 'Young Stonewall', were the three tourists who had not played at Rochdale.

The full party consisted of professionals from only four counties: Sussex and Surrey in the south, and Nottinghamshire and Yorkshire in the north. There were no amateurs in the party. Amateurs would have predominated in a rival venture that Fred Grace had been trying to organise. The Melbourne weekly newspaper, the *Australasian*, had reported in July and August of the piecemeal fashion in which Lillywhite put his team together and of Grace's agent Pickersgill attempting to undermine Lillywhite's team.

The Yorkshire contingent in the team eventually numbered five: Thomas Armitage, Andrew Greenwood, Tom Emmett, Allen Hill, and all-rounder 'Happy Jack' Ulyett. At twenty-five, George Ulyett was the youngest member. Southerton, who was forty-nine years and 119 days old at the beginning of the Melbourne match, remains the oldest test cricketer on debut. Henry Charlwood was a dashing batsman from Sussex, John Selby a batsman from Nottinghamshire, and Ted Pooley was the Surrey wicketkeeper. Ten years before, at The Oval, Pooley had caught eight and stumped four to establish a match record not equalled until Don Tallon caught nine and stumped three for Queensland at Sydney in 1938–39, a record still unsurpassed.

Lillywhite's team anchored off Glenelg, South Australia, on the evening of 6 November. The All England Eleven had a win and a draw against twenty-twos of South Australia, but fifteens defeated the tourists three times, first in Sydney, then Melbourne, then again in Sydney. When a New South Wales fifteen had a comfortable win in January 1877, it gave rise to an even greater colonial desire to meet the Englishmen on even terms.

A confrontation between the tourists and a NSW eleven took place two days later at the Albert Ground, Redfern, but was restricted to two days because of the scheduled departure of the English team to New Zealand. The game ended as a draw in the All England Eleven's favour but, before the Englishmen left to cross the Tasman, it was arranged that leading players from NSW and Victoria should form a combined eleven to play the Englishmen in March.

Historian William Mandle has argued that Australian nationalism was evident early in cricket, and the organisation of this match is sometimes put forward as evidence. Before it can be seen as an important harbinger of nationalism, however, it should be noted

JAMES LILLYWHITE'S TEAM OF 1876–77

1. *H Jupp*
2. *T Emmett*
3. *H Charlwood*
4. *J Selby*
5. *J Lillywhite*
6. *T Armitage*
7. *J Southerton*
8. *A Greenwood*
9. *G Ulyett*
10. *A Hill*
11. *A Shaw*
12. *E Pooley*

that regional rivalries were alive and kicking, as they are in Australia to this day.

The evidence of regionalism was strong. From the start, as the *Australasian* of 10 March 1877 reported, the idea of playing in Melbourne raised the ire of the Sydney press, which did its best to prevent the Sydney contingent travelling to Victoria. Through an oversight, the New South Wales Cricket Association was not formally asked to assist in the arrangements for the game. This was reported to have caused unpleasant feelings among some of the Sydney cricketers, and some diffidence on the part of the Victorian fast-medium left-hander, Frank Allan. Moreover, the supposed Australian side had two sets of selectors, from NSW and Victoria, included no players from outside those colonies, and did not practise together at any stage before the game.

In New South Wales, half the team was selected by Edwin Evans, Nathaniel Thomson, Charles Bannerman and Dave Gregory. Bannerman, Thomson, Dave Gregory and his brother Ned, William Murdoch and Frederick Spofforth all played for the Albert club in Sydney, suggesting that powerful cliques were early at work in the Australian cricket establishment.

Of the NSW players originally chosen, Spofforth and Evans declared themselves unavailable, the former because he could not have Murdoch as wicketkeeper. At this stage simply a first-rate fast bowler, Spofforth would soon enough master that variety of length and pace which made him 'The Demon' to his generation. Evans didn't want to travel six hundred miles for a game. These were cruel blows, because the pair were fine strike bowlers.

Before the Australian team could be assembled, there was further news from the Victorian selection. Frank Allan, who had been seen as indispensable in the absence of Evans and Spofforth, sent a telegram two days before the match declaring he was unavailable because he wished to meet friends at an agricultural carnival in his home town Warrnambool. The Melbourne *Argus* cricket writer said that Allan was perfectly at liberty to make his own decision, but that the would-be player might have discovered earlier that the two events clashed. Courtesy aside, the writer continued, it might be many years before eleven Australians would again meet eleven Englishmen in the field.

Two of the replacement bowlers, Tom Kendall – who would be a matchwinner – and John Hodges, made their first-class debuts in the game. Hodges, who played only two more first-class matches, was considered a 'poor substitute' for Allan. The truth of this judgement can be gauged from the fact that, when a Victorian fifteen played Lillywhite's side, Allan delivered 387 balls in taking 8-60 whereas Hodges bowled a mere sixteen balls and gave away eighteen runs. It was said in the *Australasian* that the twenty-one-year-old Hodges was nervous on this occasion, so perhaps a better guide to his quality was the 7-50 he took for Richmond against the Melbourne Cricket Club just before his selection.

When the members of the side finally assembled in Melbourne, the five NSW players practised on the Melbourne Cricket Ground in the morning, but the ten Victorians (from whom a final six would be chosen) did so in the afternoon.

Several aspects of the Australian combination finally selected deserve mention. Its average age was more than seven years younger than England's, its most senior player being Thomson at thirty-seven. Its youngest was Tom Garrett at eighteen. This differential, while usually not so marked, remains a feature of Anglo–Australian tests.

One of the players selected, John Robart Hodges, has long been a mystery man of nineteenth-century Australian cricket. Recent research by Ray Webster reveals he was born in England in 1855 before being brought to Australia by his parents in 1856, the previously-recorded year of his birth in Melbourne. Details of Nathaniel Frampton Davis Thomson's name and birth (29 May 1839, not 21 April 1838) also have been revised, his surname now being established as 'p'-less.

A unique feature was that a majority of the side were born overseas: Charles Bannerman, Hodges, Kendall, William Midwinter and Thomson in England; Tom Horan in Ireland; and Bransby Cooper in India. Cooper was the most experienced cricketer in the eleven, and its only member with overseas experience, having twice opened at The Oval with WG Grace in 1869, each time sharing century stands. The four Australian-born players were Ned and Dave Gregory, Jack Blackham and Tom Garrett.

The choice of a captain for the combined eleven posed problems. A journalist warned that 'the confidence which the public are likely to repose in the representatives of Australia will be proportionate to the good sense which they bring to the settlement of the difficulty'. New South Welshman Dave Gregory was the surprise choice: he captained his country before his colony.

A sentimental factor – the match began on Cooper's thirty-third birthday – might have seen the difficulty resolved by letting Cooper toss the coin for Australia's first test. But on this occasion, as generally in the future, sentiment was overlooked. Perhaps Gregory's full beard and physical bulk made his fellow colonials feel he had the appearance of a Grace, if not quite the class. Or perhaps what ultimately counted in Gregory's favour was his Fairy Meadow birthplace near Woollongong. Almost all Australian captains have been native-born, if not in places so quaintly named.

The birthplace issue remained a feature of early Anglo–Australian test cricket. Spofforth and Evans were native-born, like Murdoch, and all three were to tour England with the first Australian side in 1878. All but four of that thirteen-strong side would be native-born, Charles Bannerman, Horan and Midwinter being the three English-born players who kept their place from the first test of all. Blackham was the only Australian survivor of the original two teams to play in the first test in England (The Oval, 1880), Shaw being the only English survivor.

The name of the colonial team caused confusion. On 9 March

1877, the Melbourne *Argus* headlined a story 'Arrival of the Sydney cricketers', and the column was awkward about referring to the 'Australian' team. By 13 March, the *Age* referred to a 'Combined Eleven'. On 15 March, a more confident heading of 'Australia v England' appeared in the *Argus*, but the report of the first day's play on 16 March in the same paper referred to the game as 'The Combination Cricket Match'. The Melbourne papers clearly had no sense of nascent nationhood.

The English team's preparation for the Melbourne match was also far from ideal. The tourists had arrived in Melbourne only the day before the match. The team had suffered a rough passage across the Tasman Sea after a match against Eighteen of Otago at Dunedin, so the eleven who arrived were not in the best health.

Ted Pooley had been detained in Christchurch after the second of two incidents following an earlier match. In the first, Pooley had made what was known as a 'catch' bet with local surveyor Ralph Donkin. The 'catch' was that, in the match between England and Eighteen of Canterbury, Pooley had claimed he could predict every player's score. There are a couple of versions of the amounts laid. According to one, Donkin had bet him six pounds to one he could not. In another, the odds were a pound to a shilling. Pooley wrote noughts alongside each Christchurch player's name and, as might have been expected, when many of the local side managed such scores, he stood to make a good profit. The Christchurch man was upset, refused to pay, and resorted to beating Pooley with a stick, cutting his head and face. Pooley retaliated with his fists. For this assault he was fined £5 and costs in the police court – without getting his 'winnings'.

Worse was to follow. On the same day, after consuming a good deal of liquor, Pooley allegedly damaged Donkin's property at the hotel where originally the bet had been laid. The Surrey keeper was remanded on bail until 12 March, and so remained in Christchurch when the rest of the team left for Australia. Tried before the Supreme Court on 6 April and found not guilty, he returned directly to England, fortified by a public subscription from concerned inhabitants of Canterbury. Pooley's opportunity to grace the annals of test cricket were gone.

||| DAY 1

Dave Gregory won the toss and decided to bat first on the well-prepared wicket. Play began at five past one on Thursday, 15 March, a curiously late time given that play was to stop at five. A further half hour was to be deducted at two for lunch, leaving a maximum of only three-and-a-half hours' playing time. The *Argus* called it 'a spendthrift waste of an autumn day'.

The Englishmen were well received by the small crowd of 2500. Cheers followed for the first two batsmen, Bannerman and Thomson, who were at the wicket before the field had been placed. The pair played for the same club side in Sydney.

Nottinghamshire medium-pacer Alfred Shaw, renowned as the steadiest and most economical bowler of his generation, opened the bowling to Bannerman from the eastern end. According to WG Grace, Shaw had 'an easy round-arm action, kept an astonishingly good length, varied his pace from slow to medium, and made the ball break in both directions', a formidable proposition indeed.

At the opposite end, Allen Hill, a Kirkheaton-born fast round-arm bowler, operated with the wind at his back. Despite his short run, the aesthetics of the Yorkshireman's action were supposedly unparalleled in his day, and his impact as a ferocious shock bowler was considerable. After a quiet start, in which two runs came from the first three overs, Hill claimed the first test dismissal of all by clean bowling Thomson for one with the second ball of his fourth over.

The dismissal of the veteran New South Wales intercolonial player brought a Victorian, Thomas Patrick Horan, to the crease.

Horan was acknowledged as his colony's best batsman, and was later described by George Giffen as possessing a wonderfully strong defence and being unequalled as a leg-hitter. He went on to captain his country before winning more durable fame at the *Australasian* where, under the pen-name 'Felix', he became Australia's first great cricket writer and cultivated interest in the game.

Horan and Bannerman carried the total to forty. Along the way, Armitage became the first test cricketer to drop a chance, fumbling a simple chance offered off Shaw by Bannerman before he had reached double figures. Shaw eventually got a ball to turn out of a heel mark and flick Horan's glove for Hill at slip to take the catch.

Dave Gregory came in, only to make an inauspicious start as skipper. After driving the first ball he received from Shaw to long-on for a single, he made a foolish attempt to steal a run from the same bowler in his next over. His run out left Australia's total at lunch, after the first hour, at 3-41, of which Bannerman's score was 27.

The lunch interval, which was to have lasted half an hour, spun out to forty minutes, indicating that timekeeping was regarded less seriously then. By the time play resumed, the attendance had grown to 3000. Before the day was over, the numbers had risen further to about 4500. Only a small proportion of the spectators, however, patronised the grandstand. The gum trees in Yarra Park bore the usual number of free onlookers, but the elms that had grown inside the fence deprived people of the cheap view they were used to getting from Jolimont hill.

Bannerman was now joined by Cooper, who had won the first match for Victoria against Grace's eleven three years before. This time Cooper opened his score with a languid cut off Shaw for a single. Bannerman's efforts to keep the scoreboard moving, however, stood in marked contrast to Cooper's stubborn back defence. Cooper several times appeared to make up his mind to make a big hit off Shaw, only to temper his aggression. Bannerman lofted Hill to long-on for four, which brought on George Ulyett, who bowled very wildly, often ending his over with a full pitch. Hill at mid-on stopped numerous hard hits from Bannerman, who then lifted the ball over Hill's head for four. While Shaw bowled steadily and patiently to Cooper, Bannerman struck Ulyett for three and Shaw for two fours to raise the Australian century.

Two changes were now made by Lillywhite. Southerton took the ball from Ulyett and Tom Armitage relieved Shaw. From Armitage, the Sheffield lob bowler, some novelties were expected. *Wisden* used superlatives to described his 1876 performance against Surrey (13-46) but, though he brought to Australia a big reputation, it seemed he had thrown his skill overboard *en route*. In his first over three fieldsman were placed in an arc behind the bowler, but Bannerman straight-drove him twice to the boundary and placed him to square-leg for two.

In his second over, Armitage tried a typical change of tactics by attempting to pitch the ball over Bannerman's head and on to the bails, justifying one local's claim that his lobs went so high the batsmen needed a clothes prop to play them. Once he misjudged the distance and the umpire signalled 'wide'. Then Bannerman off-drove him for another four. When Cooper faced Armitage he was favoured with two grubbers, another routine Armitage tactic successful in England. The Australian met the menace with a horizontal bat and the bowler was replaced.

The sturdy Southerton broke the partnership of 77 with his off-spin, bowling Cooper for 15. The two had played with and against each other in England, Cooper having had the unusual experience during 1869 of catching Southerton in a Kent–Surrey game, and being caught off his bowling in the immediately-following Kent–Sussex game. Southerton had appeared for different sides under the more flexible county registration rules then in force.

After two hours' play Bannerman remained undefeated on 86. William Midwinter now joined him at the wicket, all six foot three inches and fourteen stone of him. Spectators prepared themselves for a treat, as the two hardest hitters of the side were together. Midwinter's style was well-enough known: after steady play for a few overs, he would launch into huge hits, hissing through his teeth, before relapsing into defence. In his first over from Lillywhite, Midwinter played so crudely at a couple of balls that the spectators must have been relieved the 'Bendigo Giant' survived them. Three more boundaries from Bannerman saw him raise his century in two hours forty minutes. In raising his three figures Bannerman put himself among an elite group of cricketers to make not just their first, but their only, first-class hundred in a test. In addition, Bannerman also made the first century by an Australian in New Zealand, in England, and North America, but none of those innings are regarded as first-class.

Midwinter attempted his own moment of glory. Stepping out to Southerton, he struck the ball through the air towards the grandstand, but picked out a man with an exceptionally safe pair of hands in George Ulyett, a former Sheffield Wednesday goalkeeper. Ulyett backed across the path marking the boundary line until, with his back to the fence curved into the form of a bow, he stretched up his hands to secure the ball, a catch to rank with his miraculous dismissal of George Bonnor at Lord's in 1884. A few inches more on this occasion, and the scorers would have awarded him five runs rather than recording the fall of the fifth Australian wicket for 142.

Poor Ned Gregory fell to Lillywhite for test cricket's first nought, though reputedly his batting had improved with age since his NSW debut in 1863. An adequate fast-medium bowler and fine fielder, he scored freely from local bowlers of the calibre of Spofforth, and could have toured England as a batsman but for age – he was in his thirty-eighth year when he made his test debut – and reluctance to leave his curatorial duties in Sydney. He was replaced by Victorian wicket-keeper Jack Blackham, who stayed with Bannerman until stumps, when the total had reached 6-166.

Charles Bannerman was plainly the hero of test cricket's first day. He hit with precision, sharpness and vigour in running up 126 in just

CHARLES BANNERMAN

Scored the first century in test cricket, and was one of Australia's first national heroes.

three-and-a-quarter hours, having kept the ball on the ground throughout. The scoreboard had a very lopsided look, with the number one having scored seventy-six per cent of the total to that stage. Only Bannerman had shown himself at home against a steady professional attack.

DAY 2

The second day's play was due to begin at half past twelve. It took a quarter of an hour for the players to come in from practice, however, so the game started at a quarter to one. About 3500 spectators were at the ground on a chilly, overcast day, and a further 500 viewed proceedings from outside the fence. Emmett and Southerton, the bowlers operating when stumps were drawn the previous day, opened the attack.

The veteran Southerton broke the ball from the off with a round-arm action, puzzling batsmen with his varied length, break, and pace, although his county keeper Pooley claimed he never 'bowled' a ball in his life, which raises questions about the legality of his action or Pooley's sense of humour. Emmett, by contrast, was a genuine fast bowler renowned for his humour and guile. Adept at using the width of the bowling crease, and not past bowling from well short of it on occasion, he was known as the 'Wide and Wicket Man' because he routinely mixed loose balls with straight ones. He toured Australia again, although he was already thirty-five in 1877 and went wicketless in the first two tests.

Although the pitch showed no ill effects from rain that had fallen during the night, Bannerman and Blackham batted cautiously for several overs. When Bannerman did begin to hit out, however, Lillywhite's defensive field cut the value of his shots. The pair added 54 before Southerton bowled Blackham off his pads. Tom Garrett joined Bannerman, and both men proved rapid scorers.

Garrett was a hard-hitting all-rounder, of whom it was said his batting was unreliable when young but improved as he aged and as his skill with the ball declined. The eighteen-year-old helped the score mount quickly to 7-232 when lunch was taken. Bannerman was then on 159.

Shortly after play resumed, a ball from Ulyett struck Bannerman's right hand. He had allowed the protective rubber on his glove to wear away, and the ball split his middle finger to the bone. He retired hurt for 165. The score was then 7-240, and he had been at the wicket for four-and-three-quarter hours. Given the assurance of Australia's eighth wicket pair, who had added 43, he might well have continued almost indefinitely.

Bannerman's unbeaten score set several records. Not only was it the first test match century, made at the very earliest opportunity, but he scored sixty-nine per cent of the runs Australia achieved from the bat, an all-time record. It would remain the highest score in test cricket until Murdoch's 211 at The Oval in 1884, and the highest test score in Australia until Syd Gregory's 201 at Sydney in 1894. It remains, even now, the highest score on debut by an Australian in test cricket. In fourteen completed innings during eight previous first-class matches, he had passed fifty three times in accumulating 307 runs at 21.92.

Kendall and Hodges did not last long in their first visits to the batting crease, leaving Garrett not out 18 when the Australian innings closed for 245. Both men were indifferent batsmen and fielders, but would have their moment of glory later in the match.

'Harry' Jupp and Selby opened for England, and the Australians were unfortunate in the first over from Hodges. The fielding side believed Jupp, having turned a ball to fine-leg, had clipped the leg bail with his foot but apparently neither umpire, Curtis Reid or Richard Benjamin Terry, saw the incident.

Nottingham-born Terry was the Richmond club professional, and later appeared for Victoria in three matches. The other umpire, Reid, who had been the presiding official at the time of the incident, was abused at the end of the day's play by spectators. From the outset, umpiring in Australia was a thankless job. The crowd's attitude was possibly provoked by players' reactions. Perhaps the combined effect of spectator outburst and player dissent led to this being Reid's only test match. On the other hand, perhaps his recent appointment as Secretary of the Melbourne Cricket Club at five pounds a week meant he preferred to devote his energies to administration.

The main contrast between the Englishmen and the Australians was in the field, where the colonial team acted as if in a reckless hurry, resulting in several overthrows. Selby's was the first wicket to fall when he gave Cooper a soft catch in the covers off Hodges at 23, but Garrett was the best of the bowlers. He had made his debut this season as an exponent of off-theory, relying more on pace from the pitch than occasional movement from the leg. After several maiden overs, the NSW fast-medium bowler was removed for the round-arm spinner Midwinter. Left-arm orthodox spinner Kendall replaced the left-hand opening bowler Hodges. The total grew rapidly as Jupp and Henry Charlwood took control and Kendall gave way to the medium-paced Thomson. Finally, when the score had reached 79, Charlwood was caught at the wicket by Blackham off Midwinter for 36.

The first case of a batsman disputing an umpiring decision in a test match arose when Ulyett, who replaced Charlwood, was given out leg before wicket after a breezy ten to make the score 3-98. He shook his head and left little doubt that he had no wish to leave the wicket. He told friends and listeners that, if they would go with him to the wicket with a tape-line, he could prove that his leg could not possibly have been in the way of the Thomson delivery that had caused his downfall.

Andrew Greenwood, another Yorkshireman, and nephew of the better known player and English umpire Luke Greenwood, was next in. No sooner had he arrived than the Australian umpires were put to the test again by the England batsmen. Jupp chose to take exception to the sudden appearance of bright light and long shadows. The contrast was unpleasant, but scarcely constituted grounds for appeal, yet Jupp consumed one of the five minutes still available for play by looking first at the sun, then shading his eyes with his left hand, before turning to the bowler and the umpire. Perhaps Jupp had picked up a few tricks from WG Grace while opening the batting with him on the previous Australian tour.

Gregory put on slow bowler Kendall. Jupp received one ball from him, called for a hat, then let the rest of the over pass without murmur. None of these delaying tactics did Greenwood any good. He was caught by Ned Gregory from Midwinter in the final over of the day, which concluded at 4-109.

DAY 3

The third day's play on Saturday had yet another starting time, twenty past noon, and attracted by far the best crowd of between 9000 and 12,000. Jupp, 54 overnight, was accompanied to the wicket by Armitage, and Kendall and Midwinter opened the bowling. England were 136 in arrears, and with their last pair of recognised batsmen in, though Emmett and Hill might be reckoned all-rounders. The game favoured Australia.

Dave Gregory, as Lillywhite had done the previous day, set a defensive field and runs came slowly in the first half hour. Kendall and Midwinter were on top and, thanks chiefly to the latter, Armitage and Shaw left as modest contributors before Jupp was the seventh man out. He went leg before wicket to Garrett for 63, with the total at 145, his nine runs in an hour and a quarter confirming his reputation as a prodigious stonewaller.

The eighth wicket, that of Emmett, fell at the same total, and England required twenty-one runs to avoid a compulsory follow-on. Lillywhite quickly set about rectifying this by placing his first ball from Midwinter to the square-leg boundary. Lillywhite and Southerton then helped the hard-hitting Hill to add 51 runs for the last two wickets. The English innings closed at 196. Midwinter was the first test bowler to achieve the equivalent of a century with figures of 5-78.

The Australian team began their second innings at half past three with a lead of forty-nine. By the end of the day, their advantage had been erased. The crowd cheered when Bannerman's name appeared at the top of the order, but his dismissal for four by Ulyett was followed by a series of mishaps. Horan again shaped well for 20 before being caught behind from a leg glance off Hill, but Thomson and most of the middle order were so ineffective that, when the fifth wicket fell at 35, there were doubts the side would reach fifty. Solid defensive play by Midwinter and Ned Gregory against some excellent bowling by Shaw retrieved the position with a stand of 25, but Ulyett got them both, and at stumps the total had just reached 83 with one wicket to fall, an overall lead of 132 runs.

DAY 4

On the fourth day most cricket judges believed the English eleven would win, and one even pronounced the result 'a moral for Lillywhite's team'.

Kendall and Hodges, the last wicket pair, added a further 21 in the first quarter of an hour before Lillywhite, in his only over of the innings, took the last wicket at 104. The visitors were left chasing a competitive, if not formidable, total by contemporary standards.

England changed its batting order, opening with the Yorkshire pair of Hill and Greenwood. Several disasters occurred at the outset. Hill was the first of three early wickets to fall to Kendall, when he lodged the second ball of the innings in Thomson's hands at mid-on: one for none. Greenwood, Jupp and Charlwood followed quickly so that the England card read 4-22, with Kendall claiming three of the four. Greenwood was also caught close in, by Midwinter at mid-off, while Jupp was lbw and Charlwood, after playing vigorously for 13, was clean-bowled.

At this point the Englishmen kept their victory hopes alive and the fifth wicket did not fall until 62 runs had been posted. Selby and Ulyett had mounted a forty-run retrieval, beginning with a four apiece off Kendall. They had raised the fifty before lunch. Even when Kendall bowled the free-scoring Ulyett for 24, Lillywhite's team still had a chance, but, when Kendall tempted Shaw from his crease, Blackham stumped him brilliantly. England were 6-68 and victory for Australia looked more certain.

England revived briefly, but it was then that Gregory, in an inspired move, brought on Hodges. This proved to be the added feather which turned the scale against England. Joined by Armitage, Selby had continued to attack Kendall, also lofting Midwinter over the bowler's head to the boundary. So long as Selby remained in this mood, the England tail might have taken the match down to the wire, but the young Victorian Hodges had him caught on the long-on boundary by Horan. The wicketkeeper's aggressive 38 had lifted England to 7-92. His side still needed over sixty to win and England's chances of winning were all but gone.

Kendall and Hodges bowled successive maidens to Armitage and Emmett, before the latter took a single from Kendall. Hodges bowled another maiden, then Armitage was beautifully caught by Blackham off the left-hander: 8-93. Emmett and Lillywhite attacked, but Hodges clean-bowled the All England captain, leaving Southerton as England's unlikely rescuer. Emmett denied him even the attempt, pulling a ball from Kendall into his stumps to be last man out at 108, leaving the combination colonial team victors by forty-five runs.

Hodges finished with 2-7 off seven overs, but the hero was Kendall who finished with 7-55 and eight wickets for the match. All accounts noted the skilful wicketkeeping from Blackham, justifying the Victorian's disputed selection over New South Welshman Billy Murdoch.

The notion of national identity certainly received a boost from the colonials' win. Reporters who had been tentative before the match in references to the 'Australian' team were less guarded afterwards, hailing Charles Bannerman as a new national hero. A letter to the editor of the *Argus* called for a testimonial for the opening batsman, arguing that the fact that Bannerman was a New South Welshman should not interfere with such a tribute. The writer felt that 'all local feeling or jealousy should be set aside', and went on to say: 'For the time being we all – Victorians and New South Welshmen – must forget our geographical distinctions, and only remember that we are of one nation, Australia.'

In this moment of triumph and self-assertion, the halo and glory belonged to a national entity, Australia, which would not have legal existence for nearly a quarter of a century to come. Bannerman, it was said, had joined the sculler Edward Trickett in showing the people of England that not only could Australians beat them on the river, but also on the cricket field. Each player received a commemorative gold medal from the Victorian Cricket Association, a slightly larger one being provided for Dave Gregory as winning captain. Bannerman's personal testimonial yielded £83, while Kendall and Blackham each received £23 apiece. On the England side, Shaw's eight wickets for 89 off eighty-nine overs went unrewarded.

The margin of the Australian victory was sufficient against the English professionals to satisfy local pride and, if the visiting eleven did not comprise all the best batsmen – since a number of these were amateurs, and not free to tour – the best bowlers and fielders were generally reckoned to have been available. Furthermore, the combined side did not include all of the best cricketing talent in Australia. Three of the best colonial bowlers – Allan, Evans, and Spofforth – were absent, as was an able player in Murdoch, and Bannerman was disabled after the first innings.

The *Australasian* newspaper warned against too much bragging, then went on to do precisely that. Shaw might be the premier bowler, it allowed, but it did not think much of Ulyett, Emmett and Hill as a pace trio. And Kendall was better than Southerton and Lillywhite, who were already *passé*. On the batting side, Ulyett was acknowledged as a brilliant hitter, but Greenwood, Charlwood and Selby were only 'good average batsmen' and England had a 'long weak tail'. The paper went on to say that Blackham was a better wicketkeeper than the absent Pooley, and that Bannerman was the best batsman on either side.

For those in the depths of defeat, there was little time for reflection, just cricket as usual. The day after the match, Lillywhite's team began a three-day match at Sandhurst, Midwinter's home town, against a Bendigo twenty-two, followed by games against similar combinations at Ballarat and Ararat. At least the anticipated long wait between eleven-a-side representative matches was quickly overcome, so the fruits of reflection could be translated into the heady brew of renewed battle.

In short, a return match was hastily arranged in Melbourne twelve days after the first, with the gatetakings going to the touring side. Although records of these takings don't exist, a crowd of between 14,000 and 19,000 would have resulted in takings of about £1000. If funds were divided equally among the players, each of the tourists would have received an extra £90, a handsome bonus.

The English fielded an unchanged team, but the Australians made three alterations, replacing batsmen Cooper, Horan, and Ned Gregory with Victorian right-hand batsman Thomas Kelly and the seemingly inseparable NSW pair of batsman Billy Murdoch and bowler Fred Spofforth. It will be recalled that the bowler had withdrawn from the first match because Murdoch was not selected as wicketkeeper. In the return game, Blackham's early stumping of Shaw off Spofforth must have assuaged the bowler's concerns.

On this occasion, the '*passé*' Lillywhite and Southerton claimed ten wickets between them. Despite a further six-wicket haul to

Kendall, five English batsmen (all from Yorkshire) managed scores of forty or more as the English turned the tables on their former conquerors to win by four wickets.

Of those who played in the first test, the oldest Australian, Nat Thomson, was dead just over a decade later. Youngest participant Tom Garrett was the last of all to die, in August 1943, just after his eighty-fifth birthday. England's longest-lived player was James Lillywhite, who died in October 1929, at eighty-seven years and eight months. The first England test player to die was that oldest of all debutants, James Southerton, who died, aged fifty-two years and seven months, in June 1880.

Southerton's death preceded by two years the public announcement of the death of English cricket. This took place in the *Sporting Times* after the ninth Anglo–Australian test, at The Oval in August 1882, when the home side's first defeat on English soil gave birth to the concept of The Ashes. Periodically since then, the death of test cricket itself has been announced, with varying degrees of self-satisfaction and an unvarying degree of delusion.

Lillywhite's team played twenty-three matches on its Australasian tour – three against elevens and twenty against odds. The results against the elevens had a neat symmetry about them, with one win, one loss and one draw. Tour organisers Lillywhite and Australian John Conway made a good profit, encouraging Lillywhite to bring four teams to Australia in the 1880s with Arthur Shrewsbury and Alfred Shaw, and to act as an agent for early Australian teams in England. Similar pecuniary considerations no doubt influenced Conway to promote an Australian tour of England the following year.

•SYDNEY 1894•

'CRUEL LUCK! CRUEL LUCK!'

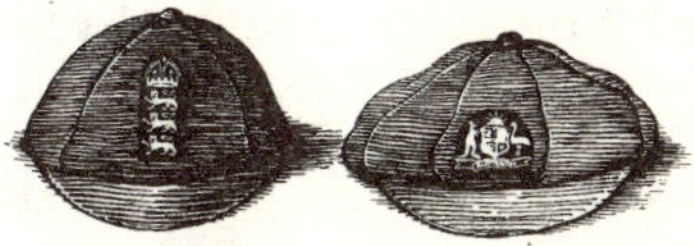

Chapter two picks up the threads of the nationalism-regionalism debate in a reappraisal of a remarkable match which Australia lost after England had been forced to follow on. This account attempts to balance the view that 'Australia was robbed' by suggesting that danger signs were apparent in the weather much earlier than has previously been considered. While Australia has three heroes – George Giffen, Syd Gregory, and a Sydney batmaker – the financial rewards for local hero Gregory are considerably greater than for South Australian Giffen. The weather, an uncovered wicket, and England spinners Bobby Peel and Johnny Briggs finally conspire to spoil Australia's party.

AUSTRALIA v ENGLAND 1894 (1st Test)

Played at Sydney Cricket Ground on 14, 15, 17, 18, 19, 20 December.
Toss: Australia. Result: ENGLAND won by 10 runs.

AUSTRALIA

JJ Lyons	b Richardson	1	b Richardson	25
GHS Trott	b Richardson	12	c Gay b Peel	8
G Giffen	c Ford b Brockwell	161	lbw b Briggs	41
J Darling	b Richardson	0	c Brockwell b Peel	53
FA Iredale	c Stoddart b Ford	81	(6) c and b Briggs	5
SE Gregory	c Peel b Stoddart	201	(5) c Gay b Peel	16
JC Reedman	c Ford b Peel	17	st Gay b Peel	4
CE McLeod	b Richardson	15	not out	2
CTB Turner	c Gay b Peel	1	c Briggs b Peel	2
JM Blackham*†	b Richardson	74	(11) c and b Peel	2
E Jones	not out	11	(10) c MacLaren b Briggs	1
Extras	(B 8, LB 3, W 1)	12	(B 2, LB 1, NB 4)	7
Total		**586**		**166**

ENGLAND

AC MacLaren	c Reedman b Turner	4	b Giffen	20
A Ward	c Iredale b Turner	75	b Giffen	117
AE Stoddart*	c Jones b Giffen	12	c Giffen b Turner	36
JT Brown	run out	22	c Jones b Giffen	53
W Brockwell	c Blackham b Jones	49	b Jones	37
R Peel	c Gregory b Giffen	4	b Giffen	17
FGJ Ford	st Blackham b Giffen	30	c and b Mc Leod	48
J Briggs	b Giffen	57	b McLeod	42
WH Lockwood	c Giffen b Trott	18	b Trott	29
LH Gay†	c Gregory b Reedman	33	b Trott	4
T Richardson	not out	0	not out	12
Extras	(B17, LB 3, W 1)	21	(B 14, LB 8)	22
Total		**325**		**437**

ENGLAND	O	M	R	W	O	M	R	W
Richardson	55.3	13	181	5	11	3	27	1
Peel	53	14	140	2	30	9	67	6
Briggs	25	4	96	0	11	2	25	3
Brockwell	22	7	78	1				
Lockwood	3	2	1	0	16	3	40	0
Ford	11	2	47	1				
Stoddart	3	0	31	1				
AUSTRALIA								
Turner	44	16	89	2	35	14	78	1
Jones	18	6	44	1	19	0	57	1
Giffen	43	17	75	4	75	25	164	4
McLeod	14	2	25	0	30	6	67	2
Trott	15	4	59	1	12.4	3	22	2
Reedman	3.3	1	12	1	6	1	12	0
Lyons	2	2	0	0	2	0	12	0
Iredale					2	1	3	0

FALL OF WICKETS

	A	E	E	A
Wkt	**1st**	**1st**	**2nd**	**2nd**
1st	10	14	44	26
2nd	21	43	115	45
3rd	21	78	217	130
4th	192	149	245	135
5th	331	155	290	147
6th	379	211	296	158
7th	400	211	385	159
8th	409	252	398	161
9th	563	325	420	162
10th	586	325	437	166

Umpires: J Phillips and C Bannerman.

Syd Gregory

Bobby Peel

George Giffen

In the days leading up to the opening match of the 1894–95 series, South Australian George Giffen, a selector with Jack Blackham (Victoria) and Charles Turner (New South Wales), made no secret of the fact he wanted five of his colony's representatives in the side. South Australian claims must have been based on their success in claiming the Sheffield Shield during the previous season, a feat they would not repeat until NSW had taken ten titles and Victoria another five.

Giffen's preference revealed that, in the Australian test cricket team, regional allegiances were still as strong as any nationalistic spirit. Moves toward federating the Australian colonies might have begun in 1883 with an intercolonial conference, and gained momentum with federal councils, national conventions and federation leagues being formed to draft a constitution, but cricket rivalries remained.

As in 1877, the team did not practise together as a unit, even though several members had toured England together. New South Welshmen Syd Gregory and Charles Turner had been twice, in 1890 and 1893; Joe Lyons (SA) and Harry Trott (Victoria) had toured in 1888, 1890 and 1893; Giffen had made four trips (1882, 1884, 1886, 1893); and Blackham eight, including the first two tours of all, 1878 and 1880. The experienced nucleus of the team must have seemed an impenetrable clique to outsiders and newcomers.

Two days before the test, three of the four Victorian representatives (Blackham excepted) – Trott, Charles McLeod and Harry Graham – and five South Australians – Giffen, Joe Darling, Lyons, Jack Reedman, and Ernest Jones – practised in the morning, while New South Welshmen Turner, Frank Iredale and Gregory, plus Victoria's Trott and Graham, practised in the afternoon. The hard-hitting Graham was attempting to impress, but to no avail. He had made 107 in his test debut at Lord's in 1893, but he ended up twelfth man in this match. Such was the presumed strength of the Australian batting or the power of intercolonial rivalries that he was not required to play until the fourth test of the series, again in Sydney, whereupon he made 105.

The Sydney Cricket Ground wicket was still being made with Melbourne's Merri Creek soil, even though the first loads of nearby Bulli soil had been shipped to the ground in 1894. The curator, former test player Ned Gregory, was confident that, given good weather, both teams would be satisfied. Merri Creek soil already had the reputation of the finest wicket-making material in the country. Ned might well have passed on some fatherly advice to Syd, given his son's spectacular success in this match.

Early in the season, a Mr A Dye of Cleveland Street, Redfern, had presented to Syd Gregory one of the bats he was making in competition with established English firms like Gunn and Moore. Gregory scored an unbeaten 201 not out with it the first time he used it in a match, against a Combined Country team. He went on to make a succession of big scores with it, including 153 not out and 87 before the test, and 101 and 42 thereafter. In all, he scored 855 runs with the bat at an average of 85.5 runs per innings. A number of other Australian players, including Alick Bannerman, Frank Iredale, and Harry Donnan also used Dye bats at this time.

The Sydney Cricket Ground had been considerably refurbished for its eleventh test. An awning along the eastern side afforded shade to spectators and a new Smokers' stand accommodated six hundred people. The Fresh Food and Ice Company announced that they would supply iced water free of charge, which, at this distance, sounds a generous gesture, but was doubtless a new form of advertising for the recently-introduced commercial refrigeration. Lovers of music were entertained by bands. What batsmen thought of musical accompaniment to and from and at the crease is unclear.

Andrew Stoddart's England team was a powerful one. On paper, the Surrey combination of 'Long Tom' Richardson and Bill Lockwood looked a more hostile opening attack than had hitherto appeared in Australia, though the fact that Richardson's first three wickets on the tour had cost him 263 runs meant local opinion was confident of an Australian triumph. Bobby Peel of Yorkshire and Johnny Briggs of Lancashire were the outstanding left-arm spin bowlers of their generation in English conditions. Supporting them was the right-arm fast-medium bowling of Surrey all-rounder William Brockwell.

In addition to the stylish batting of Stoddart himself, new opening batsmen Albert Ward and Archie MacLaren of Lancashire, and Jack Brown of Yorkshire, would prove worthy replacements for WG Grace, Bobby Abel and Arthur Shrewsbury from the previous tour. In the middle order, left-hander Francis Ford was a legendary hitter, and all-rounders Briggs and Peel could be expected to make runs.

Even before it began, the First Test was remarkable for the

presence of nine debutants. Middle-order batsman Iredale and Darling, all-rounders McLeod and Reedman, and fast bowler Jones were the five Australians, while batsmen MacLaren, Brown and Ford, and wicketkeeper Leslie Gay, were the four making their first appearance for England.

DAY 1

A crowd of 10,917 was present when the Australian team met just after noon and Jack Blackham, the only survivor in the two teams from the 1877 tests, was reappointed captain by the players. After leading the Australian team to victory over Lord Sheffield's team in Australia three years earlier, but then to defeat in England in 1893, there had been some speculation the veteran might be replaced.

Blackham won the toss and elected to bat. Charles Bannerman, the hero of the first-ever test, appeared as the Australian-nominated umpire beside Jim Phillips, who was nominated by Stoddart's team.

Play began twelve minutes after noon when the burly South Australian, Lyons, and the Victorian, Trott, opened against the fast right-hander Richardson and slow left-hand spinner Peel, in what was regarded at the time as an ideal combination. Had Stoddart allowed Richardson to operate with a fast bowler at the other end, as he and Lockwood did for Surrey, the match might have opened, and concluded, quite differently.

As it was, Richardson made the initial break after just ten minutes. The 'Surrey Catapult' set the Australian innings in a spin in the first half hour, doubling his tour tally by removing three of its top-order batsmen. Lyons, who had flayed Lord Sheffield's bowlers on the previous tour, struck his knee with his bat as he moved forward and the ball glanced his leg stump when he had only one run. Trott lost his off stump to a good length ball to make the team total 2-21. This brought two South Australians together, George Giffen being joined by Joe Darling, who had made a century against the tourists in

Adelaide. This time he did not disturb the scorers, losing his middle and off stumps to a first ball yorker.

The Australian collapse must have seemed incredible to the spectators who clustered around the newspaper offices and those who read the news flashed in on the wires were said to have regarded one another with 'blank astonishment'.

This was the performance of a truly great fast bowler, whose arm was poetically described as like 'the thong of a stock-whip' and whose back, from which he generated his pace, was fancied, in a mechanical metaphor typical of its time, to be equipped with 'double-action, Damascus-steel fittings'. In the preceding English season, Richardson had bowled 936 overs for 196 wickets at ten apiece and, after an arduous tour – 265 overs for 68 wickets – would bowl another 690 overs for 290 wickets at fourteen in 1895. Between 1894 and 1897, he captured 1005 wickets, bowling as if he wanted to operate from both ends. He was not reckoned as great as Australia's Fred Spofforth but, as a purely fast bowler, many authorities consistently described him as 'the finest that ever bowled'.

Bad as things looked for Australia after Richardson's onslaught, the bowling side was allowed only one new ball per innings, and it soon lost its potency on the shirt-front Australian wickets of the period.

Lionhearted George Giffen had much to prove. He had achieved outstanding scores at intercolonial level, but had never dominated with the bat in tests. He had followed his phenomenal performance in 1891–92 of scoring 271 in a single innings against Victoria, during a match in which he also took 16 wickets for 166 runs, with only 138 runs in eight innings against Lord Sheffield's team that tour.

Iredale came in at the fall of Darling's wicket to join Giffen. Until this point in his career, he had been regarded as a batsman 'slightly above the average'. Following the innings upon which Iredale now embarked, Giffen later called him one of the three best in Australia. Together, the pair broke the back of the bowling.

Iredale struck a boundary to square-leg off Richardson, then both batsmen attacked Peel. Giffen straight-drove fours off consecutive balls, and in subsequent overs a glance by Iredale and a cut by Giffen also registered boundaries.

The score was fifty by one o'clock, when Giffen made an examination of the pitch. He felt that there was a rise about midway between the wickets, and that Richardson's bowling was lifting unpleasantly as a consequence. Richardson was in fact renowned for bowling a consistently full length and not at the body, even moderating his attack when batsmen showed themselves in difficulties on imperfect pitches, so it may be that this was a nice piece of tactics by the batsman.

Giffen helped himself to four with a hook when Richardson pitched on the leg stump. The only half chance came when a bumper from the fast-medium bowling of Bill Lockwood looped off the handle of Giffen's bat to the left hand of wicketkeeper Gay, who was unable to hold it.

The Cambridge wicketkeeper was playing in his only test, and had an unhappy time of it. Nevertheless, Patrick Murphy's claim that his 'status as England's worst wicketkeeper seems imperishable' is harsh. Three catches and a stumping off Peel suggests that he may simply have been better close-up than standing back.

Giffen had made exactly half the lunch score of 3-78. When the batsmen resumed, Iredale began confidently with two fours off the Lancashire left-arm spinner Johnny Briggs. The hundred came soon afterwards and Giffen celebrated by jumping down the wicket to straight-drive Briggs over the fence for five. The batsmen scored at a run per minute, and England's prospects seemed bleak when Lockwood left the field with a ricked back.

At ninety Giffen gave a chance to the wicketkeeper off Richardson but Gay let it drop on the second attempt, a crucial miss in more ways than one. The keeper had already dropped Giffen twice at 75, and had fumbled a return when Giffen and Iredale were both at the bowler's end. Stoddart seemed to have exhausted most of his options but, either at a loss or with a stroke of genius, brought on Frank Ford with his occasional left-arm spin. The Cambridge man made a vital break, securing his only test wicket when Iredale was caught at mid-on by the captain for 81 with the score at 4-192. Tea was taken with Giffen three short of his century.

Giffen and Iredale had added 171 in 149 minutes. Their fourth-wicket partnership was not surpassed by Australia against England until Neil Harvey and Graeme Hole added 173 together at Manchester in 1953. Worse was to come for England, however, for Sydney in 1894 was to be a match of big partnerships.

Syd Gregory joined Giffen after the break. A few minutes later, the South Australian brought up three figures with a pull to the square-leg boundary off Richardson. After the 200 was raised, the scoring became very rapid, Gregory reaching his fifty in just over even time, and the third century was passed at half past five. Giffen had plenty of time to form the opinion he later offered that 'no colonial executes a greater variety of strokes'. He thought Gregory late-cut beautifully, jumped to meet the ball and drove well, leg-glanced to a nicety, and loved a good pull or hook, building these strokes on the firm foundation of his splendid defence.

Runs came more slowly at the end of the day. Just when it seemed as though Giffen would bat through the day, he snicked a fast ball from Brockwell and was caught in the slips for 161 at 331. His innings lasted four-and-a-quarter hours and included twenty-two fours and one five. Gregory outscored Giffen in their stand of 139 and had reached 85 by the close. He remained united overnight with test debutant Jack Reedman, who would play first-class cricket for fourteen more years without another test. At stumps Australia were 5-346.

DAY 2

The first day was dominated by Giffen, but Gregory's innings on the second was even more remarkable. Resuming on 85, before a record crowd for Sydney of 24,120, he brought up his century in 129 minutes after half an hour. Like Charles Bannerman, Gregory thus made his maiden first-class hundred in a test match, though not in his first test. Unlike Bannerman, he would go on to make more first-class hundreds – three in tests, and twenty-four more in a career that extended to 1912.

Peel and Richardson bowled unchanged in the morning session, during which they took three wickets and Peel had Gregory dropped behind the wicket. This further fielding mishap occurred just before lunch, when Gregory's score was 131. The loss of Reedman and McLeod in the teens, and Turner for a single, might have seemed to signal the approaching end of the innings. With the score at 8-409, however, great deeds were yet to be achieved.

The same bowlers continued into the afternoon as Blackham supported Gregory. Briggs replaced Richardson at 478. Blackham back-cut him for two to raise the 500. Stoddart rung the bowling changes to no effect. Gregory passed Giffen's tally and proceeded towards his double-century; crowds gathered at newspaper offices in breathless interest. Blackham himself stopped his innings to catch his breath, before returning to the crease with renewed vigour.

Stoddart's appearance at the bowling crease increased the tempo, with three overs of his medium-pace yielding 31 runs, until he enticed Gregory to give a catch to Peel on the square-leg boundary. Gregory's score was 201, made in one minute over four hours with twenty-eight fours. The total had reached 9-563. In the period after lunch Gregory added 67 out of 121 in only fifty-eight minutes. His partnership with Blackham of 154 in seventy-six minutes remains the Australian ninth wicket test record a century later, and was the world test record until 1967. The Australian total was already the highest score then achieved in test cricket, and Ernest Jones helped

Blackham advance it even further, to 586, before Richardson took his fifth wicket of the innings.

The English team began their innings seven minutes before four o'clock with MacLaren and Ward taking strike against Jones and Turner. Blackham was behind the wickets. Regardless of knocks, and despite thin pads and gloves, he was reputed to take the fastest bowling with 'marvellous dexterity'. Blackham on this occasion stood well back to Jones, whom observers rated as being as quick through the air as Richardson.

It was not pace, however, which brought about the fall in English wickets, but the medium-paced off-cutters of Turner and the slow-medium off-breaks of Giffen. Turner induced a false stroke from MacLaren, who was caught for four at 1-14.

The English captain came in to face Giffen. Stoddart, right hand gripped low down on the bat-handle, was generally reckoned a magnificent bat, a very hard hitter and an excellent defender, whose driving was safe and hard. Giffen, on the other hand, was a bowler who did not mind being hit, one who bowled long spells of flighted deliveries, intent on deep-field catches. They were well matched, but the bowler's nagging accuracy accounted for Stoddart to make the score 2-43.

Ward and Brown added 35 before a quick return by Lyons brought about Brown's downfall. Australia seemed to be gaining the ascendancy, but then the attack received a check. Despite changes in bowling, Ward and Brockwell took the score to 130 at stumps, when the former was 67 and the latter 18.

The players returned to the pavilion to witness a ceremony that demonstrated the financial benefits that could accrue to a local hero, and revealed how politicians could milk such situations to their advantage. Syd Gregory's batting had so delighted the spectators that Alderman Waine and a Mr Abrams took up subscriptions for him. They quickly collected £103 10s, the equivalent of the annual minimum wage of an adult male. It was even more valuable when high unemployment was producing massive social dislocation in Australia.

George Reid, President of the New South Wales Cricket Association and for the previous few months NSW Premier, presented this award. Reid was remarkably prescient in his speech when he said, 'I suppose you will admit that we are having one of the grandest matches we have ever witnessed.' But he was then quick to note his political constituents, adding:

> When I saw Giffen play his magnificent innings of 161 I thought it would be impossible to surpass it, but for once the champion of Australia has been surpassed by the champion of New South Wales, and he will shortly – and I feel sure, with Giffen's approbation and consent – become the champion of Australian batsmen.

A more expert cricketer than Reid, Giffen himself, thought Gregory's 201 was one of the most brilliant innings he had seen, full of strokes played with a 'remarkable precision'. Reid obviously had an eye on the political clock: his five-year premiership, which extended until 1899, was a long time in nineteenth-century colonial politics. But Reid was also a man with national aspirations and British roots. Later during the long speech he said:

> There is one thing I want to add, and that is that the bat he played with was made by a Sydney man, Mr Dye, so it is all true colonial from beginning to end. I am sure our English friends will be the first to admire his performance, and you must never forget that it was the men of the old country who were the first to teach us to play cricket.

Reid then called for three cheers for Gregory, adding, 'Don't let us forget Giffen,' and the cheers rang out once more. Cheers for Giffen – but little cash! As for Reid himself, it can hardly have surprised onlookers when he became the fourth Australian Prime Minister ten years later.

Giffen, like Gregory, Reedman and Trott, a postal worker between cricket engagements, would no doubt have liked his share of the £100. As it is, he would have received £10 offered by the brewer Mr Toohey for making a century, although Gregory trebled that figure from the brewer. Toohey donated a further £10 for anyone who passed Giffen, and £10 more for scoring a double century.

A testimonial fund eventually opened for Giffen in Adelaide but failed to boom. He had changed his club, losing him all his Norwood supporters, especially the wealthy and locally influential Edwin Smith (another brewer) who might have been expected to subscribe £10 but did not. As the *Bulletin* recorded, 'Giffen has been sinned against as much as sinning.'

||| DAY 3

Rain fell during Saturday night and Sunday morning, but Monday was generally fine, and the wicket, though slower, was undamaged. A sharp shower once drove the cricketers into the grandstand, but play resumed a quarter of an hour before lunch before a crowd of 11,606. The wicket was slightly sticky at mid-day, but played fairly in the afternoon, and the only disadvantage to the batsmen was that the ball travelled slowly in the field. Neither of the overnight batsmen Ward and Brockwell were disturbed before lunch, which was taken at 3-140, with Ward on 70 and Brockwell 21.

Their stubborn stand of 71 was broken after the interval when Ward, on 75, lofted a drive off Turner. Peel, who replaced him, did not last long. Brockwell and Ford then took the total to 211, at which score both wickets fell. Some doubts were cast over Blackham's involvement in both dismissals. Ford had made 30 when he went down the wicket to Giffen. Blackham was credited with stumping him. The *Sydney Morning Herald*, however, noted that Blackham had barely removed the bails before he dropped the ball. The batsman seemed disconcerted by the umpire's decision. The paper was casual about Brockwell's dismissal for 49, describing how Blackham, standing back to Jones, tossed the ball up for a catch, with the umpire nodding in reply. Blackman's actions reveal, perhaps, that cricketers have never been averse to playing confidence tricks on umpires.

At 7-211, England were in danger of collapse, but Briggs had yet to be reckoned with. At tea, he had taken England to 7-246, with his own score on 22 and Lockwood on 13. He and Lockwood carried the score past 250 before Briggs and Gay scattered the Australian bowling in an aggressive stand of 73. A slow ball from Giffen eventually broke Briggs' stumps for 57, and no sooner had last man Richardson gone in than Gay was caught off Reedman's bowling. This final dismissal provided a nice irony, since both Gay and Reedman were making their solitary test appearance, and each won greater renown as footballers. Gay was already a soccer international for England, and Reedman appeared regularly in intercolonial games of Australian Rules football.

England's final score of 325 meant that it had to follow on, since this rule was compulsory and the 261-run deficit was much greater than the 120-run margin required. As the time was then twelve minutes to six, and a changeover of innings took fifteen minutes, play ended for the day.

Giffen was the best of the seven bowlers used, taking 4-75, but the fielding, with the exception of Trott and Gregory, was poor. Blackham had cracked the top joint of the thumb on his right hand so seriously when taking a ball from Lyons that he was forced to surrender the gloves to McLeod. He did not keep wickets again in the match.

DAY 4

Tuesday dawned cool and cloudy, and the outfield was heavy. It was six minutes past midday, and 8034 spectators were present, when Ward and MacLaren set about the huge task facing England. The Australians were without Blackham, his role as captain being taken by Giffen with twelfth man Graham fielding as substitute.

As Jones was erratic, Giffen quickly brought himself on, and a flighted delivery struck the top of MacLaren's middle stump when the batsman had made 20 and the total was 44. Stoddart, who replaced him, then played carefully against Giffen. Ward should have followed suit, and was fortunate at 28 when the bowler deceived him but McLeod, snatching at a catch, could only deflect it toward slip. It fell short of Jones. Ward remained. The miss proved costly.

At lunch the score stood in the mid-sixties with Ward on 32, and Stoddart just in double figures. Forty overs had been bowled with only one change. Jones returned to the attack after the break, but pitched too short, so that both batsmen cut him with ease. Ward brought up his fifty in two hours and twelve minutes but Stoddart, cutting once too often at Turner, skied the ball to cover. At 2-116, the deficit was still 146.

Brown, who came in to partner Ward, made a careful inspection of the wicket before he took block, but both batsmen were still in command at tea, when the total had reached 2-183. Ward was approaching his century, and Brown in the twenties.

Following the interval, McLeod bowled and Reedman took the gloves. After a couple of overs, Ward brought up his century in seventeen minutes over three hours. He did not survive long afterwards as Giffen bowled him for 117. Ward and Brown had put on 102 at better than a run a minute for the third wicket, the best English partnership in the match, but it seemed insufficient.

Brown completed his fifty with a four off Giffen, but immediately afterwards skied a ball to the on-side where Jones made a good running catch to leave the score 4-245. England were still sixteen runs behind and MacLaren, Stoddart, Ward and Brown had departed. It was a stiff handicap. Peel and Brockwell pushed their team in front so that, by the close, the score had reached 4-268 with Brockwell 20 and Peel nine. England were seven runs on with six wickets left.

The Bulletin

Registered at the General Post Office, Sydney, for transmission by post as a Newspaper.

Vol. 14—No. 776 **SATURDAY, DECEMBER 22, 1894.** Price, 6p

THE RELATIVE SIZES OF THINGS JUST NOW.

DAY 5

England's occupation of the crease throughout Tuesday had allowed the wicket to ease further and, on Wednesday, the batsmen added a further 169 for the last six wickets.

Punctuality remained a problem. Play started eight minutes late but still too early for Turner, who had not arrived at the ground. With McLeod again keeping wicket, Johnny Briggs (who was still to bat for England) acted as a substitute fielder for the Australians.

Jones pitched the ball up early in the day, and was rewarded when he bowled Brockwell. When Giffen got rid of Peel in the same way, six wickets were down for 297, a lead of only thirty-six. Briggs joined Ford, and there was speculation whether he would match his first innings half-century. From the outset the Lancashire all-rounder showed that he was determined to remain as long as possible.

Giffen continued to suffer at the hands of his field when McLeod missed stumping Ford, who then put Jones away for two boundaries in one over when that bowler reverted to bowling short.

At lunch the score had advanced to 6-344. Afterwards, Ford struck Trott straight over the fence for five, and Briggs took two boundaries from an over by Giffen. The batsmen were pacing each other until McLeod made a double break. First, Ford pushed the ball back to him, and left at 7-385. With the wicket still wearing well, Ford's 48 (his highest test score) had helped add 89, though both batsmen had been missed. Then McLeod bowled Briggs thirteen runs later. The Australians must have hoped to wind the innings up quickly, but a hard-hitting 29 by Lockwood carried the total to 437.

Australia's second innings began at four o'clock and it faced the comparatively light task of scoring 177 runs to win. Lyons and Trott again opened against Richardson and Peel, and Lyons began as though he wanted to finish the match that night. This was in keeping with his customary style – contemporary comment marvelled at his scoring rate. Few balls, whatever their length, escaped punishment and no ground, whatever its size, seemed too big for him. This time, he bludgeoned his way to 25 out of 26 in a quarter-hour, but his innings proved only a miniature. Slashing out recklessly at Richardson, he was bowled off his pads for the second time in the match. A tame end for the powerful Lyons.

Giffen, next in, was much more circumspect. There was later a feeling that the match might have been lost in this period, as Giffen and the stodgy Trott played a succession of maidens while black clouds formed overhead. One opinion was that if Australia did not pass 130 by the close, they could lose the next day. Had Gregory and Iredale been at the crease, the game might even have been won that night. The Australian team watching in the grandstand, chafed at the tardiness of the play.

With the score at 32, Richardson retired ill with a chill and Lockwood took up the attack. This change prompted Giffen to take six runs from the first over but, when the score had reached 45, Trott hit out at Peel and was caught at the wicket.

This was a poor start by Australia, but Giffen and Darling put a different complexion on the game. Darling, in particular, having escaped his pair and been dropped by Stoddart, decided to chance his arm. In the last hour, the batsmen scored at a run a minute against some slack fielding so that the overnight score reached 2-113. The score was marginally short of the anticipated 130 but, with Darling on 44 and Giffen 30, victory must have seemed a formality. After all, Australia needed just sixty-four with eight wickets in hand.

DAY 6

Unfortunately for the Australians, it rained heavily during the night, and it needed no prophet to predict that they would struggle to win. One look at the pitch justified their fears. A famous anecdote tells of how Giffen, having slept soundly, greeted Blackham cheerily at breakfast, only to meet an extremely gloomy face. Blackham was always reckoned a captain who tended to worry and magnify temporary misfortunes, but on this occasion his worst fears were well-enough founded. Curator Ned Gregory, who was up before the larks, gave the opinion before play began that the Australians would be beaten. Who knows what batting instruction he gave his son at this time? The pavilion end had suffered badly, and was so soft you could stick a finger in it, whereas the other end was hard and dry.

Darling and Giffen, however, resumed confidently and Australian hopes were raised when Stoddart surprisingly put Richardson on at the pavilion end instead of Briggs. Peel was bowling to the troublesome end. Darling roused the small crowd of 1268 when he lofted Peel over the fence for five but in trying to repeat the stroke he was caught by Brockwell for 53 on the long-on boundary. The score was now 3-130, and there were forty-seven to get.

On the previous evening, Peel had conceded defeat, and attempted to drown its sting in copious quaffings of beer. When, next morning, the changed conditions became apparent to his teammates, they stood Peel in the showers until he was able to predict that the wicket would be unplayable within twenty minutes, and the game would be over by lunch. He was regarded as having less resource and devil than Briggs, but was steadier. Although Briggs reputedly possessed a larger repertoire of tricks, and seldom sent down a loose ball, both left-handers had marvellous command of pace, length, and break, and were unplayable on sticky wickets of the kind they encountered in Sydney. Sadly, Peel would drink himself out of the game within five years, though he lived until 1941.

The career of his slow-bowling partner would similarly come to an abrupt and more tragic end before the end of the century. But Charles Fry left a superb pen-portrait of the bowler in his heyday, recording how Briggs would beam upon incoming batsmen before and after their innings in such conditions. The shorter their innings, Fry noted, the happier he was toward them. He would pass a cheery time of day, inquire with feeling after a player's health and form, take two steps, and deliver a fast yorker instead of the high-tossed slow ball expected. As the batsman retired, discomfited, Briggs smiled once more. 'What could be pleasanter?' Fry asked ironically.

This combination, then, was what faced the Australians when Briggs replaced Richardson. Varying the order of the first innings, Blackham sent Gregory in next to get the runs quickly before the pitch deteriorated, a commission the batsman immediately set about discharging. By now, the tension was getting to both sides. Giffen had enjoyed a life at 41 when Brown put down a simple catch at point off Peel, but fell leg before wicket to the first ball from Briggs.

The margin had been reduced by five. Iredale was next in, but saw only eleven runs added before spooning the ball back to Briggs. Reedman then shaped awkwardly, and it was mainly due to the aggression of Syd Gregory, who hit each bowler for four, that another eleven runs were added.

The match virtually ended when Gregory was dismissed, deceived in flight by Peel, though the board showed 6-158 and only nineteen runs were required. McLeod played carefully but lost Reedman, stumped by Gay. Turner made two before giving Briggs an easy catch at cover off Peel. Jones came in and began hitting hard in agricultural fashion, but paid the penalty when caught in the outfield for a single. Fourteen runs were still needed when captain Blackham, amid cheers, made his way to the wicket.

Blackham had said on Tuesday, as he nursed his split thumb, that he would not play again in the match unless a few runs were required and he had to go in. Such was now the situation, but would he be the man for the moment? Never a reliable run-getter, he could demoralise bowling, as he had in the first innings. On the debit side, he could never bear to watch an exciting finish.

There was a single to McLeod to open his account and another for Blackham when he popped a ball up between MacLaren and Peel. The Englishmen were aware of Blackham's ability to take quick singles and, when a ball was hit away from the pitch, half a dozen of them converged on it. The end came when Blackham pushed a catch back to Peel. The bowler took off his cap and jumped in the air with joy. England had won by ten runs.

The scene at the finish was almost indescribable, but 'Observer' of the *Australasian* did his best to oblige in one of the most dramatic pieces of cricket reportage:

> The crowd were all on their feet, yet the silence, except for the roar when a wicket fell, was the tragic stillness of death, and for an hour people suffered, in silence, that unpleasant sinking about the waistband which is a manifestation of anxiety, and almost painful while it lasts. Blackham walked up and down the balcony like a caged tiger, muttering, 'Cruel luck – cruel luck,' and George Giffen, half dressed, stood with a singlet in one hand and a shirt in the other, blankly watching the procession . . . In short, the team were thoroughly cut up seeing victory thus snatched away . . . 'The rain beat us,' said some of them. 'No! the sun beat us,' said Blackham. Those who bet were heavy losers, a well known Sydney jockey dropping £100, while another was fool enough to lay £40 to £5 on the Australians on Thursday morning. He was an admirable judge of horses but a poor judge of cricket.

It would be unfair to detract from the merit of the English team's play on the final day, but the change in weather brought about a remarkable change in fortune. The headlines were modest in size, and ingeniously worded. Until the end, the two heroes of the game had been Australians. As batsman, bowler, and even fielder, Giffen won the admiration of critics. Gregory made the sensational score of the match, but to Giffen belonged the credit of having beaten down the bowling. With two left-handers like Peel and Briggs bowling on a line and turning from the leg on a pasty pitch, there was little way of judging the behaviour of the ball. Peel, who until the final morning had experienced a trying match, was almost unplayable, while Briggs bowled well to the end better for the batsmen.

One result of the game was a call for covered wickets, a call which fell on deaf ears. A George Crowley, writing to the Sydney *Daily Telegraph* on 21 December 1894, declared that the so-called glorious uncertainty of cricket was 'glorious humbug' and questioned the received wisdom that winning the toss meant winning the game. He suggested the game should be played from start to finish under conditions which would 'leave the most finished exponents the victors at termination'.

The match created a number of world records. It was the first test to last into a sixth day, during which time the attendance reached 62,113, the gate receipts £2835, and the aggregate number of runs scored 1514.

The immediate impact of the game was that Giffen was rewarded for his grand efforts when he replaced the injured Blackham as test captain. He proceeded to lead Australia perhaps too much from the front. Not only did he achieve a phenomenal season in the tests with 475 runs and 34 wickets, still the only player to top the aggregates in both departments for both sides, but his astonishing first-class season saw him make 902 runs and take 93 wickets in only eleven games. Despite his individual efforts, England still won the series. The Australians lost the next match at Melbourne, drew level after winning the Third Test in Adelaide and the Fourth in the return Sydney match, only for England to win the deciding Fifth Test in Melbourne.

The day after winning the First Test, Stoddart's team played Eighteen Sydney Juniors, who scored over 400 against them, and managed a draw. Among this team were two players who were quick to serve notice of greater deeds to follow. Monty Noble made 152 runs, and the seventeen-year-old Victor Trumper 67 in slashing style. Their influence on future Ashes battles would be enormous.

•MANCHESTER 1902•

TRAGIC HEROES

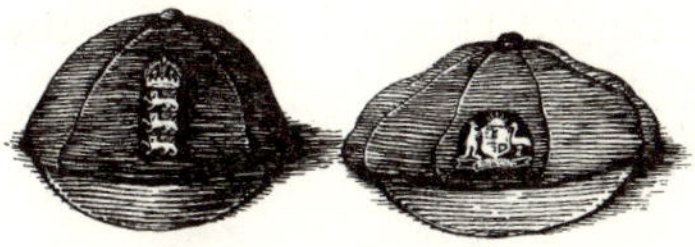

This game has been widely reported, most often following Neville Cardus, as Fred Tate's tragedy. Although a charming approach, sporting contests are rarely decided in their final moments; there are many contributing factors throughout the play. Rather than treating Tate as merely an old pro out of his depth, we show him as one of a number of curious selections by England, the defeat in part arising from a situation where parochial feelings were put before national interest. Conversely, a tragic-hero-to-be, Victor Trumper, who will die thirteen years later at the age of thirty-eight, establishes the foundations for Australia's victory with a brilliant century before lunch on the first day. Perhaps the moral is that few of us can be sure how we would react when put to the test, and none can know what will follow today – triumph after tragedy, the reverse, or merely more of the same?

ENGLAND v AUSTRALIA 1902 (4th Test)

Played at Old Trafford, Manchester, on 24, 25, 26 July.
Toss: Australia. Result: AUSTRALIA won by 3 runs.

AUSTRALIA

VT Trumper	c Lilley b Rhodes	104	c Braund b Lockwood	4
RA Duff	c Lilley b Lockwood	54	b Lockwood	3
C Hill	c Rhodes b Lockwood	65	b Lockwood	0
MA Noble	c and b Rhodes	2	(6) c Lilley b Lockwood	4
SE Gregory	c Lilley b Rhodes	3	lbw b Tate	24
J Darling*	c MacLaren b Rhodes	51	(4) c Palairet b Rhodes	37
AJY Hopkins	c Palairet b Lockwood	0	c Tate b Lockwood	2
WW Armstrong	b Lockwood	5	b Rhodes	3
JJ Kelly†	not out	4	not out	2
H Trumble	c Tate b Lockwood	0	lbw b Tate	4
JV Saunders	b Lockwood	3	c Tyldesley b Rhodes	0
Extras	(B 5, LB 2, W 1)	8	(B 1, LB 1, NB 1)	3
Total		**299**		**86**

ENGLAND

LCH Palairet	c Noble b Saunders	6	b Saunders	17
R Abel	c Armstrong b Saunders	6	(5) b Trumble	21
JT Tyldesley	c Hopkins b Saunders	22	c Armstrong b Saunders	16
AC MacLaren*	b Trumble	1	(2) c Duff b Trumble	35
KS Ranjitsinhji	lbw b Trumble	2	(4) lbw b Trumble	4
FS Jackson	c Duff b Trumble	128	c Gregory b Saunders	7
LC Braund	b Noble	65	st Kelly b Trumble	3
AFA Lilley†	b Noble	7	c Hill b Trumble	4
WH Lockwood	run out	7	b Trumble	0
W Rhodes	c and b Trumble	5	not out	4
FW Tate	not out	5	b Saunders	4
Extras	(B 6, LB 2)	8	(B 5)	5
Total		**262**		**120**

ENGLAND	**O**	**M**	**R**	**W**	**O**	**M**	**R**	**W**
Rhodes	25	3	104	4	14.4	5	26	3
Jackson	11	0	58	0				
Tate	11	1	44	0	5	3	7	2
Braund	9	0	37	0	11	3	22	0
Lockwood	20.1	5	48	6	17	5	28	5
AUSTRALIA								
Trumble	43	16	75	4	25	9	53	6
Saunders	34	5	104	3	19.4	4	52	4
Noble	24	8	47	2	5	3	10	0
Trumper	6	4	6	0				
Armstrong	5	2	19	0				
Hopkins	2	0	3	0				

FALL OF WICKETS

	A	E	A	E
Wkt	**1st**	**1st**	**2nd**	**2nd**
1st	135	12	7	44
2nd	175	13	9	68
3rd	179	14	10	72
4th	183	30	64	92
5th	256	44	74	97
6th	256	185	76	107
7th	288	203	77	109
8th	292	214	79	109
9th	292	235	85	116
10th	299	262	86	120

Umpires: J Moss and T Mycroft.

Fred Tate

Victor Trumper

By any definition, 'tragedy' as popularly used would be too trite a term with which to typify the Old Trafford test of 1902. Yet most people with even a trivial knowledge of the history of Anglo–Australian tests probably think this word fits the match to a 't' – Fred T. Frederick William Tate has gone down in the annals of cricket as the man who muffed *the* catch, the catch which cost England the Ashes. He is possibly second-best remembered for a despairing spur-of-the-moment remark, first reported by Len Braund to John Arlott a half-century later. According to Braund, Tate supposedly said, 'I've got a little kid at home there who'll make it up for me', a comment which has been seen in hindsight as prophetic rather than as pathetic.

What matters is what did happen. 'Observer' of the Melbourne *Argus* was able to comment that 'there have been several remarkable test matches, but nothing to equal the everchanging sensationalism of the game which Australia has just won by three runs'. That outcome was as bruising for England's pride as Australia's batting had been for the England fielders' palms on that first morning, and as baffling as what onlookers made of the England selections. Allen Synge's *Sins of Omission*, a witty analysis of England selection to 1990, makes it difficult to call the resulting eleven a team. Annihilated by Trumper and Hill with the bat and Noble, Saunders and Trumble with the ball on a wearing Sheffield wicket in the Third Test three weeks before, England may have regrouped for Manchester but had scarcely recovered in that time.

First, the England batting. After leading the 1901 English averages, Charles Fry's scores of 0, 0, 1 and 4 in the first three tests of 1902 meant he was replaced by Lionel Palairet, an Old Reptonian and Oxford cricket blue. The selectors' apparent preference for an amateur like Palairet over the professionalism of Surrey's Tom Hayward, roughly his equal in age but far more experienced and in better form, would have gone unquestioned by most at this time. Fry's Sussex amateur teammate KS Ranjitsinjhi had topped the England averages in 1896 and 1900, but had been bowled for 13 and 0 in the first two tests. The selectors had at least replaced him at Sheffield with Surrey professional Bobby Abel, who remained in the side for Manchester following a century against the tourists for his county side, but then brought back Ranji to replace amateur all-rounder Gilbert Jessop. Despite taking 8-58 at Lord's for Gloucestershire against Middlesex, Jessop had scored only six (batting at number eight) at Birmingham, 12 (batting at number nine) and a rapid 55 (opening with Abel) in the tests.

The selectors themselves – Martin Bladen Hawke (Yorkshire and England), former England wicketkeeper Gregor McGregor (Middlesex) and Herbert William Bainbridge (Warwickshire) – were all moderate batsmen but capable fielders. This made an outstanding cover point like Jessop all the more surprised that 'no English team can ever have been picked with less regard for its fielding capabilities'. He noted that three fielders 'had not thrown a cricket ball fifty yards for quite a number of years'. Abel, Bill Lockwood and Fred Tate were the three who could not field in the deep, in a side which already included three slip specialists in Len Braund, Ranji, and the captain, Archie MacLaren.

Rain during the Tuesday and Wednesday prior to the match had meant repeated recalculations about the attack. One contemporary account plausibly suggested Surrey all-rounder and opening bowler Lockwood replace Yorkshire all-rounder George Hirst, who had played at Sheffield. A second account nominated middle-aged medium-paced off-spinner Tate to replace Hirst. Since Tate was picked as a wet wicket bowler, it could be argued the weather forced his selection in the final eleven.

On a third reading (Fry's) of the situation, the Lancastrian MacLaren preferred Sussex's Tate to Yorkshire's Hirst, who had taken over sixty wickets and was averaging thirty with the bat. Yet another interpretation suggests Hirst could have been replaced by Sydney Barnes, who had taken seven wickets in the previous test. Perhaps ignoring reports Barnes was not fully fit with a knee injury, Lionel Brown has argued Barnes was possibly omitted because MacLaren had picked him for Sheffield without consulting the selectors.

Synge suggests that these selectorial difficulties all arose because Lord Hawke, the Yorkshire captain, wouldn't release another bowler, Schofield Haigh, for England duty. Haigh claimed a wicket every 30.34 balls during the season to top the national averages with final figures of 158 wickets at an average of 12.55. Tate took more wickets (180) but at a higher cost (15.71) and strike-rate (39.44 balls per wicket) than Haigh. The politics of national selection, at a time when the county championship outranked test cricket in importance, were never more apparent.

The remainder of this bowling quintet were more obvious choices than Tate. Stanley Jackson had taken four wickets in five balls at

Headingley against the Australians earlier in their tour as he and Hirst dismissed the tourists for twenty-three. Wilfred Rhodes had topped the averages with over 250 wickets in each of the preceding two seasons, so his inclusion in any representative eleven of the day was automatic. Braund, a right-hand batsman and slow-medium leg-spinner, achieved the double each year from 1901 to 1903. Reputedly a big-occasion player, he made fourteen hundred runs and took 172 wickets at under twenty runs apiece in the 1902 season. Manchester would prove Bill Lockwood's penultimate test of twelve. The thirty-four-year-old, equipped at his peak with an unpickable slower ball and a formidable bodybreak, would take seventeen of his forty-three test wickets in his last two games.

With respect to the England bowling, 'Observer' thought the inclusion of Jackson in the English squad 'strengthens a very strong main attack', consisting of Rhodes, Tate, Braund and Lockwood. Later events and interpretation have conspired to make this seem a very contentious remark, particularly regarding Tate.

Despite the difficulties, the right captain could have made this into a formidable England combination. The eleventh Australian team to England already was a formidable combination and, by contrast, Australian selection seems to have been a formality. The touring party had been chosen by Clem Hill, Monty Noble and Hugh Trumble, and was thought to have virtually picked itself. Only the choice of Hanson Carter as second wicketkeeper had been considered a surprise, and Australia introduced no newcomers to the test scene in this entire series as part of a record eleven-test sequence between May 1902 and January 1904 in which the side consisted entirely of 'old hands'. It was already harder to get out of the Australian side than to get in to it.

Of the party of fourteen, there were five newcomers to England: Carter, Warwick Armstrong, Reg Duff, Bert Hopkins, and Jack Saunders. Noble, Victor Trumper, and Bill Howell had toured in 1899; the South Australian trio of captain Joe Darling, Hill, and Ernie

Jones were making their third trip. Hugh Trumble and Syd Gregory were on their fifth tour.

The Australian batting relied on Trumper, Duff, Hill, Darling, Gregory and Noble, although only Hill and Gregory had enjoyed productive seasons in 1901–02 against MacLaren's touring team. Duff had shaped well after his century on debut at Melbourne.

Noble and Trumble, who had carried the bowling attack in Australia, were again expected to be the spearheads in England. Left-hander Saunders had taken nine wickets on his Sydney debut. Jones and Howell had proved ineffective during the Australian summer, so it was feared their best days were behind them.

An outstanding omission from the Australian side was the Aboriginal fast bowler and off-spinner Jack Marsh. Ostensibly this was because his bowling action was supposed to be suspect, and the 1902 tour was held against the background of a recent throwing controversy that had ended the career of Lancashire and England fast bowler Arthur Mold. The irony was that the Australian attack already contained three suspect bowlers. Former Australian all-rounder Jack Worrall, then Victorian captain, had already warned Australian umpire Jim Phillips in England he 'could make a name for himself by calling Noble and Saunders', as he had already done with Jones. In fact, Marsh's absence from the tour was not surprising since sole New South Wales selector Noble refused to pick him for the state side. He was not selected for New South Wales until an Easter match against Queensland, by which time the Australian and England sides had departed for England together on the *Omrah*.

On the tour itself, Australia drew the first two tests and won the third despite a series of illnesses and injuries. The first match at Edgbaston saw England dominate, scoring 376 before Rhodes took 7-17 to dismiss Australia for its lowest-ever test score of 36. Australia, following on, was 2-46 when the match ended. When the Lord's Test ended, England had reached 2-102 in the only innings started.

Jack Saunders had suffered from tonsilitis at Lord's but, recovered, kept South Australian fast bowler Ernest Jones out of the following tests. Hopkins, playing as an all-rounder at Sheffield, retained his place for the rest of the series. Darling and Noble at Lord's had barely shaken off the flu, and at Sheffield Darling became the first Australian captain to achieve a pair, where his side won by 143 runs, thanks to Hill's almost even-time hundred and Noble's eleven wickets. Trumble had overcome injury to take 4-70 in that match after missing the first two tests, and thereafter kept out Howell.

Of the other players, Trumper had made 92 (in seventy-two minutes) at Bristol and 85 in even time at The Oval following the 62 in under an hour with which he had paved the way for the Third Test triumph.

DAY 1

Twenty thousand watched the first day, despite initial reports that the Old Trafford ground was saturated. The wicket was accordingly slow and easy at the start, and the run-ups were predicted to remain greasy for at least the first hour of play. MacLaren hoped to restrict Australia to around eighty runs before lunch but, recalling Trumper's efforts on a wearing wicket in the previous test, such optimism seems extreme.

After two overs from Rhodes and Jackson, Trumper was already seven and Duff two. Two fours off the first two balls of another Rhodes over, a drive behind point and then, next ball, through the leg side for another four, heralded the onslaught. With Rhodes in his next over twice being lofted over the sightscreen into the practice ground. Australia had put 42 on the board in twenty-five minutes with Duff outscoring Trumper 24 to 18.

Not yet twenty-four, Reg Duff scored test hundreds in his first and last innings in a nineteen-test Ashes career which ended before he reached the age of twenty-seven, and averaged thirty-five in his twenty-two tests. BJ Wakley, in his *Classic Centuries*, a compendium of Ashes hundreds to 1964, identifies him as 'a forcing batsman' best known as the 'junior partner' to Trumper, to whom he nevertheless 'could bear comparison'. Duff could 'on occasion bat even more brilliantly' than his state and test colleague, as in his last test, at The Oval in 1905, where he reached his century in 129 minutes. A willing and ideal foil for Trumper, and described by Fry as 'full of sunshine', his career declined precipitately, ending in 1907, and he died in 1911.

Tate replaced Jackson soon afterwards. His first four-over visit to the bowling crease yielded thirteen runs, a tally immediately doubled by Trumper off Tate's fifth over. After the fifty arrived in thirty minutes, Braund was brought on, with Duff still outstripping Trumper by two runs. Trumper romped to his fifty in two minutes over even time, the Australian score then being 92 without loss. MacLaren's plans were already defeated, whatever he did with his bowlers and wherever he placed his fielders.

The opening partnership reached three figures in three minutes under the hour. It remains the fastest century opening partnership recorded in all test history. MacLaren's comments and calculations at this point remain unreported. At 119, with Duff having reached his only half-century of the series, MacLaren brought back Jackson and Lockwood.

Braund dived, but failed to snare a slip catch from Duff who, however, was soon dismissed, edging to Lockwood while playing for a breakback, the delivery achieved by body-action rather than the use of fingers or wrist for the cutter. Trumper was 80 and the partnership had realised 135 runs in seventy-eight minutes. The stand surpassed Australia's first wicket record of 116, set by Jack Worrall and Charlie McLeod at The Oval in August 1899. The record remained intact until 1909, when Warren Bardsley and Syd Gregory mustered 180 together against a friendlier attack. Bardsley on that occasion became the first player to make twin hundreds in the one test. The Trumper–Duff total remained the ground record for Manchester until 1936.

MacLaren must have been looking forward to lunch, but still there was no respite. Instead, the Australian 150 having been posted in ninety minutes, Rhodes replaced Jackson. A pull and hook (Trumper's thirteenth and fourteenth boundaries) off Lockwood took Trumper to his hundred out of 168 in 108 minutes.

Despite the delayed start, Australia went to lunch at 1-173 with Trumper 103 and Hill 14. The score was more than twice the maximum Maclaren had been aiming to allow. Australia had already got the better of England and enjoyed the best of the wicket.

Considerable dispute about its behaviour ensued after the break, when things soon improved for England. 'Observer' remarked that 'a turf wicket is not like a quick-change artist. It cannot be a favouring angel one instant, and a demon of destruction the next. The slow change from good to bad is, indeed, fairly reflected in the progress of the game'. Nevertheless, Trumper managed but a solitary post-prandial single off Lockwood before he changed his mind as he tried to back-cut and Lilley caught him right-handed low off Rhodes' fifth ball after lunch.

Trumper made his 104 in five minutes short of two hours, in a total of 175. It took his tour tally to 1423 runs, and was the second of his six hundreds against England. It was also Australia's twenty-ninth test hundred in its sixty-fifth Ashes test.

Rhodes continued the improvement. The umpires sent Noble on his way for two after he had disputed a caught-and-bowled decision, claiming it was a bump ball. When Gregory went cutting, the Yorkshire left-hander had claimed three wickets for six runs in a four-over spell. Contemporary comments suggest that the wicket only thereafter began to dry out and become more difficult!

Australian captain Darling entered at 4-183 to mount a recovery for his side. At 212, when Tate replaced Lockwood, he had reached 11. Hill was then 34. The two South Australians proceeded to add 73 in forty-five minutes as the sun started to affect the surface even more.

At 238 Jackson replaced Rhodes, by which time Hill was one

short of reaching his fifty in one hundred minutes, and Darling was 22. The latter twice hit Rhodes out of the ground for six toward the Warwick Road end, once off the fifth ball of his eighteenth over and again in his twenty-first over, these being the first sixes ever scored in England. Darling had hit the first six in Australia, to reach his hundred at Adelaide in January 1898. This day he interspersed his sixes with three balls dispatched for four on the full pitch out of the playing arena itself, shots which would have counted as six under later rules.

MacLaren brought Lockwood back in place of Tate. Hill, having achieved a statistical milestone in overhauling Maclaren's record test aggregate, left for 65 to a gentle catch to mid-off. His scoring shots included five boundaries and his departure signalled the start of an England fightback. Bert Hopkins was caught in his first over, fending a short one to the on-side, where leg-side fielding specialist Palairet ran in from short-leg.

The Australian situation, with six wickets lost for 256, was now serious. 'Observer' imagined the tourists deciding in their dressing room that a typically steady not out Armstrong innings might help his average rather more than his side in such circumstances, and that therefore he, like Darling, should also aim to hit Rhodes out of Old Trafford. Lockwood yorked Armstrong for five before he could succeed in this aim and Darling, after ninety-five minutes (two sixes, five fours) at the crease, miscued Rhodes to MacLaren at mid-off. From twenty-three overs, Rhodes had claimed 4-99.

Perhaps the Australian dressing room now decided it was misdirected ambition for Jack Kelly, Hugh Trumble and Jack Saunders to waste time in trying to get runs, when they might be better employed trying to get wickets. Whatever was thought or said, Trumble was soon enough caught low at slip and Saunders bowled off stump by Lockwood, whose final eight-over spell included five wickets for eight runs. Kelly remained not out.

The Australian innings ended for 299. It had lasted fifteen

minutes over four hours. England accordingly had seventy-five minutes to play that first night. The situation allowed contemporary reporters to wax eloquent. 'Sunshine after rain sounds poetical enough, but there is no poetry in it for the batsmen who have to wait their chance of an innings,' said 'Observer'.

Trumble and Saunders, right-hand medium-paced off-spin and left-hand medium-paced spin respectively, were a classic combination on rain-affected wickets, and they opened the attack to Palairet and Abel. Contemporary accounts reckoned Saunders the more difficult. Jack Fingleton, over fifty years later, told a delightful anecdote where a laughing Trumper, beaten twice by Saunders in his opening over on a sticky wicket at Sydney, reckoned 'It's you or me for it, Jack' and proceeded to ensure it was the bowler who suffered.

The left-hander claimed Abel, caught at first slip off a top-edge in his fourth over, and Palairet was caught by backward point off the same bowler a run later. The England card read 2-13. When MacLaren was bowled through the gap, playing forward to Trumble, and Ranji was adjudged leg before wicket playing back to the tall off-spinner, each bowler had two wickets and the score had slumped to 4-30 after thirty-five minutes.

An England recovery of sorts began when Lancastrian professional John Tyldesley, claimed by many contemporaries as the best bad-wicket batsman in England, was joined by Jackson the Yorkshire amateur at ten to six. The top of the England order had played what would later be derided as 'festival cricket' and, despite the perilous score, did not cease to do so. Fifteen minutes and fourteen runs later, Tyldesley cut high over gully to be caught at third man.

The fall of the fifth wicket at five past six brought in Braund to join Jackson, then seven. By close of play at 6.30, Jackson had reached 16 and Braund 13, which indicates they did not 'play for stumps'. Even-time scoring in the final twenty-five minutes saw England leave the field at 5-70, 229 in arrears.

||| DAY 2

Friday dawned fine following a clear night, with prospects of the pitch proving firmer on resumption than it had been through the first day's play. Trumble and Noble opened the bowling to Jackson and Braund, who took fourteen runs from the first three overs of the day. With the score at 5-84, Jackson was already 27, Braund 16. At 86, Darling replaced Noble with Saunders and, shortly after, Trumble went round the wicket, but the England hundred accrued without further loss after thirty-five minutes. England thus added thirty in just under even time. How serious can they have thought the situation was? Their approach was in marked contrast to safety-first tactics adopted in later times.

At 114, the situation could have become considerably more serious had Saunders not dropped Jackson, then 41, from a sharp caught and bowled. In the first hour, the sixth-wicket pair added 54 runs. Five minutes later, Jackson completed his fifty in 105 minutes. Ever alert to the tactical niceties of the situation, Darling made a number of quick bowling changes: medium-pace Noble for medium-pace Trumper, leg-spinner Armstrong for left-armer Saunders.

Appreciating the latter move, Braund took sixteen off an Armstrong over, through a seven-man leg-side field, to reach his fifty. At 58, however, and five minutes shy of lunch, he swiped at Noble's outcurve, and pulled the ball onto his stumps. Jackson and Braund had added 141 in fifteen minutes short of three hours, a historic effort not surpassed by England at Manchester until 1934.

England lunched more comfortably at 6-186, with Jackson 78 and Dick Lilley yet to score. Wicketkeeper Lilley soon after played forward to Noble and lost his leg stump. He was replaced by Lockwood. Noble continued to extract something from the wicket, and almost extracted Jackson when the Yorkshireman was eight runs short of his century. Jackson cut Noble to Duff at short third man, but Duff misfielded – or pretended to – and the pair found themselves stranded mid-wicket. Like a good lad, lower order and lower class, Lockwood sacrificed himself to a round of applause: 8-214.

Jackson reached the third of his five test hundreds – all against Australia in England – with a single at five past three, before Rhodes was caught and bowled by a Trumble slower ball. Jackson's century took 225 minutes. It was England's thirtieth test century against Australia. Jackson, later Sir Stanley, marched on until he was caught for 128 by the running Duff at deep mid-wicket, shortly after being dropped off Noble.

England's reply of 262 meant a draw was the great probability given the game lasted only three days. The chances were that Darling would close his innings late on Saturday on the remote possibility of an English collapse. Betting men among the crowd of 25,000, taking the chance of one side winning as against the draw, would have asked for odds of ten to one at least.

Australia went in again at 4.15, enjoying a thirty-seven-run lead. Leg-spinner Braund opened with a maiden to Trumper, an achievement hard to conceive today after his first innings effort. From the Warwick Road end, Lockwood bowled to three slips, a gully, and short forward and backward legs. Duff took a single. Trumper, beaten first ball, then pulled his second from Lockwood for four through mid-wicket. He miscued an out-swinger next ball along the ground to Braund, fielding at second slip. Duff took two runs through mid-wicket in the next, Braund over. From the next Lockwood over, Trumper miscut the fourth ball to second slip. Braund parried it, then caught the rebound. The great opener was gone, with only seven runs on the board, and was replaced by Hill.

Duff played back to Lockwood's off-cutter, which he dragged onto his stumps from a thick inside edge. The score was 2-9 when Darling promoted himself two places in the order – but the two South Australian left-handers were not to repeat their first innings salvo. Hill was bowled off stump by Lockwood through the gap so that Australia were 3-10, forty-seven ahead. The right-hander Gregory then came in at his normal position of number five.

'Whoop!' The Kangaroo Rejoices.

(*Melbourne* Punch)

Braund bowled on, amid the wreckage being wrought from the Warwick Road end. At 3-16, with left-hander Darling on strike, he proposed to move his Somerset teammate Palairet to deep square-leg; instead, Tate was moved there by MacLaren for the last ball of the over, which Darling duly lofted in Tate's direction. Tate, needless to say, got the fingers of his left hand to it but could not complete the catch.

For most commentators, this was the turning-point of the match, but quite what events created the situation remains unclear. According to Harry Altham, whose first edition of *A History of Cricket* was published in 1926, 'at [Braund's] special request, Palairet, who was fielding deep on the leg side, was brought up to short-leg, his normal place in Somerset matches, and Tate was dropped back in his stead'. For Gerald Brodribb, writing fifty years after Altham, Palairet, who 'usually fielded deep at square-leg for Braund . . . was about to move across the wicket' but Tate was sent from slips and could not cope with the catch as the ball curved in the air on him. John Marshall's history, *Old Trafford*, even provides a hypothetical MacLaren–Braund conversation to the effect that Old Harrovians don't ask Old Reptonians to cross the field for one delivery at the suggestion of a professional.

Whatever the events, the outcome was quite decisive: Darling hit Braund out of the ground and into the station in his next over and went on to play a vital captain's innings for Australia.

At 64, Tate got Gregory lbw with his off-cutter, after the only two Australians to reach double figures in this innings had added 54 in the hour. Ten runs later, Palairet ran backwards at long-on to catch Darling from a low raking drive off Rhodes. By then, Tate's efforts were all a bit late, and Australia overnight were 8-85, Trumble four and Kelly one, giving their side a lead of 122 with the third day to play.

DAY 3

Five hours' rain on the third morning had delayed play till noon and it took but fifteen minutes further to terminate the Australian innings. This was time enough to witness a display of petulance by Trumble – the second time in the match when an Australian had shown dissent – against umpire Moss, and for Saunders to be caught at long-on. Trumble obviously wanted to stay and bat, Saunders to go and bowl. Australia's second innings ended fourteen short of the hundred, a lead of 123.

Palairet came in again at 12.40, this time accompanied by England captain MacLaren instead of Abel. Four byes in Noble's second over opened the scoring before Saunders replaced Noble. Gregory nearly ran out MacLaren in one over, and in the next, from Saunders, dived but just missed Palairet. Despite such minor alarms, England went to lunch with 36 on the board, MacLaren and Palairet level on 16 runs apiece in fifty minutes. MacLaren must have thought England had the game in its keeping, whatever the state of the wicket. Just eighty-eight runs to get with all wickets intact.

Eight runs off the first two overs following the break was a sign of renewed aggression, but also saw Palairet's removal by Saunders. The score was 1-44, and England's target was eighty with two Lancastrians, MacLaren and Tyldesley, at the wickets.The pair, amateur and professional county colleagues, continued aggressively, Tyldesley adding sixteen in fourteen minutes while MacLaren added eight before the former was caught at slip. Only fifty-six runs were needed, with eight wickets in hand.

Ranji came in at 2-68, MacLaren off-drove Trumble for four to reach 35 and a record test aggregate of 1531 runs against Australia. Statistical thoughts were probably far from MacLaren's mind, and farther still as he lifted Trumble's next ball – slower, loftier, delivered from round the wicket – toward the Australian deep mid-on, who did his duty.

Abel joined Ranji at 3-72, and Saunders nearly caught him at mid-on. After a boundary from Abel, rain stopped play for fifteen minutes. Abel then hit two fours off Trumble, in the process rather riskily beating Hill at mid-on with one that went into the crowd. In the light of later events and Abel's natural cautious game, this seems poor tactics.

Given Ranji's natural game, his timorous batting seemed equally inept. Trumble's tactics perhaps explain it. He had placed extra men on the leg side to cramp Ranji. The field moved as the bowler brought his arm over, and the batsman would have been unsure where each fielder was. Trumble had the uncertain Ranji leg before to his third appeal in an over, and England were 4-92. When Abel was bowled through the gap five runs later, half the side were gone and thirty-two runs were still to be obtained.

A Braund snick between keeper and slip off Saunders for three brought up the England hundred, before Jackson, driving a welcome full toss from Saunders, saw Gregory, after many attempts, finally make his only catch for the match, diving to his right at cover point: 6-107.

None of the match accounts mentions tea but, refreshed or not, Trumble beat Braund with a straight ball that went between bat and pad. It missed the stumps but, the batsman having lifted his toe, Kelly stumped him. Seven for 109 became 8-109 as Lockwood was dismissed third ball by Trumble. Rain twice drove the players off, before Rhodes raised the score and England's hopes with a boundary off Saunders over the mid-on rope.

Lilley nearly ran himself out scoring a single, then made a two before he hit the second ball of Trumble's twenty-fifth over to leg, over the umpire's head. The shot, described as a 'hard skimming pull', looked likely to clear Clem Hill too. He sprinted more than a pitch length at deep backward square-leg. The great South Australian's spectacular diving catch reduced England to 9-116.

There may well have been a breathless hush at Old Trafford that night, eight to make and a match to win, an indifferent pitch and poor light, plenty of time to play and last pair in, to paraphrase a famous poem – but rain drove players off again, this time for forty-five minutes.

At the resumption, Trumble delivered the last three balls of his incomplete over to Rhodes. From the other end, Saunders bowled his first ball to Tate. He played it through Duff's legs, the ball beating Armstrong, running from slip, to the boundary and saving the field all sorts of instantaneous tactical decisions about conceding runs to keep the weaker player at the striker's wicket.

Tate played an effective forward defensive stroke to the second Saunders delivery, and survived the third. The fourth ball bowled him middle and leg. It was a shooter, according to some accounts. According to others, it was Saunders' quicker ball, delivered with a suspect arm action, an allegation which adds a whole new touch to the drama.

Tate is said to have been booed from the ground, and rain fell shortly thereafter. Had it fallen sooner, Tate's reputation, and the match, might have been retrieved.

Brodribb, as one might expect of the biographer of Fred Tate's son Maurice, sagely observed that 'the only difference between Tate's sad moments at Manchester in July 1902 and that of the humblest player on every day of the season is that Tate's misfortunes have been recorded and retold over and over again, while that of others has soon faded into merciful oblivion'. This merciful judgement deserves emphasis.

On the 'little kid at home' story told at the start of the chapter, Brodribb shows fine historical detachment in counterpointing the observation that the seven-year-old Maurice 'had shown no aptitude whatever for cricket' to that point, and refrains from suggesting it was this event which prompted his advance.

In the event, Fred Tate returned to Sussex, and partly consoled himself with figures of 8-145 in a Middlesex total of 401 at Eastbourne, further restoring his self-image by top-scoring with 22 not out against the Australians at Brighton, exactly a week after his

Manchester demise. He was obviously not the duffer he is so often portrayed to be. Brodribb cites Fry, in his *Book of Cricket*, as characterising Tate as a 'useful bat on fast wickets, neat catch at slip, clever extra cover, cannot throw', all sound observations borne out in the Manchester Test of 1902.

Neville Cardus, in typical fashion, wrote that Tate 'was a capital bowler, but as soon as he was seen in the company of the great, the question went out: "What is he doing in this galley?" Tate had not the stern fibre of character that can survive in an air of high tragedy'. Cardus thought that Tate's 'bent was for pastoral comedy down at Horsham' in his native Sussex, where he could play the rustic clown without criticism.

The point about Tate's place in the scheme of things appears well made. This was a player who appeared in over three hundred matches, coached Western Province in 1898–99 and public schoolboys at Oundle in 1907, and graduated to coach the Derbyshire County Club between 1921 and 1925. He died in 1943. Unlike most of the other players with whom he took the field during those fateful days of the Golden Age at Old Trafford, Fred Tate was asked to do more than might reasonably have been expected of him.

Perhaps some final words from 'Observer' are most appropriate. In assessing that Saturday's play, he remarked for the benefit of *Argus* readers that the inclusion of Jackson and Rhodes, who had not toured Australia, meant even greater satisfaction in winning by what he described as 'even so narrow a margin as three runs'. The outcome meant, in his view, that England's long-held advantage was steadily diminishing to such an extent that it had almost reached the disappearing point. He believed 'another such victory will do more to bring England's best eleven out to Australia next trip than anything else'. By the same token, such victories also helped ensure the omission from tests of the Fred Tates of the world.

•ADELAIDE 1929•

THE BALANCE OF THE YEARS

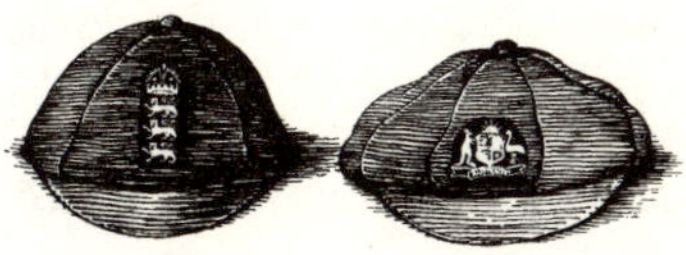

When this match ends, Australia has won forty-seven test matches to England's forty-six, so the first fifty years of competition are decidedly even. The game can be read in terms of the merits of youth versus the experience of the participants. Of the young, the genius of Archie Jackson is on show, for the first time at test level, beside the continuing excellence of Walter Hammond, and the emergence of Don Bradman. Of the seasoned players, Jack White and Clarrie Grimmett turn in marathon performances. Key players in the Bodyline Test of four years later – Bradman, Douglas Jardine, and Harold Larwood – are also present, but who could predict the mammoth proportions of Bradman's appetite for runs, and the measures which would be taken to control him? In this match the notion of the tragic hero is extended through Jackson, and we see English gentlemen cricketers in contrasting roles. Jardine shows his contempt for the crowd by wearing his Harlequin cap, while Somerset left-hand spinner 'Farmer' White appears in the unaccustomed role – for a gentleman – of 'worker'.

AUSTRALIA v ENGLAND 1929 (4th Test)

Played at Adelaide Oval on 1, 2, 4, 5, 6, 7, 8 February.
Toss: England. Result: ENGLAND won by 12 runs.

ENGLAND

JB Hobbs	c Ryder b Hendry	74	c Oldfield b Hendry	1
H Sutcliffe	st Oldfield b Grimmett	64	c Oldfield b a'Beckett	17
WR Hammond	not out	119	c and b Ryder	177
DR Jardine	lbw b Grimmett	1	c Woodfull b Oxenham	98
EH Hendren	b Blackie	13	c Bradman b Blackie	11
APF Chapman*	c a'Beckett b Ryder	39	c Woodfull b Blackie	0
G Duckworth†	c Ryder b Grimmett	5	(11) lbw b Oxenham	1
H Larwood	b Hendry	3	(7) lbw b Oxenham	5
G Geary	run out	3	(8) c and b Grimmett	6
MW Tate	b Grimmett	2	(9) lbw b Oxenham	47
JC White	c Ryder b Grimmett	0	(10) not out	4
Extras	(B 3, LB 7, W 1)	11	(B 6, LB 10)	16
Total		**334**		**383**

AUSTRALIA

WM Woodfull	c Duckworth b Tate	1	c Geary b White	30
A Jackson	lbw b White	164	c Duckworth b Geary	36
HSTL Hendry	c Duckworth b Larwood	2	c Tate b White	5
AF Kippax	b White	3	c Hendren b White	51
J Ryder*	lbw b White	63	c and b White	87
DG Bradman	c Larwood b Tate	40	run out	58
EL a'Beckett	hit wkt b White	36	c Hammond b White	21
RK Oxenham	c Chapman b White	15	c Chapman b White	12
WAS Oldfield†	b Tate	32	not out	15
CV Grimmett	b Tate	4	c Tate b White	9
DD Blackie	not out	3	c Larwood b White	0
Extras	(LB 5, W 1)	6	(B 9, LB 3)	12
Total		**369**		**336**

AUSTRALIA	**O**	**M**	**R**	**W**	**O**	**M**	**R**	**W**
a'Beckett	31	8	44	0	27	9	41	1
Hendry	31	14	49	2	28	11	56	1
Grimmett	52.1	12	102	5	52	15	117	1
Oxenham	35	14	51	0	47.4	21	67	4
Blackie	29	6	57	1	39	11	70	2
Ryder	5	1	20	1	5	1	13	1
Kippax					2	0	3	0
ENGLAND								
Larwood	37	6	92	1	20	4	60	0
Tate	42	10	77	4	37	9	75	0
White	60	16	130	5	64.5	21	126	8
Geary	12	3	32	0	16	2	42	1
Hammond	9	1	32	0	14	3	21	0

FALL OF WICKETS

	E	A	E	A
Wkt	**1st**	**1st**	**2nd**	**2nd**
1st	143	1	1	65
2nd	143	6	21	71
3rd	149	19	283	74
4th	179	145	296	211
5th	246	227	297	224
6th	263	287	302	258
7th	270	323	327	308
8th	308	336	337	320
9th	312	365	381	336
10th	334	369	383	336

Umpires: D Elder and GA Hele.

This match featured three outstanding individual performances in an absorbing contest. Walter Hammond, on his first tour of Australia, made two centuries as part of his record breaking summer of 905 test runs at 113.2. Somerset captain, Jack 'Farmer' White, on his only Australian tour at the age of thirty-seven, gathered thirteen wickets from his 124.5 overs of left-arm spin. In the view of former Australian captain Monty Noble, White was 'the only man who truly and actually won the Ashes'.

The third great performance was by Archie Jackson. This was the one and only time the majesty of Jackson's batting was given free rein in a test match. Hammond's glorious play extended in tests from 1927 to 1947, and his were just two among a plethora of epic innings, although his splendour in its turn was overshadowed by the sheer abundance of Bradman runs.

Archie Jackson must have been one of the most graceful batsmen in cricket history. According to Johnny Moyes, he was second in beauty and artistry only to Victor Trumper, and ahead of his contemporaries. Sir Donald Bradman, in his foreword for the 1981 book *Bradman's First Tour*, described Jackson as 'this gloriously talented youngster' and recalled, 'I batted with Jackson on that memorable occasion and can vouch for the worthiness of the plaudits showered upon him.'

Jackson's death at twenty-three from tuberculosis inspired Moyes to write that the young Scots-born batsman 'flashed across the sky with all the brilliance of a meteor but before we had fully glimpsed the radiance of his batting he had gone'.

As David Frith has recorded in his biography, *Archie Jackson: the Keats of Cricket*, Jackson was born in 1909 near Glasgow to a Scot who had lived as a child in Australia during the 1880s. He grew up within a long hit of Birchgrove Park, home of Balmain District Cricket Club, for whom he first demonstrated his batting brilliance at fifteen. Mentored initially by his club captain, the immortal Arthur Mailey, no less a person that Herbert Vere Evatt, the MLA for Balmain, also took an interest in the youngster. Evatt – who later became Chief Justice of New South Wales, a High Court judge, leader of the Australian Labor Party, and President of the United Nations Assembly – was an avid cricket-lover, and paid Jackson's fares to district matches and his membership and match fees. At fifteen Jackson was working for NSW batsman Alan Kippax, with whom he was often later compared, and playing for Balmain against test veteran bowlers Jack Gregory and Charles Kelleway. At seventeen he made his debut for New South Wales. His first season of 1926–27 brought him 464 runs at 58.00. Jackson was still only nineteen when the selectors picked him for the Adelaide Test of 1928–29, having played less than forty first-class innings and already made six of his final tally of eleven first-class centuries.

His selection was a belated recognition of an error in previous

Australian thinking, which valued mature experience too highly and youthful ability too little. Five of Warwick Armstrong's 1921 eleven took the field at Brisbane for the opening match of the 1928–29 series but thereafter, with Gregory and Kelleway eliminating themselves permanently through injury, only Ryder and Oldfield survived the series, Hendry having been discarded *en route*. A number of young bloods made the side in their stead. Bradman's place became permanent following the Third Test after some Second Test experience as drink-waiter and substitute field.

England and Australia had similar commitments to mature expertise around this time. All but two of the teams for the opening test of the previous (1926) series had been aged at least thirty, and during that series England's median age hovered around thirty-six. In the first test of the 1928–29 series, the median age of the Australians was only one year less.

The seventeen-strong English touring party included four batsmen in their twenties: the captain, Percy Chapman, and Douglas Jardine, both amateurs, and Hammond and Morris Leyland, professionals. Five other batting tourists were older professionals: Herbert Sutcliffe in his mid-thirties, 'Patsy' Hendren thirty-nine, Jack Hobbs, Phil Mead and Ernest Tyldesley in their forties. Les Ames and George Duckworth, the wicketkeepers, were twenty-three and twenty-eight respectively. Of the bowlers, Larwood was twenty-four, but the other quicker bowlers, Maurice Tate and George Geary, were in their thirties, with Hammond in support. The slow attack, discounting forty-year-old 'Tich' Freeman as ineffective in Australia despite taking 304 wickets in the preceding English season, consisted of the thirty-seven-year-old Somerset left-hander White.

The Adelaide Test, unusually, was the fourth rather than the third match of the series. It was preceded by Brisbane's first ever test match at the Exhibition Ground, and by tests in Sydney and Melbourne.

Percy Chapman and his English team had wasted little time in asserting their authority in Brisbane, and their 675-run win weighed heavily on Australian minds through the summer. The match was also remarkable for the inauspicious debut of Don Bradman, who made 18 (lbw Tate) and one (c Chapman b White) out of Australia's innings of 122 and 66, and for Tate's unfortunate remark to White: 'What's the idea of getting my rabbit?' It was a remark Bradman would later make him rue.

For the First Test, the Australian selectors – South Australia's Dr Charles Dolling, Victorian Ernest Bean, New South Welshman Warren Bardsley, and Queenslander John Silvester Hutcheon – revealed their preference for experience when they picked the forty-five-year-old Victorian left-arm orthodox spinner Bert Ironmonger to partner leg-spinner Clarrie Grimmett, then a mere thirty-seven. For the Second Test, at Sydney, they selected off-spinner Don Blackie, Ironmonger's forty-six-year-old state and St Kilda colleague. At this distance in time, it's customary to criticise these decisions, but Blackie and Ironmonger were still a class act. Ironmonger had originally come to notice as early as 1905 when he was described by the Ipswich newspaper, the *Queensland Times,* as the 'Wilfred Rhodes of the Albert Club', but his debut for Queensland was delayed until 1909–10. Playing for Victoria from 1913–14, and for Australia on a New Zealand tour in 1920–21, he had taken 199 wickets at 21.52. Although Blackie had not been picked for his state until the age of forty-two years and 294 days in 1924–25, in four complete seasons he had taken 105 wickets at 26.41. There was not much joy for them at the Sydney bowling creases, however, as England's massive score of 636 set it up for an eight wicket Second Test win.

Australia reduced the margin of defeat at Melbourne, where four home batsmen scored centuries against two by the tourists. These included Bradman's 112, his first test century, in the second innings, but not even the late loss of four wickets for ten runs could avert the victory which gave England the series.

Australia's changes for the Adelaide Test included the introduction of young Archie Jackson to replace a South Australian stalwart.

Vic Richardson exchanged his bat for a pen as a reporter for the Adelaide *Register*, and for a microphone as a commentator with local radio station 5CL. Richardson had not made many runs – 35 in four innings – but it was felt to be a surprise that he was omitted after his wonderful fielding in previous matches. At thirty-four, he was reckoned to save a run for every year of his age during each innings in the field. Richardson was also unfortunate in that he had been forced to open the innings with Bill Woodfull due to Bill Ponsford's absence.

Another player had been tried as an opener since the Melbourne Test. Bradman had gone in first at Adelaide for New South Wales but had failed twice against Tim Wall. The Don scored five and two, one of the only two matches in which he was dismissed for less than double figures in both innings. NSW opener Jackson made 162 and 90 in his two innings to secure his spot.

Before the match began, Adelaide Oval curator Albert Wright predicted that the wicket would be easy-paced to begin but, with the drying effects of sun and wind, would become faster as the game proceeded.

Motorists who travelled to the ground were advised that, unlike in Melbourne, there would be no charge for admission to parking areas. Ground authorities had provided extra seating, with the expectation that 45,000 to 50,000 people would be able to view the match in comfort. There were early indications that the attendance would be excellent. Hundreds of motorists had arrived from the country, and reports showed that accommodation at Adelaide's hotels and boarding houses was at a premium.

Cricket permeated the atmosphere of the city. The Humphrey Bishop Musical Comedy Company's production at the Garden Theatre of 'The Sixth Test Match' proved popular, with actor 'Scratcher' Ross playing the part of the Australian captain, Jack Ryder. He defended his huge wicket against the visitors with an outsize bat and, thanks to the umpire, Australia won the Ashes. This sally may not have sat well with umpires David Elder and George Hele, but it reflected touring teams' perennial perception that umpires remain the home side's most effective allies. English batsman Patsy Hendren received mention in several numbers and it was reported that a special birthday presentation would be made to him on the Monday night, when both teams would be present.

The idea of opposing teams socialising together after the third day of a test contrasts with the bitter atmosphere of the Bodyline Test at Adelaide four years later. In order to keep the spirit between the team's harmonious, an English sweets manufacturer, John Mackintosh and Sons Limited, had even sent gifts to the cricketers and officials of each team before the match with the following message:

> Convey to members of English and Australian Elevens our best wishes for a pleasant and closely-fought match, and give each a small parcel of our toffee as a reminder that we are taking a keen interest in the game.

They wore hats in those days.

DAY 1

When English captain Percy Chapman called correctly, both countries had been favoured by the spin fifty-nine times. Hobbs and Sutcliffe opened the batting for England, and the game began sensationally when Hobbs missed medium-pacer Ted a'Beckett's opening delivery from the river end as it flew over the head of wicketkeeper Bert Oldfield for three byes. Runs then came easily against the friendly attack, with Hunter 'Stork' Hendry bowling from the Cathedral end.

Apart from leg-spinner Grimmett, introduced after twenty minutes, there was no sting in the Australian bowling. Fifty runs came up just after the first hour, and ten minutes later Hobbs scored his first boundary by off-driving Grimmett. Both batsmen played correctly against Australian skipper Jack Ryder's frequent changes, so that at lunch, after a ninety-minute opening session, the score was 0-77 with Hobbs on 41 and Sutcliffe 31.

Before an afternoon crowd of 21,380, the pair continued to show perfect understanding, each giving a masterly display of patient, restrained batting, and 'delaying' their strokes. By this means, they were able to play a ball slowly from the bat and pick up a number of quick singles although, untypically, on three occasions they went close to running each other out.

The crowd cheered Hobbs when he reached his fifty with the score at 94, but gasped when he was missed off a return catch to Blackie shortly afterwards. Sutcliffe reached a chanceless half-century after nearly two-and-a-half hours and it seemed the openers would never be separated. Half an hour before tea, however, with the score on 143, Hobbs tried to cut Hendry and was caught by Ryder low down to his left at slip. Without addition to the score, Sutcliffe went down the wicket to Grimmett and was stumped by Oldfield. After just six more runs, Jardine fell lbw attempting to glide Grimmett to the leg side off the last ball before tea. Hammond was on five at the interval.

The question of dissent was raised by Jardine's dismissal. Jardine, in a manner supposedly untypical of an English amateur, appeared loath to leave the wicket. Only during the adjournment, when he asked umpire Elder, did he learn how he had been given out. The Englishmen were apparently surprised by the decision since, as Christopher Douglas records in his biography, *Douglas Jardine: Spartan Cricketer*, 'Jardine was given out lbw to a ball he was clearly heard to play'.

Honours were even during the final session, during which Australia collected two wickets and England ninety-three runs.

Hammond and Hendren ran brilliantly between the wickets before Hendren fell, reaching forward to a medium-paced off-spinner from Blackie, for 13 at 4-179. Former England player Percy Fender asked incredulously how anyone could have beaten the bat on such a wicket. Hammond, meanwhile, was showing excellent judgement in using his feet to counteract Grimmett's menace. His eleventh run raised his thousand for the tour, and he had reached 21 when Chapman entered.

Captain Chapman played attractively, though with more restraint than usual. After nearly chopping a ball from Hendry onto his stumps, he began to hit more freely, making beautiful off-side shots until Ryder brought himself on two overs before stumps and induced him to snick a wide ball low to second slip from an attempted off-drive. Chapman had made 39 and the score was 5-246. George Duckworth, the Lancashire wicketkeeper, went in as nightwatchman, and he and Hammond played out time without addition to the score. Hammond was on 47. The *Yorkshire Post* headlined its report 'England's Mixed Fortunes', concluding that on balance it had not been 'a good day'.

||| DAY 2

On the Saturday, Hammond took twenty-one minutes to reach 50 and Duckworth dawdled for half an hour. The English wicketkeeper was intent on running only for Hammond's singles at the end of each over, but Grimmett trapped him into giving a catch at forward short-leg after seventeen runs had been added.

Grimmett sent down eleven overs for seven runs in his first spell of the day. The little leg-spinner packed his leg side on the drive and bowled on and outside the leg stump to Hammond with the object of giving the batsman a single except at the end of an over. Relying mainly on his back-foot forcing shot for runs, with the leg-glance his other scoring avenue, Hammond made little attempt to force the pace, although he dominated the batting by making seventy-two of the last eighty-eight runs. Writing in the 1966 *Wisden*, Neville Cardus noted that on the field Hammond was 'seldom disturbed from his balance of skill and poise' and, finding his only form of self-expression in his artistry, did not gladly suffer boredom. At lunch, he was 85.

Larwood and Tate did not last long: Tate was missed twice off Grimmett before being bowled around his legs. Geary and White then hung around, in the former's case for forty-two minutes for three until run out. White arrived when Hammond was on 97 and helped the score reach 334, by dint of the centurion taking a single off the last ball of seven successive overs. The number eleven was no mean batsman, actually achieving the double in the next two English seasons, but Grimmett's first ball to him was enough to claim his wicket.

Hammond carried his bat for a serene 119 in 263 minutes, including nine fours. He later described this innings as one of the hardest of his career. He fought a keen duel with Grimmett but strangely, given the bowler's line and the absence of boundary fielders at or behind square-leg, never attempted to sweep him. Grimmett was rewarded for his clever flight and fully deserved his five wickets.

Jackson opened for Australia with Bill Woodfull, the sturdy Melbourne schoolteacher sometimes known as 'The Rock' but more often as 'The Unbowlable', an especially appropriate title at this time, when he had not been bowled in over two years of first-class cricket. Jackson's slender, frail appearance seemed to pose no threat to the fierce England attack as he stood at the crease, his hands high on the bat handle, but it was Woodfull who departed first. Duckworth caught him brilliantly down the leg side off Tate's fourth ball with only a run on the board, the stroke being more of a glance than a nick.

Hendry then gave Duckworth his second catch off Larwood to make the score 2-6, and Kippax was yorked by White. Chapman had brought on the spinner merely to allow Tate and Larwood to change ends, but the dismissal left Australia 3-19. To such accidents is 'tactical acumen' attributed. Jackson, meanwhile, was imperturbable in the crisis. He opened his account with three off his body from a short-pitched ball from Larwood, and then twice turned Tate neatly to the square-leg fence, the first time playing the shot so typically late that Tate had appealed for lbw before realising umpire George Hele had signalled the boundary. He had reached 13 when captain Jack Ryder came in.

The two batsmen set about rebuilding the innings. Jackson timed the ball splendidly, with freedom and elegance in all his movements, and displayed excellent placement. Ryder, even though Tate had all but bowled him three times in as many overs, showed aggression, abetted by Chapman's failure to use his great quick bowler Larwood against him for the first hour of his innings. Though Ryder hit hard, he found it difficult at first to penetrate the field. Neither batsmen took risks, but attacked the loose balls to post 50 in seventy-six minutes and 100 in 125 minutes, raising their own century partnership in just over even time. Ryder was willing to go down the wicket to break up left-arm spinner White's length and later repeatedly drove him through the off and pulled him to leg. Chapman changed his field, but Geary's leg strain, and Hammond's exhaustion from his long innings, forced him to rely mostly upon Larwood, Tate, and White at the bowling crease.

Jackson brought up his half-century with a leg glance off Geary at twenty minutes past five. Often said to be reminiscent of Alan Kippax, who was more than twelve years his senior, Jackson was freer and more forceful in his play than English observers had witnessed in the older man. At the close he had moved along to 70, with only one false stroke, a glide to leg off Larwood which took the leading edge but fell short of Hobbs at cover. Jackson was understandably exhausted when he got to the Australian dressing room. With Ryder contributing 54, an enthralled crowd of 37,700 had watched Australia recover to 3-131.

||| DAY 3

The weekend's excitement burst into full bloom on Monday. It was Jackson's day. The headlines screamed 'Young Sydney Colt, Australian Hero of the Test Series'; 'Wild Cheering Greets Century by Youthful Batsman', 'A Champion Class Batsman'. The journalists predicted a long career for him as Australian opening batsman, while Charles Macartney observed that Jackson and Bradman (nineteen and twenty respectively) were two of the finest young batsmen to have appeared in test cricket together. Bradman was playing in only his fifteenth first-class match; Jackson had appeared for New South Wales a season earlier than Bradman, touring New Zealand at the end of the 1927–28 season.

On the third day, 23,800 spectators had the opportunity to judge for themselves. When Ryder misread White and departed early for 63 at 4-145, Jackson was 75 and the partnership with his captain had yielded 126 in two hours and twenty-nine minutes. The youngsters were then associated in an eighty-two-run partnership, Larwood during this time bowling to what David Frith describes – in italics, but without further comment – as 'a concentrated leg-side field of four between fine and square-leg'. Bradman at first had trouble timing his drives and skied one just out of reach of Chapman at mid-off shortly after his arrival. Fender's match account in his book *The Turn of the Wheel* is notable for the way he stresses errors by Bradman, which could indicate either that Bradman felt under pressure to perform or that Fender was fault-finding. Thus he records six mis-hits which might have accounted for Bradman in this period.

Jackson, similarly, edged the ball wide of close-in fielders twice before he settled down. For the most part, however, he remained fluent, despite a slow start (twenty runs) in the first ninety-minute session, and escaped criticism. This was, after all, a timeless test, and in his first test Jackson needed to overcome his reputation as a second-innings centurion.

At lunch Jackson was 97 and Bradman 34, with 4-201 on the board. Both batsmen had pleased the crowd by using their feet to White and hitting him forcefully.

There are several versions of what passed between them over lunch. In one account, Bradman supposedly advised Jackson along the lines of 'get 'em in singles, sport'. In his own *Farewell to Cricket*, Bradman suggests that he told Jackson to take his time and the century would come. On resumption, Bradman played a maiden from Tate. It was then that the great test came. Could Jackson survive Larwood with the new ball? The answer was swift. From the first ball he faced after the interval Jackson raised his century with a rocket-like crack past point to the boundary in front of the George Giffen stand. His century, with seven fours, took 250 minutes.

Reaching three figures was the signal for Jackson to begin plundering the bowling. Bradman left for 40 at 5-227 to a catch at second slip off Tate, the ball deflecting from Duckworth's gloves. Despite what Wakley described as his 'rather streakily' played innings, he had managed to eclipse Trumper's record seasonal aggregate.

Jackson, undeterred, scored sixty-seven in seventy minutes in the afternoon while shepherding the strike from his partner a'Beckett. His perfect timing and the certainty of his crisp stroke-play stamped him a champion in many spectators' eyes, his repeated square-cutting just wide of second slip reminding some of Charlie Macartney. Perhaps the saddest aspect of Jackson's premature demise was that he reminded onlookers so often of someone else. His aesthetic appeal was compared with Trumper's, but, like Ross Gregory a decade later, he lasted too short a time at the top to leave anything like a similar legacy to the next generation. They might revel in the 'flay' of Bradman's bat, in one famous phrase, and Bradman might point to the quality of Stan McCabe, but there was never any jostling to be a junior Jackson as there was to be for the title of the next Bradman.

Jackson was especially severe on Hammond during the afternoon session. With his score on 147 he late-cut that bowler through the slips for three and then hit him for four, two, and three off successive balls. The fielding at this point grew ragged. Returns to Duckworth came at varying heights and it seemed the only way to dismiss the tyro would be by running him out. After banging White to the square-leg boundary, however, he came a long way down the wicket but played over a ball from that bowler and was out lbw. His long and brilliant innings of 164 had been brought to a close. It had taken 318 minutes, included fourteen fours, and the Australian score stood at 6-287.

The plaudits continued, Monty Noble rated it the 'greatest knock of the series', and the presentations began that night on the stage of Adelaide's Garden Theatre. Later the South Australian Cricket Association presented Jackson with a set of cut glass, while well-wishers gave him gifts and started a 'shilling fund' that eventually totalled £200. When Jackson returned home, the Balmain mayor honoured him with a public meeting at which he received an inscribed silver tea service, and made a speech in which Jackson was linked by name with such cricketing luminaries as former England captains Stanley Jackson and Archie MacLaren. Sydney Methodists gathered in the Town Hall to celebrate the feats of one of their faithful.

DAY 4

Ted a'Beckett, Ron Oxenham and Bert Oldfield all made useful contributions before White and Tate wheedled them out on the fourth morning with the Australians reaching 369. Geary was unable to bowl effectively, but Hammond, recovered from exhaustion, played his part. White took the bowling honours with 5-130 from sixty overs, figures testifying to his superlative accuracy and length against batsmen ready to use their feet and, in Jackson's case, in full cry. White's variations of flight and pace, his substitute for great powers of spin, led Noble to rank the Somerset amateur as one of England's 'most tireless workers with muscle and brain', attributes perhaps gained from toil on his Stogumber farm.

Even such a tireless worker as White no doubt expected his professional colleagues Hobbs and Sutcliffe to do the right thing in England's reply, especially as he was the only fully-fit bowler left to Chapman.

For once, though, the great men failed. Hobbs was out to Hendry for the second time in the match with one run on the board, and, when Oldfield took his second catch, both the openers were back in the pavilion for 21. Now, with a first innings lead of thirty-five, Australia must have sniffed the chance of a win. Hammond was three, and there were eight minutes to play before lunch.

At times such as this, some captains would have sent in a good attacking player like Hendren, with instructions to hit the side out of trouble. Chapman instead sent out vice-captain Jardine in his usual position, perhaps because Hendren had other matters on his mind.

It was Hendren's fortieth birthday. Such was his popularity that a ceremony was held during lunch in the visitors dressing rooms, during which he was handed a cheque, a tray and a walking-stick made from Australian timber. The presents were handed to Hendren by the South Australian Cricket Association president, Harold Fisher, after a number of admirers of Hendren had subscribed £13 6s to a fund opened by the local newspaper, the *News*.

Hendren's local popularity stemmed from the five months he had spent the previous Australian summer as SACA coach and captain of the 'Colts' district team. In his history of the Association, Chris Harte has recorded:

> Patsy Hendren was a great success during his stay in South Australia and is warmly remembered by those members of the Colts team who are still alive. He topped the Colts and District cricket averages with 146.50; coached the state team four evenings a week, and University the other; visited various schools for morning coaching; gave lectures to city clubs and country associations; and was generally helpful to all those who sought his advice or assistance.

Hendren returned to England in April 1928, having signed a contract with the SACA to coach for a further three years, but cancelled this when he was chosen as a member of Chapman's tour party.

Hammond and Jardine struggled to the long break, by which time only 42 runs were on the board. Play brightened after lunch as Hammond opened up against Grimmett and a'Beckett. He added twenty-one in the first twenty minutes and reached his fifty in just over two hours, but Jardine's score remained stationary. In one forty-minute period, he scored just seven from the fifteen balls Hammond allowed him to face. As in every other test during the series, one or other of the English team had come to the rescue either in the bowling or batting department. Hammond had helped save the situation in the first innings of the present match and now, with Jardine, he was performing a similar role in the second.

At tea, after a substitute ball had replaced the damaged ball in use, and twelfth man Andrews had replaced Jackson in the field, the score was 2-129. Jardine was then 39 to Hammond's 61, the latter having just broken Sutcliffe's four-year-old record series aggregate of 734. Hammond might have been out when stranded down the wicket but, at 5.30, a single helped him reach his second hundred of the match, scored in ten minutes under four hours. In the next half hour he could add only another five runs as all-rounder Oxenham restricted his off-side strokes. By stumps, England had reached a total of 2-206 with Hammond 105 and Jardine 73.

The batting was slow but deliberate, the wicket perfect, the heat extreme. Hammond, like Sutcliffe, had registered his fourth century in the series. He was advancing his claim as the greatest living batsman, though critics noted that, throughout his Adelaide innings, he eliminated many of the audacious strokes he had displayed before his test debut, and restricted those he made to a narrow segment of the arc available to him. Whatever the origin of these limitations, many of the crowd of 15,250 were more critical of Jardine, even though he outscored Hammond in terms of runs per deliveries faced. The crowd's hostility to Jardine is not difficult to fathom. The Harlequin cap he wore was unconventional by English amateur standards and provocative by local ones.

An anecdote may help illustrate contemporary local attitudes toward such headgear. During Hendren's time as state coach, he had taken the Colts grade team, which he captained, to a fixture at the Alberton Oval, home ground of the determinedly working-class Port Adelaide District Cricket Club. Making his Colts debut in this match was the scion of a proud Adelaide family, the product of one of the prestigious private schools, who proudly wore his multi-hued school first eleven cap to the wicket.

Greeted by a crescendo of cat-calls, the college boy was dismissed instantaneously by Norm Williams, a legendary grade leg-spin bowler after whom the ground scoreboard is still named. The youth retired to the depths of the dressing room, contemplating the crushing of his cricketing hopes. There Hendren consoled him, taking all the blame for the reception he had received, and proposing he might choose to wear some less ostentatious headgear in the second innings. Success attended this sartorial change, and the youth prospered thereafter.

Perhaps Jardine underestimated the wit of Australian working-class crowds, perhaps not – but it still seems unfortunate that, had Hendren ever ventured to offer similar advice to Jardine, the patrician would have been unlikely to have heeded the professional.

Walter Hammond

DAY 5

In the morning session, under a blazing sun, Jardine could add only seventeen runs against Grimmett's leg stump attack, while Hammond scratched thirty-seven from a greater share of the strike. When Oxenham, the Queensland slow-medium bowler, ended Jardine's 345 minute vigil at 2.40 by inducing a catch to Woodfull at silly point from a slower delivery, the batsman was only two short of his first test century. He had faced 378 balls, while Hammond had scored 156 off 581 deliveries. The stand of 262, scored at forty-four runs per hour, had put England nearly 250 ahead, and should have paved the way for the hitters to entertain the crowd and further demoralise the fielders.

Instead the score slumped. Hendren replaced Jardine and in turn was replaced by Chapman. With six wickets falling for 54 runs, Chapman's among them for a duck, the bowlers must have thought the end was in sight. When Hammond's marathon innings ended at 177, caught and bowled by Ryder from an exhausted stroke, the score was 7-327. The twenty-five-year-old had thus compiled 296 runs in the match for once out, forty-two per cent of England's final tally from the bat, while batting the equivalent of nearly two entire days.

A hard-hitting innings of 47 (off fifty balls) by Tate, dubbed 'a tonic after the day's dreariness', carried England to 383, and set Australia a target of 349. It was a realistic challenge on a pitch curator Albert Wright declared to be one of the best he had ever prepared.

DAY 6

The home team made a gallant start, this time against White and Larwood. Larwood had a couple of times bowled medium-paced spells during the first innings, when Duckworth had stood up to the wicket to him, and this occurred at the start of the second innings as well. Beginning the day at 0-24, Australia went to lunch at 2-74. Leicestershire fast-medium bowler George Geary had Jackson caught behind by Duckworth after the batsman had several times taken near-fatal liberties with White in following Monty Noble's advice to use his feet to the left-hander. The former Australian captain had criticised Woodfull from the press box for appearing to caution Jackson, though umpire Hele later said that Woodfull had actually been encouraging his partner's aggressive tactics. Geary was also involved in the second dismissal, catching Woodfull off White from a ball that jumped sharply from a worn spot on the wicket.

After lunch, White induced Hendry to mis-time a pull shot in the first over to be caught at mid-on, but Ryder joined Alan Kippax to turn the tide in a partnership of 137 in even time. By the tea interval, White had operated virtually unchanged throughout the day against the wind, beguiling the batsmen to dance to his tune. Tate, Larwood and Geary supported White in turn downwind. Tate had injured his back and, for him, bowled comparatively little and none too well, while Geary and Larwood also carried niggling injuries into the field. Much therefore hinged upon the left-hander's stamina and success.

Fortunes changed again when Hendren caught Kippax from a

juggled chance in the slips off White. White then accepted a hard return catch from Ryder, and Hammond, three paces from the bat at slip, dived to get his hand under an edge from a'Beckett to another ball that White landed on a worn spot. From 3-211 Australia had slipped to 6-260, with Bradman on 16 after sixty-eight minutes and Oxenham on two. At the end of the day. Australia needed eighty-nine to win.

DAY 7

Percy Fender has provided an understated description of the last day, enthralling in its laconic attention to the tactical conundrums Chapman had to solve. These included tired bowlers, who took much more time than could be spared to settle down, a tricky cross-wind, and inflexibility in the fielding side. Chapman wasted himself by maintaining his station at silly point to the upper-order batsmen. He kept both Hammond and Hendren in the slips and Tate at leg-slip when they might have been better employed elsewhere.

In the first session, before 13,700 spectators, Bradman and Oxenham pushed thirty runs in the direction of the square-leg umpire, while Tate was positioned to restrict the riskier glances off White. Finally, when Chapman at silly point caught Oxenham at 7-308, fifty runs had been added.

Only forty-one were needed to win as keeper Oldfield entered. Bradman had reached his fifty in the first three-quarters of an hour and, such was his youthful assurance, anything seemed possible. The mature Bradman would almost certainly have won the test from this position but, after adding twelve with Oldfield, he responded to the striker's call for a single off the last ball of an over, played directly to Hobbs at cover, and was run out in what he later termed 'a hair-splitting decision'. Australia were now 8-320.

Runs still came through forward short-leg as Oldfield and Grimmett added six of the twenty-nine needed but, after lunch, Chapman at last moved Tate to cut off the supply line. Tate was also used to contain Oldfield, and reckoned his four-over spell was among the most important he ever bowled. The only score in those overs was four byes from a ball that beat both Oldfield and keeper Duckworth. Grimmett's innings ended when he was caught by Tate at the second attempt as the batsman launched himself at White, and Blackie was dismissed in similar style. The nature of the final dismissal bears retelling.

Patsy Hendren, many years later, told David Sheppard that, when he saw the forty-six-year-old left-handed number eleven, Don Blackie, drop his bat three times as he came down the Adelaide pavilion steps, he said, 'We've won.' So nervous was Blackie that he couldn't hold his bat to take guard to White. He faced four balls without scoring, and Hendren from short-leg helped things along by telling the batsman to hit White out of the ground.

Was this sledging of a sort? Bradman certainly reported that Blackie himself, when questioned about his thoughts as he hit the final shot, replied he was envisioning the boys cheering as they saw him hit White for six. The side's most mature player might have shown more of the supposed discretion and focus on the moment which comes with experience but who, in the circumstances, could blame the number eleven? For such moments, heroes are made – and Fred Tates and Blackies born.

Blackie's moment came after Maurice Tate bowled another maiden to Oldfield. In a nice clash of colours, White bowled four balls to Blackie, then, off the fifth, the Victorian took Hendren's ironic advice, hitting hard and high. For a long moment, the fielder must have regretted his riposte, but Larwood took the catch, sprinting round from mid-wicket to square-leg in front of the pavilion. White picked up the last two men in his sixty-fourth and sixty-fifth to give him eight wickets for the innings, thirteen for the match, the record number of deliveries in a match (not exceeded for a decade), and England victory by twelve runs.

One English writer described Jack White as 'between the reigns' of Yorkshire professional left-handers Wilfred Rhodes and Hedley Verity, but this is to draw a false comparison and unjustly downgrade the Somerset amateur. The original intention may have been for White to bowl, a yard shorter than his English length, endless overs at a pace described as ' slow to stationary' and with minimal spin, to allow the quicker bowlers a break. In fact, White averaged a hundred overs per match in the last four tests. By contrast, Tate averaged eighty-five, and Larwood and Geary sixty. It was a war of attrition. The tests averaged seven days' play after the Brisbane debacle, and White took 25 wickets at 30 apiece as he wore down his opponents, for easily the best figures of any bowler in the series.

With the rubber at 4–0 it seemed as though Australia might go down in total defeat, and England might revenge its five–nil defeat by Australia eight years before. After the Adelaide game the margin of tests between Australia and England was one: Australia 47 and England 46. Many expected it to be even after the final match in Melbourne, despite Australia's far better showing in this match at Adelaide, but the home side managed to snatch the game after an eight-day marathon. Australia won this game with the twenty-four-year-old Tim Wall and Alan Fairfax, twenty-two, joining Jackson and Bradman in the team.

England's overall ascendancy in 1928–29 was built around the magnificent form of the twenty-five-year-old Hammond. He went home to an April wedding, and a marital relationship which, his personal letters indicate, would affect his form adversely until he retired after the war. Hammond's mood-swings and introspection, coupled with his reportedly poor communication skills, clouded much of his subsequent life though his biographer, Ronald Mason, believed he had enjoyed his cricket. The inevitable comparison with Bradman also affected him, as it did Bill Ponsford. The apparent promise of this England side was thus rendered illusory by several factors: Hammond's relative decline, the age of many of its participants, and changes in the captaincy.

A key factor would become the general failure against Bradman of its attack, for all that on this tour Chapman could depend on a strong quartet of bowlers, of whom White was the pick.

Australia's problems began with errors made at the selection table. Australia's final series statistics showed two youngsters – Jackson with 69.00 and Bradman 66.85 – atop the batting averages and Fifth Test debutant Tim Wall heading the bowling, but the selectors were too slow in giving youth a chance.

Within four years, England manager Sir Pelham Warner would be broadcasting a funeral address for Archie Jackson from the Balmain Methodist Mission as the eulogies became elegies following his premature death. A subscription fund raised £453 for a headstone, carved by test player Tommy Andrews, who had substituted in the field for Jackson at Adelaide, and the Balmain Club established a memorial shield in his honour.

Bradman's monumental scoring began in earnest in that 1928–29 season and his total first-class runs for the summer were 1690 at 93.88 with seven centuries. That record still stands. No one, however, least of all the English, was prepared for the extent of his dominance in the years to come.

•LEEDS 1938•

DARK VICTORY

The dark clouds of the second world war hang in the background and dark storm clouds hang over Headingley throughout this test. It is a match in which Australia's heaviest artillery – its greatest batsman Don Bradman, and greatest bowler Bill O'Reilly – demonstrate their mastery. Bradman sets up the victory with a small century (103) which, like his 103 at Melbourne in 1932, was one of his most valuable. O'Reilly takes ten wickets, as he also did in that Melbourne match, won by Australia. The turning point in this match is O'Reilly's first ball dismissal of Walter Hammond in England's second innings, although a crucial thirty by the young Lindsay Hassett weighs heavily in the final result. England has the better balanced attack, but Hammond does not manage his resources as well as Bradman marshals his.

ENGLAND v AUSTRALIA 1938 (4th Test)

Played at Headingley, Leeds, on 22, 23, 25 July.
Toss: England. Result: AUSTRALIA won by five wickets.

ENGLAND

WJ Edrich	b O'Reilly	12	st Barnett b F'wood-Smith	28
CJ Barnett	c Barnett b McCormick	30	c Barnett b McCormick	29
J Hardstaff, jr	run out	4	b O'Reilly	11
WR Hammond*	b O'Reilly	76	c Brown b O'Reilly	0
E Paynter	st Barnett b F'wood-Smith	28	not out	21
DCS Compton	b O'Reilly	14	c Barnett b O'Reilly	15
WFF Price†	c McCabe b O'Reilly	0	lbw b Fleetwood-Smith	6
H Verity	not out	25	b Fleetwood-Smith	0
DVP Wright	c Fingleton b F'wood-Smith	22	c Waite b F'wood-Smith	0
K Farnes	c Fingleton b F'wood-Smith	2	b O'Reilly	7
WE Bowes	b O'Reilly	3	lbw b O'Reilly	0
Extras	(LB 4, NB 3)	7	(LB 4, W 1, NB 1)	6
Total		**223**		**123**

AUSTRALIA

JHW Fingleton	b Verity	30	lbw b Verity	9
WA Brown	b Wright	22	lbw b Farnes	9
BA Barnett†	c Price b Farnes	57	(7) not out	15
DG Bradman*	b Bowes	103	(3) c Verity b Wright	16
SJ McCabe	b Farnes	1	(4) c Barnett b Wright	15
CL Badcock	b Bowes	4	not out	5
AL Hassett	c Hammond b Wright	13	(5) c Edrich b Wright	33
MG Waite	c Price b Farnes	3		
WJ O'Reilly	c Hammond b Farnes	2		
EL McCormick	b Bowes	0		
LO'B Fleetwood -Smith	not out	2		
Extras	(B 2, LB 3)	5	(B 4 NB 1)	5
Total		**242**	(5 wickets)	**107**

AUSTRALIA	O	M	R	W	O	M	R	W
McCormick	20	6	46	1	11	4	18	1
Waite	18	7	31	0	2	0	9	0
O'Reilly	34.1	17	66	5	21.5	8	56	5
F'wood-Smith	25	7	73	3	16	4	34	4
McCabe	1	1	0	0				
ENGLAND								
Farnes	26	3	77	4	11.3	4	17	1
Bowes	35.4	6	79	3	11	0	35	0
Wright	15	4	38	2	5	0	26	3
Verity	19	6	30	1	5	2	24	1
Edrich	3	0	13	0				

FALL OF WICKETS

	E	A	E	A
Wkt	1st	1st	2nd	2nd
1st	29	28	60	17
2nd	34	87	73	32
3rd	88	128	73	50
4th	142	136	73	61
5th	171	145	96	91
6th	171	195	116	
7th	172	232	116	
8th	213	240	116	
9th	215	240	123	
10th	223	242	123	

Umpires: F Chester and EJ Smith.

Don Bradman

Lindsay Hassett

Bill O'Reilly

Leeds' last inter-war test was its eighth to entertain the Australians, and its thirteenth overall since 1899. The late Jim Kilburn's official *History of Yorkshire Cricket 1921–1949* encapsulated the game as 'a close approach to the perfect test match, a game full of incident and uncertainty, remembered affectionately by all who played in it or watched'.

More prosaically, Ralph Barker and Irving Rosenwater twenty years later characterised the match as 'one of the most thrilling tests ever played', and the background to England's third defeat by Australia at the ground as being 'as fascinating as the match itself'. Sir Donald Bradman himself described the game within a decade of its decision as 'the greatest test match of modern times'. The on-field details confirm Lindsay Hassett's opinion that 'the most gripping test matches have been the low-scoring ones'. As participants at Leeds, Bradman and Hassett were well-placed to comment.

The test was played against the backdrop of intense political tension in Europe. The March *Anschluss*, when Germany invaded Austria, had been succeeded in April by an Anglo–Italian treaty that defused possible disagreements in the Mediterranean. From May onwards, events escalated in Czechoslovakia, with demands for an independent German state in the Sudeten. Within a month of the end of the Leeds test, the British government had persuaded the Czech government to concede autonomy to the Sudeten Germans. In mid and late September, the British Prime Minister Neville Chamberlain flew to Germany to negotiate a historic agreement which he believed would secure 'peace in our time'.

Under gathering war-clouds, the nineteenth Australian team to tour England played out an international contest that served as light relief. Newspaper accounts of political events routinely occupied the same page of the *Yorkshire Post* as Jim Kilburn's reports of the play at Headingley, scheduled as the venue for the Fourth Test.

The First Test at Trent Bridge had been a draw, as had the Second (Lord's) Test in late June. Lord's had witnessed double hundreds by Wally Hammond, the ninety-ninth century for England against Australia, and Bill Brown, the hundredth for Australia against England, and a Bradman hundred (142 minutes, fifteen fours), the two hundredth in Anglo–Australian tests. In his forty-fourth innings, The Don had taken his Anglo–Australian test aggregate past the record established by Hobbs (3636 in seventy-one innings) in 1930. He had now scored a thousand runs in his last eight test innings.

Persistent rain had prevented the captains even tossing on any of the four days in July of the Third Test at Manchester. In the absence of results, it was a season for setting statistical benchmarks, which are worth summarising here because they indicate the extent of the Bradman ascendancy.

Already, during the First Test, Bradman had completed two thousand runs for the tour in fewer visits to the wicket – twenty-one – than anyone else has required to record this amount. After the Manchester wash-out, Bradman hit hundreds against Warwickshire (135 in 163 minutes) and Nottinghamshire (144 in a minute under three hours). This latter innings was his eleventh hundred of the tour, equalling Trumper's 1902 record. His eighty-fourth innings in England set a new record for hundreds by Australians in that country, twenty-eight; Warren Bardsley had needed more than double the number of innings to establish the old record. It was Bradman's seventy-ninth first-class hundred, already twenty-six ahead of Bardsley, the previous Australian leader. Finally, Bradman became the first Australian to aggregate twenty thousand runs, reaching this target in his 243rd innings, over a hundred innings quicker than any other Australian player.

The world's greatest batsman was thus in good standing, statistically, for whatever England might have in store for him at Headingley, especially bearing in mind that his two previous visits to the crease in tests there had yielded over six hundred runs.

Following two draws and a wash-out, skipper Bradman had a clear strategic priority: winning at Leeds would guarantee that the tourists retained the Ashes, whatever the outcome of the final test at The Oval. To let everything ride on that match would be to invite an outcome similar to the experience of Bert Collins in 1926, when England had regained the Ashes in the final test, the only decided match in that series. Bradman's imperative was obvious: to win.

The team which England fielded is often said to have been selected for the same purpose. The Manchester thirteen had excluded Essex express Ken Farnes and sent six-hitting Somerset medium-pacer Arthur Wellard back to the cider country. Two all-rounders and an off-spinner, Tom Goddard of Gloucestershire, had been chosen to bolster the attack. Norman Yardley, a Yorkshire batsman and Cambridge University blue, had been introduced to the thirteen.

For Leeds, Goddard and Yardley were omitted and the all-rounders disappeared; Farnes and Bill Bowes, back from a damaged knee, were brought in to strengthen the England pace attack on an under-prepared pitch.

Their presence weakened the batting, already disarrayed by a dramatic county game at Lord's in the week prior to the Leeds test. In his report of the match, chairman of selectors Sir Pelham Warner remarked that 'it was said at the time that there was a "ridge" at the Nursery End just short of a good length', without obviously being moved to do anything about it. Because of the ridge, opener Len Hutton had fractured the middle finger of his right hand, and this kept him out of the England side. Yorkshire and England stalwart Morris Leyland had fractured his left (bottom) thumb. Yorkshire's wicketkeeper-batsman Paul Gibb had also been injured, so that Warner's panel brought Fred Price, aged 36, into the England side as wicketkeeper for his first test, knowing full well his inclusion would further weaken the batting. In the absence of Hutton and Gibb, Warner was later certain the selectors erred in not playing the regular Yorkshire wicketkeeper Arthur Wood, for Wood 'was the sort of a man who would have risen to the occasion, and *he was a Yorkshireman*, which means a lot'.

In the event, the selectors promoted Bill Edrich to open with Charles Barnett, replaced Hutton with the Nottinghamshire professional Joe Hardstaff junior, and gave England captain Walter Hammond a four-member specialist attack: two quick bowlers, Bowes and Farnes, and two spinners, Yorkshire left-hand orthodox Hedley Verity and Kent's medium-paced leg-spinner Doug Wright.

Australia opened with Ernie McCormick (express), supported by Merv Waite and Stan McCabe (medium-pacers). Two spinners, medium-paced leg-spinner Bill 'Tiger' O'Reilly and unorthodox left-hander Leslie O'Brien 'Chuck' Fleetwood-Smith, completed the Irish-Australian attack. Fleetwood-Smith and O'Reilly were Australia's counterparts to Verity and Wright.

Frank Chester, who umpired the Leeds test with 'Tiger' Smith, described Verity as faster through the air than Wilfred Rhodes, able to make the ball pop disconcertingly, but less able to spin or flight the ball than his great Yorkshire predecessor. Other authorities suggest he was equally able to do the one while his greater height made the other less necessary. The Australians described Wright as 'the best bowler in England', perhaps an instance of what their opening batsman at Leeds, Jack Fingleton, later alleged was an Australian predilection for trying to play certain bowlers into England sides to suit themselves.

Writing his autobiography two decades later, Chester regretted Wright's indecision about the length of his run-up, given that the shorter the run he used, the greater the degree of control he could achieve. The trade-off between control and capturing wickets proved a key factor in the tactical battle during the fourth innings of this match.

Headingley, Leeds 1938

DAY 1

Some members of the first-day crowd of nearly 24,000 had begun to queue at 6.30 for the gates to open at 9.15. Their numbers included an un-named Australian clergyman intent on spending his vacation at the tests, regardless of the Leeds weather or the worsening political climate in Europe. The crowd braved a heavy atmosphere, a dull misty morning, a heavy outfield and an underprepared pitch that Headingley curator Dick Moulton had been forced to change late. His prediction that 'Bradman won't get three hundred this time' would have left the clergyman with mixed feelings: if The Don was going to struggle in the conditions, what might lesser mortals manage or witness?

When Hammond won the toss for England that Friday morning, he had the usual two choices. His powerful opening attack could use both atmosphere and wicket, so bowling first must have appealed. But Australia's less than powerful opening attack gave batting first greater appeal.

Bill Edrich and Charles Barnett opened to McCormick, coming downwind from the Main stand end, with Waite operating at the Kirkstall Lane end. The latter, swinging the ball a good deal, had Barnett several times edging the ball through the slips and missed twice. The first was a so-called easy chance, by O'Reilly stationed at second slip, with the score at 14. Five runs later Bill Brown, having replaced O'Reilly at second slip, made Waite wait a month and another test to claim his only test wicket (Compton).

Barker and Rosenwater suggest that 'Bradman seems to have appreciated from the start that Australia's chance had come'. After twenty-nine runs had come in the first hour, the ball was already beginning to turn in conditions expected to favour the England pace attack. Edrich was out to a wrong'un, delivered from the Kirkstall Lane end, which gave O'Reilly his first wicket in the match for four runs in eleven overs. Sightscreen difficulties may have contributed to another in Edrich's string of dismal dismissals – 5, 0 and now 12 – in the series so far, but the quality of the idiosyncratic Australian spinners was evident in the conditions.

To help Australia along, Barnett ran out his partner Hardstaff, backing up for a stroke played wide of mid-on. Hardstaff tried what was described as a baseball slide, but he found himself well out of his ground. Barnett almost repeated the effort with his own county captain Hammond, who restrained him in the face of typically alert and accurate Australian ground fielding. By lunch, England were 2-62. O'Reilly's figures read 14-11-4-1, two of those runs resulting from overstepping the crease while attempting to further intimidate the batsman. Although the ground fielding was brilliant, three chances had already been missed.

Charles Barnett had finished the first session of the Trent Bridge Test with his own score just short of three figures. At Headingley, his dismissal at 2.25 for just 30 – caught one-handed by his wicket-keeping namesake Ben flicking at a wide delivery from McCormick – indicates how different the conditions and scoring opportunities were at Headingley. England were 3-88.

Hammond now played and displayed strokes of power and grace. A four past cover from McCormick and a six over mid-off into the stand came from two of the many no balls McCormick delivered on the tour. Two on-driven boundaries and two off-drives wide of extra cover, each pair of strokes from consecutive O'Reilly deliveries, ran Hammond to his half-century in ninety-five minutes.

At the other end meanwhile, Fleetwood-Smith, Hammond's nemesis in a crucial Australian win at Adelaide in 1937, repeatedly made the England number four stretch for him, and kept quiet the England number five, Paynter. When Waite relieved O'Reilly, Hammond drove the ball back so hard that umpire Chester was endangered, only saving himself from injury by diving to the ground.

Jim Kilburn left readers in little doubt concerning the wicket's respectability or the boundary's proximity as Hammond continued to treat the bowling with majestic contempt. He rated the innings as 'at once the joy and condemnation of his colleagues'. Wilfred Rhodes, however, commented in the *Yorkshire Post* that few well-pitched-up deliveries reached the boundary, first because those colleagues mostly drove with little power, second because Bradman could afford to field his players deeper than England because of their superior throwing arms.

Paynter finally cut Fleetwood-Smith for another four, and England had added 63 in the hour since lunch. Drinks were taken seven runs later but, immediately afterwards, Hammond played forward to a leg-break from O'Reilly to be sent back after what contemporary newspaper accounts called a 'truly splendid innings of 76', scored out of 108, with a six and twelve fours.

Paynter and Compton proceeded, if not smoothly, at least without loss, until the junior partner, trying to run an O'Reilly leg-spinner between keeper and slip off the edge, played back, was deceived in flight, and bowled. There is some hesitation in describing the delivery in question as a 'routine' or 'orthodox' leg-spinner, so the adjectives are omitted to acknowledge that nothing about O'Reilly justifies their use.

Umpire Chester was well positioned to comment on that experience. Leeds was the fifth test in which he had watched O'Reilly bowl. He reported that O'Reilly never spun the ball more than he needed to find the edge of the bat, rap the batsman's pads, or rattle his stumps. O'Reilly, face contorted by the cosmic injustice of it all, cocked his wrist to such an extent the ball almost brushed the inside of his forearm. This master of the bowling crease then windmilled his lumbering way to the wicket for another tilt at the giants he opposed. Sacrificing height to a stooped front leg at the crucial moment of delivery, but never length, he varied pace and flight with virtually indiscernable changes of action, getting the ball to lift and turn. Chester believed that O'Reilly seldom bowled successive deliveries alike, was never off the wicket, and was always prepared to appeal.

A stump-rattling O'Reilly delivery broke the crucial fifth wicket partnership between Paynter and Compton. At the other end, Paynter promptly overbalanced while trying to off-drive a flighted delivery from Fleetwood-Smith and was stumped, whereupon tea was taken at 6-171.

Middlesex man had succeeded Middlesex man before the interval, Yorkshire man succeeded Lancashire man after it. With but a run added, Price was caught at short slip without scoring. Chairman of selectors Warner might well have then asked what price the Yorkshire wicketkeeper Arthur Wood? Verity was joined by Wright, England's supposed answer to O'Reilly with the ball. Missed by that worthy from his own bowling, Wright managed two or three well-timed pulls before being caught by a very deep mid-off to end the forty-one-run stand. Ten more runs were added before Farnes was caught by a sprinting Fingleton off Fleetwood-Smith, and Bowes bowled by O'Reilly in his thirty-fifth over. Verity, having square-cut and hooked – according to Barker – 'as a man unconscious of the sorrows around him', remained unbeaten on 25 when England closed for 223.

Australia faced a brief interlude in fading light. Openers Fingleton and Brown did not have the benefit of Kilburn's or Warner's assessment that the wicket was 'kindly' or 'easy-paced'. Though the Australian spinners had made the ball turn occasionally, McCormick could not make it bounce. For his part, Waite had swung it both ways a little, though the ordinariness of his action was all that Warner considered noteworthy about him.

The England opening attack was of a different calibre. Fingleton faced Farnes coming downwind from the Main stand end without the benefit of a sightboard behind the Essex paceman. Twice beaten by Farnes, Fingleton would have derived little comfort from seeing Brown beaten once before he was bowled leg stump trying to hook Wright's first ball after the Kent man had replaced Bowes from the Kirkstall Lane end.

Although Wright almost yorked nightwatchman Barnett, Australia went in overnight at 1-32. Warner and Chester both commented that time had been wasted by the inadequate screens, but downplayed Australian objections to the Headingley gloom.

In the wider world, the political gloom descending over Europe politically was momentarily lifted by an impressive unveiling ceremony at Villiers-Bretonneux, seen in France as 'an act of faith'. Ex-AIF members, Australian Deputy Prime Minister Sir Earle Page, Mr RG Menzies, High Commissioner Mr SM Bruce, and the Australian Governor-General, Lord Gowrie, paid tribute to 11,000 Australian dead of the first world war.

DAY 2

Saturday's crowd of nearly 37,000 showed great restraint as they watched even the quiestest periods of play with intense interest. Included in their number were a number of Australians: the *Yorkshire Post* reported that the vacationing clergyman had been joined by Sydneysider Mr JW Sullivan, who had landed at Southampton on the Wednesday and hitched to Leeds. Arriving in the early hours of the second day, he would have seen Fingleton and Barnett add a further 55. Wright twice beat Barnett with wrong'uns, but both batsmen hit Wright for fours. Bowes troubled Fingleton before Verity bowled him as he tried to force a good-length ball wide of mid-on: 2-87.

Verity almost got Bradman immediately he came in at 12.55, and the left-hander's length allowed him to bowl thereafter with only one deep fielder to Bradman, while his accuracy allowed him to dispense with even that protection when bowling to the other Australian batsmen. He conceded just 30 runs in nineteen overs. Wright troubled Bradman once, and a better throw from Hardstaff might have found him short of his crease as he came back for a fourth run off a late-cut.

England may have gained some illusory pre-lunch consolation at seeing the back of Barnett. After taking eleven off an over by Farnes, all on the leg side, the wicketkeeper was caught in Farnes's next over for 57. This was Barnett's only test fifty, and more than double his final test average. He had helped the Australian score to 3-128, ninety-five behind England, and must have been well satisfied with his work.

Bradman was 17 at lunch. The innings that followed remains 'one of his greatest'. Aside from a boundary edged through the slips off Bowes and an inside edge that flew almost within reach of the square-leg fielder, 'perhaps in no other [innings] was his superiority to his fellow batsmen quite so pronounced'.

The preceding citations, and the facts that follow, come largely from one of the greatest books of cricket statistics ever written, *Bradman the Great*, now an oldie but still a goldie. While it would stretch the analogy to Bradman's innings to write that in perhaps no other book does BJ Wakley's superiority to his fellow statisticians seem quite so pronounced, such was the youthful reaction of one of the authors when he bought the book thirty years after the events revisited in this chapter. The disproportion between the three lines here allowed to Barnett, and the three paragraphs allocated to Bradman, reflect the considered evaluation of many mature admirers of the player considered the world's best batsman. That Bradman performed so well in these conditions offsets admitted lapses, such as Lord's in 1934, where his cheap dismissal helped England enforce the follow-on and defeat Australia for the only time on the ground during this century.

At Leeds in 1938, Bradman scored the fifteenth of his nineteen hundreds against England, his twelfth of the season, his third of the current series, his third in successive innings at Leeds, and his sixth in successive Ashes tests. This innings meant he had scored over a thousand runs in the six tests played since the Third Test of the 1936–37 series. He became the first Australian to complete five thousand runs in tests, the third player to do so, in his fifty-sixth innings. At twenty-nine he was the youngest. Hobbs had taken ninety-one innings, and Hammond ninety-seven at thirty-three years of age; Hutton would take ninety-eight innings, Compton 113. This was Australia's 102nd century; England would equal the tally with three centurions (Hutton, Leyland and Hardstaff) in the last inter-war Anglo–Australian test at The Oval, the 143rd between the sides.

These considerations were in the future. On that historic second day at Headingley, the Australians had to confront a damp wicket which assisted a dangerous attack, and light that steadily worsened as thunder haze closed in on Headingley from the west. Bradman himself wrote that he chose not to appeal against the 'darkest in which I have ever batted' in order not to extend the Australian innings and risk possible rain-damage to the wicket.

Having to bat on a spoiled surface held no appeal for Bradman, but batting in bad light held fewer fears for him than for lesser mortals. So Stygean became the surroundings, however, that 'matches lit in the grandstand were plainly visible from the centre'. At the same time, so Olympian were Bradman's attributes that his judicious blend of defensive and offensive stroke-play allowed him to manipulate the strike and justify his opinion, expressed in *Farewell to Cricket*, that 'we would make more runs in that light on a dry pitch than in a good light on a wet one'.

Shortly after lunch, lesser mortals among Bradman's teammates began to succumb to the conditions. McCabe was bowled playing back, 'sightless and strokeless', by a ball from Farnes that kept low and left him. Jack Badcock played back rather than forward to a ball from Bowes that pitched on middle and hit off. With the score reading 5-145 and the light 'very bad', Bradman went to his half-century in ninety-two minutes.

Hassett was next out, caught at slip off a beautiful leg-break by Wright, but not before he and his captain had added forty. Waite's survival was assisted by a brief stoppage of play for bad light, Bradman finally appealing when Hammond decided to take the new ball at 6-205. Bradman was then 71. Waite was caught at the wicket after the partnership had added thirty-seven, taking Austraia to the lead. Bradman was 97, the score was 7-232, with only the tail and the fourth innings to follow.

Bradman reached his hundred with a single. It had taken him ten minutes less than three hours. Eight minutes on, from the 187th ball he faced, he was bowled middle stump, trying to drive a delivery with the new ball that Bowes moved in on him from leg. In scoring 103 of the 153 Australia added while he was at the crease, he equalled his own record for the best proportion of runs during a test innings of a hundred or over. More importantly, Australia had a lead of seventeen. If it rained, England would have to cope with O'Reilly on a damaged wicket, as Australia had been forced to face Verity at Lord's in 1934. Bradman's tactics in batting on were paying off.

In short order, Hammond caught O'Reilly at knee-height, Farnes missed catching Fleetwood-Smith off his own bowling from a skier, and Bowes bowled McCormick. Warner in his match report sounds as though he was writing a half-term report: Hammond had 'worked his bowling admirably; the field was well placed', and the England fielding had been high class. He commended Bowes at fast-medium for always doing something with the ball, Farnes for his 'great fire and zest' during the afternoon, and Verity for his accuracy. Wright he had thought 'valuable'. The focus of his praise for the spinners perhaps says it all: he was quiet about their strike-rate.

By the close, England had gone thirty ahead at 0-49 after eighteen overs, with Barnett 20 and Edrich 25, both unbeaten. Edrich had been dropped twice off McCormick, whom he also hooked for four. He had also hit O'Reilly first bounce to the sight-screen, but had been worried by both spinners. Barnett, by contrast, was lordly and unhurried, three times reaching the cover boundary. The pair batted a mere fifty minutes, after a delay for bad light. Wilfred Rhodes thought it too early to be optimistic about the outcome, but believed England were better placed over the weekend than in any test of the series.

Newspaper reports indicated that Europe was no differently placed over this weekend than on any weekend of the summer.

Field Marshal Goering arrived at Elsinore in Denmark to watch a German cast present *Hamlet* at Kronborg Castle, and Chancellor of Germany Hitler left Berchtesgaden to visit naval installations at Kiel. Elsewhere, two German and two Austrian climbers teamed together to make a historic first ascent of the north face of the 13,038-foot-high Eiger in Switzerland. The heights that the England and Australian teams would have to scale on the Monday were set aside as the teams were entertained during the rest day at Harewood House by the Princess Royal and the Earl of Harewood, the *Yorkshire Post* noting that cricket was not discussed.

||| DAY 3

A sunny and warm start to Monday's proceedings, after a Sunday with rain always in the offing but avoiding Headingley itself, brought a crowd approaching 39,000 and meant the gates were closed before 11.30. Neville Cardus was apprehensive in his newspaper column about O'Reilly on a pitch unrefreshed by rain, but Kilburn reported that it 'never emphatically ill-behaved'.

McCormick from the Main stand end continued to bowl very fast, while O'Reilly again bowled from the Kirkstall Lane end. By now, the pitch had crumbled at both ends. There was a hint of thunder on high, and not only in the warm air. Len Hutton commented in his autobiography that Rhodes 'declared roundly, flatly, and in every sort of way, that England lost through deplorable batting, timidity and incompetence, nearly all round'. Rhodes also complained about England's batting tactics against O'Reilly: 'Why don't they play at the ball?' he asked. But then Rhodes never faced the 'Tiger'.

Two quick fours off O'Reilly might have temporarily assuaged the non-combatants' anxieties but, with sixty on the board, Barnett shaped badly to a short-pitched delivery on his body and was caught by his namesake off McCormick, the same combination as in the first innings. McCormick was raising dust where the ball pitched, showing how dry the wicket was, so Bradman replaced him with O'Reilly, Fleetwood-Smith going on at the Kirkstall Lane end instead. It proved a match-winning move.

Five runs on, Hardstaff attempted to attack O'Reilly by hooking him for four, then got the bowler's Irish up by on-driving a boundary off a faster no ball: 1-73. But O'Reilly countered quickly, pitching an express on leg stump and taking Hardstaff's off-bail to claim his ninety-fifth test wicket. In umpire Chester's view, the ball moved so quickly that no one could have stopped it.

Warner noted Bradman in 'earnest consultation' with O'Reilly, perhaps the moment when, according to legend, Bradman told his star bowler that, if he took his hundredth wicket in the current match, he could be spared from bowling on The Oval featherbed in the final test. (O'Reilly's figures in that game, his last against England, would be 85-26-178-3.) Such an arrangement required O'Reilly to remove five of the final eight wickets, perhaps a not unreasonable ask on a pitch assisting him, and with Australia wanting to chase only a small total for victory.

Hammond came in, and Brown and Fingleton were brought in to the double leg-trap O'Reilly had developed successfully under Vic Richardson's captaincy in South Africa in 1935–36. Hammond was averaging 86 for the season, as far ahead of any other England player as Bradman was of the tourists. Cardus, writing in the 1966 *Wisden*, thought Hammond experienced 'only two major frustrations' as a batsman, one of them being that whenever O'Reilly's leg stump attack confined him in 'sweaty durance', his batting became 'sullen, a slow but combustible fire, ready to blaze and devour'. Writing in the English press just before Headingley, Cardus thought that O'Reilly had been played 'almost with ease', with the implication that he had become just another brand for the Hammond burning.

At 2-73, England were fifty-four runs on. Jack Hobbs thought that another two hundred runs might ensure an England win and Frank Chester that, had Australia been set even 170, they would have failed. The stage was set for Hammond to break free from O'Reilly's toils and assert both his mastery over the Australian bowling and his parity with Bradman.

First ball to Hammond, O'Reilly pitched his wrong'un on leg and middle. It ran up the England captain's bat from his half-cocked defensive shot, lobbing toward a slightly backward short-leg whose right hand was at least sufficiently forward to complete the catch a yard from the probing bat. Hammond's first duck against Australia in England was only his second in forty-nine innings against the old enemy while scoring 2625 runs. Hammond's slow fire had been damped by two will-powers equal to his own, by two cricket intellects whose tigerish qualities had calculated his dismissal to a nicety. In the words of one of the 36,000 onlookers, there followed 'a silence that could be felt'. As Chester later wrote, this was all too obviously the turning point of a close match. England were 3-73.

O'Reilly's analysis read 7-2-15-2, eight of those runs coming from two no-balls. Surrounded by fielders, including a silly point, Paynter saved the hat-trick, but nothing could save England. Three wickets down became four in the next over when Bill Edrich, having achieved what would remain his best score against Australia until December 1946, was stumped off a Fleetwood-Smith wrong'un without addition to the score. Three wickets had fallen for no runs in five minutes.

Compton got the board moving when he found a four past third man off Fleewood-Smith. He on-drove O'Reilly for two more fours, one off another no-ball. We can only assume the bowler shrugged off such infringements. He had a more pressing concerns than to worry about where he put his feet.

Compton, trying to hit O'Reilly to leg, was hit on the glove by a kicking wrong'un, and could only offer an easy catch at the wicket: 5-96. The England lead was now seventy-seven. Paynter and Price added twenty but Fleetwood-Smith ensured there was to be no recovery: 6-116, 7-116, 8-116. In three swift strikes he dismissed Price leg before, and then Verity and Wright in successive balls. Paynter was left unbeaten, having, like Edrich earlier, played O'Reilly onto his stumps without disturbing the bails. O'Reilly finished the innings with successive balls to Farnes and Bowes: 9-123, all out 123. England were out for their lowest total since Trent Bridge in 1921. O'Reilly's ten-wicket tally included Hammond and Compton twice, and Edrich and Hardstaff once each, so six of his wickets were specialist batsmen. O'Reilly finished one short of his hundredth wicket, necessitating a date with destiny and Bill Edrich at The Oval to secure that victim.

Australia, needing 105, opened again with Fingleton and Brown. Hammond had three options: giving three overs each to the opening bowlers, as opener Bowes himself recommended, then asking spinners Verity and Wright to bowl Australia out. Alternatively, he could have relied on Bowes and Verity to contain the Australians and force them into error, essentially a policy of attrition. Finally, he could wait for a winning opportunity to present itself before going on the attack. This he seems to have preferred to do, though such opportunities mostly have to be made by captains, not waylaid.

Hammond began with Farnes and Bowes against Fingleton and Brown. The latter was palpably leg before to Farnes, but Bowes seemed to bowl well within himself, so the policy seemed to be attack at one end and containment at the other. Bradman entered with seventeen runs on the board, in what Kilburn described as 'a thunderous afternoon of increasing darkness and gathering storm'. Bradman had again forbidden his batsman to appeal against the light. He was at once himself nearly yorked in the gloom, then survived an appeal for lbw from Farnes. Perhaps music-lovers like Cardus could hear the Valkyries riding high overhead, but this occasion was being scripted for England by Warner, in his dual role of selector and newspaper correspondent, not Wagner, whose mythical Teutonic warrior maidens would not carry dead soldiers to their rest for another thirteen months.

Douglas Wright, whose run-up was described by Ray Robinson as 'a cross between a swallow-dive and a barn dance'.

With fifteen runs added, Verity replaced Farnes and had Fingleton lbw: 2-32. Bowes continued to bowl well within himself from the Main stand end but, after Verity upset Hammond's niggardly plan of containment by conceding fourteen runs in his next over, Hammond, with fifty-seven runs to spare, replaced Bowes with Wright: 2-48.

Some critics believed Hammond should have introduced Wright sooner, a view Warner shared, although he also commented that Wright's 'mixture of difficult balls and occasional short balls make him an awkward problem of captaincy'. The light was by now really bad. Bradman edged a two between Hammond and Verity in the slips from Wright's first ball, attempted to drive the next, a good-length leg-break, then was caught at second slip, cutting at a leg-break. Did a score of 3-50 represent a breakthrough for England? McCabe was the only experienced batsman to come.

Bradman subsequently admitted that from that point on, and 'for the only time in my life I could not bear to watch the play'. Instead, 'consuming copious supplies of bread and jam augmented by a liberal quantity of tea', he paced the dressing room floor as others bore the burden that had so often been his lot. O'Reilly, padded up, also paced and sipped.

Hassett on-drove his first ball, a no-ball from Wright, for four, snicked the next – and was missed as slip moved to his right instead of standing still. Non-playing pundits agreed with Warner that slips should not move to good-length balls from leg-spinners, as fielders could not anticipate the course of a false stroke from the bat's edge. Verity's was a vital miss, because rain was close and conditions were getting worse. Hassett's instructions were unchanged: go for the doctor.

Wright had McCabe caught at mid-wicket, trying to hook a characteristic long-hop. After three expensive overs, Wright had taken two wickets, but at a cost Hammond could ill afford. What price success? As always, Wright was a mixture: the great and the gruesome. At 4-61, perhaps Hammond should resort to his successful bowlers of the first innings, and keep Wright in reserve?

Badcock had his off stump shaved by a leg-break from Wright, but Hassett hooked him for four. Hammond brought back Bowes to replace Wright, finally finding the cost too high. Hassett responded by hooking Bowes for four, on-driving Verity, and pushing the left-hander off his pads for two more boundaries. The young man who would become an Australian 'great' asserted himself at a crucial time.

Farnes relieved Verity. So much for accuracy.

The Hammond plan of attack-cum-containment was falling apart as quickly as the rain was starting to fall. Bowes could not contain Hassett, though Badcock continued to concentrate on defence. With the score at 91, Hammond brought Wright back to replace Bowes for one final attempt to break through. The Kent leg-spinner had Hassett caught in his first over, the Victorian skying a leg-break to silly point after a match-deciding 33 out of forty-one scored while he was at the wicket. Though the storm seemed imminent, Hassett had so hectically ridden the tempest that England's chances were now full fathom five down – and almost out.

Australia needed only fourteen to win. Some said Hammond should have persevered with Wright throughout, others that he should have been saved for some psychological moment which had never quite arrived. Whatever the merits of the case, it was too late for any bowler to rescue England from defeat.

Barnett, who had played so sensibly at number three in the first innings, came in at number seven to join Badcock. He hooked a short Wright ball for four, only for rain to start falling with nine runs or five wickets needed to finish the game. This match, however, ended at four o'clock without further loss, Australia winning with Barnett and Badcock together. The latter had made five of Australia's last forty-six runs while Hassett and Barnett went for the long handle.

Though the fourth day was not needed, total crowd numbers reached 99,614. Frank Chester argued, on the basis of this game, that three days should be sufficient for any match, believing the batsman had to produce every reserve of skill and concentration to survive on such a wicket against the intriguing variety and guile of the bowlers on display. On the Headingley wickets experienced by Australians in 1938 and often since – 1956, 1961, 1972 – there are grounds for accepting this view, although only the 1961 game ended in three days.

In 1938, the Australians read and reacted to the conditions better than England and attacked whenever opportunity presented. Against pre-match expectation, it was the slower bowlers for both sides who did the real damage at Headingley, although the captains deployed them differently. The Australian spinners took 17-229 from ninety-seven overs in the match, compared to their England counterparts' 7-118 from forty-four overs. The quicker Australian bowlers by contrast delivered only fifty-two overs to claim 2-104 while the England opening bowlers returned figures of 8-221 from eighty-seven overs.

England were caught in a tactical trilemma arising from their team selection. Had the selectors recast the original side in the light of the withdrawals, the weather and the wicket, rather than making piecemeal repairs to whatever their original plan was, Hammond may have had a better chance. The final margin between success and failure was sufficiently small to suggest even a little luck might have tipped the balance his way. Had Hammond, on the other hand, been able to emulate Bradman in showing his side the way against hostile bowling and difficult conditions, he might not have had to rely on luck. Again, had England's premier batsman been as well supported with the bat as Barnett and Hassett supported Bradman, England might have had a greater margin than the one with which Hammond was asked to manage during the fourth innings.

The Australian team held a celebratory team dinner at its Harrogate hotel. Ben Barnett, with seventy-two runs for once out, five dismissals, and no byes, had enjoyed a good match. He would play only one more test, though his fitful first-class career lasted until 1961. His England namesake was dropped for The Oval to make way for Hutton, and Leyland returned. With Wright sick, and Wood coming in for Price, five Yorkshiremen were in the team. Between them, they made over six hundred runs – including Hutton's Ashes record score of 364 – took ten wickets and three catches. England won by the greatest margin in Ashes tests, an innings and 579 runs, to draw the 1938 series.

EW Swanton wrote that the result in the 1934 series, when Bill Woodfull's team regained the Ashes for Australia, 'could only have been different if Bradman's birthplace had been Banbury as distinct from Bowral; and if the parents of O'Reilly had arranged for his arrival in their native Ireland'. His comments were even more true for Headingley in 1938.

Bradman later remarked that, in normal circumstances, 1938 would have been his last England tour of England. He was nearing thirty, and had a living to make. Eight years had passed by the time the teams next met. Farnes and Verity had been killed in the war, as had Australia's Ross Gregory and Charles Walker, deputy gloveman on the 1930 and 1938 tours. O'Reilly gave test cricket one last go, at Wellington in early 1946, but his knees forced him to give the game away and retire to the press box. With the need to develop a new Australian side, and despite his own ill-health, Bradman batted on, returning to England for his triumphant 1948 tour. Hassett became his deputy, and Australia's next captain after Bradman retired.

After the war, Hammond's best years were behind him and Hutton, following injury to his left forearm, took a while to recover his form against a more formidable Australian pace attack, in Lindwall and Miller, than he had ever encountered before the break. Compton remained England's hero, with Edrich briefly bringing sunshine after rain. The clouds of war that had hung over Leeds in 1938 had dissipated, though there remained a shadow over post-war English hopes for three series to come.

·SYDNEY 1954·

THE TYPHOON OF CHANGE

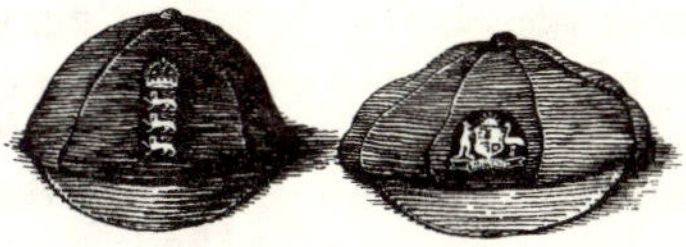

Explosive fast bowling by Frank Tyson confirms England captain Len Hutton's resolve that he can win with pace, enabling England to re-establish itself for the next four years as the world's premier cricket power. Hutton, as England's first professional captain in the twentieth century, shows a tough-minded approach, in some ways reminiscent of the amateur Douglas Jardine, England's Bodyline captain, twenty-two years earlier. Like Jardine, who did not call on the services of the great medium-pacer Maurice Tate, Hutton dispenses with the services of Alec Bedser, then England's greatest test wicket-taking bowler, after the first test of the series. But Hutton's captaincy is important for other reasons. Slow over rates, the bane of the modern game, become an attacking instrument. He also inspires the best of England's amateur batsmen, Peter May and Colin Cowdrey, to add grit to their game. Australia, by contrast, is unsettled. Arthur Morris is a stand-in captain and the team seems to have too many all-rounders. Young players Alan Davidson and Richie Benaud are yet to hit their straps.

AUSTRALIA v ENGLAND 1954 (2nd Test)

Played at Sydney Cricket Ground on 17, 18, 20, 21, 22 December.
Toss: Australia. Result: ENGLAND won by 38 runs.

ENGLAND

L Hutton*	c Davidson b Johnston	30	c Benaud b Johnston	28
TE Bailey	b Lindwall	0	c Langley b Archer	6
PBH May	c Johnston b Archer	5	b Lindwall	104
TW Graveney	c Favell b Johnston	21	c Langley b Johnston	0
MC Cowdrey	c Langley b Davidson	23	c Archer b Benaud	54
WJ Edrich	c Benaud b Archer	10	b Archer	29
FH Tyson	b Lindwall	0	b Lindwall	9
TG Evans†	c Langley b Archer	3	c Lindwall b Archer	4
JH Wardle	c Burke b Johnson	35	lbw b Lindwall	8
R Appleyard	c Hole b Davidson	8	not out	19
JB Statham	not out	14	c Langley b Johnston	25
Extras	(LB 5)	5	(LB 6, NB 4)	10
Total		**154**		**296**

AUSTRALIA

LE Favell	c Graveney b Bailey	26	c Edrich b Tyson	16
AR Morris*	c Hutton b Bailey	12	lbw b Statham	10
JW Burke	c Graveney b Bailey	44	b Tyson	14
RN Harvey	c Cowdrey b Tyson	12	not out	92
GB Hole	b Tyson	12	b Tyson	0
R Benaud	lbw b Statham	20	c Tyson b Appleyard	12
RG Archer	c Hutton b Tyson	49	b Tyson	6
AK Davidson	b Statham	20	c Evans b Statham	5
RR Lindwall	c Evans b Tyson	19	b Tyson	8
GRA Langley†	b Bailey	5	b Statham	0
WA Johnston	not out	0	c Evans b Tyson	11
Extras	(B 5, LB 2, NB 2)	9	(LB 7, NB 3)	10
Total		**228**		**184**

AUSTRALIA	O	M	R	W	O	M	R	W
Lindwall	17	3	47	2	31	10	69	3
Archer	12	7	12	3	22	9	53	3
Davidson	12	3	34	2	13	2	52	0
Johnston	13.3	1	56	3	19.3	2	70	3
Benaud					19	3	42	1
ENGLAND								
Statham	18	1	83	2	19	6	45	3
Bailey	17.4	3	59	4	6	0	21	0
Tyson	13	2	45	4	18.4	1	85	6
Appleyard	7	1	32	0	6	1	12	1
Wardle					4	2	11	0

FALL OF WICKETS

	E	A	E	A
Wkt	1st	1st	2nd	2nd
1st	14	18	18	27
2nd	19	65	55	34
3rd	58	100	55	77
4th	63	104	171	77
5th	84	122	222	102
6th	85	141	232	122
7th	88	193	239	127
8th	99	213	249	136
9th	111	224	250	145
10th	154	228	296	184

Umpires: MJ McInnes and R Wright.

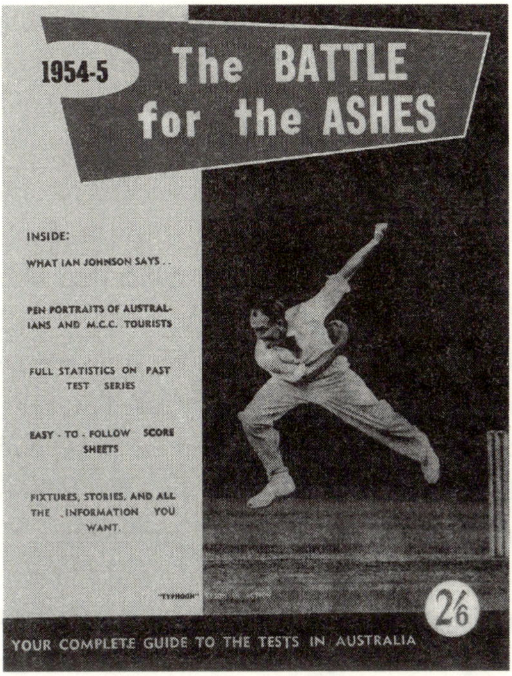

The second match of the 1954–55 series was a high point among England's fifties successes, and a low point in Australia's rebuilding in the post-Bradman era.

In the post-war period, Bradman and Hassett had led Australia through eight rubbers against all countries, winning all but the two most recent. The Australian season of 1954–55 would be the first under a new captain. Though transitional difficulties were experienced until 1958–59, the process of choosing Australian captains seems to have been less complicated than in England during the same period.

England, constrained by the tradition that selectors and captains alike were amateurs, had called upon ten captains in sixteen post-war series for seven wins and five losses. Although the old story of amateur unavailability for tours had made things tricky in 1950–51, the forty-year-old Freddie Brown had turned up trumps, and played on as captain in 1951. There followed in 1952 an elaborate game of cricket politics, involving the young Cambridge-educated amateur David Sheppard and the thirty-six-year-old Yorkshire professional Len Hutton. The drama surrounding the choice of captain is well summarised by Allen Synge in *Sins of Omission* and recorded at considerable length by Sheppard in *Parson's Pitch*, but the final outcome was that the England captaincy for the Australian tour went to Hutton.

Another key issue of the 1954–55 tour was the England opening attack, and much ink has been expended over its composition. Equal amounts of hot air have probably been released over the selection for Sydney of 'The Typhoon', Frank Tyson, at the expense of Alec Bedser.

In a nutshell, events prior to the Sydney test followed England's usual pattern in the post-war period of annihilation by Australia at Brisbane. The England loss by an innings and 154 runs was largely due to the unbalanced attack of four opening bowlers (Bedser, Tyson, Brian Statham, Trevor Bailey), and no spinners. Bedser had taken 1-131 and Tyson 1-160 out of Australia's 8-601 declared, but after that match Tyson had returned figures of 6-101 against Victoria at Melbourne.

Team selection is a collective exercise, although the captain's views obviously carry great weight. The 1954–55 touring selectors were batsmen Hutton, vice-captain Peter May and Bill Edrich, with wicketkeeper Godfrey Evans and tour manager Geoffrey Howard completing a mixture of amateurs and professionals. Bedser's omission attracted mixed reactions, with Bill O'Reilly describing it as an ill-timed blow to cricket lovers who had admired his skill in carrying England's bowling responsibilities almost alone. Such a comment neglected the fact that England picked its attack to win the test, not to entertain cricket lovers. It also overlooked the fact that Bedser had not recovered from illness suffered earlier in the tour. Thus his previous skills and successes were not necessarily germane to what he could have achieved in Sydney.

Bedser certainly should not have been shocked by his omission.

If he read Tom Goodman's report in the Friday morning's *Sydney Morning Herald*, he would have discovered that he was likely to be out of the side, and spinners Bob Appleyard and Johnny Wardle in. Subsequent accounts that depict his omission as a last minute manoeuvre by Hutton seem fanciful.

England made four changes from Brisbane and Australia two. Wardle and Appleyard replaced Bedser and batsman Reg Simpson, and the injured Denis Compton made way for Tom Graveney, while Godfrey Evans took over the wicketkeeping duties from Keith Andrew. For Australia, Jim Burke and Alan Davidson replaced captain Ian Johnson and Keith Miller, who were injured. Arthur Morris took over the captaincy for this test.

The vice-captains were Peter May and Richie Benaud. Fifteen years later, Benaud wrote that being made vice-captain for this match remained 'one of the most astonishing things that had ever happened' to him. To that time, he had only captained his club side and saw Neil Harvey, Ray Lindwall, or even Bill Johnston as more serious candidates for the role.

The absence of Keith Miller from the Australian line-up reduced both its strength and spectator appeal. Yet after the tour English umpire Frank Chester wrote that many critics identified Australia's lack of specialists as a problem. The inclusion of too many all-rounders – at various times Johnson, Miller, Lindwall, Benaud, Davidson, and Ron Archer – was said to have weakened the side. In this side Benaud, Archer, Davidson and Lindwall batted at numbers six, seven, eight and nine in the batting order.

DAY 1

Hutton and Morris tossed on a gloomy Sydney day and Morris chose to bowl on a greentop. Typically, the pitch had been covered from five on the evening preceding the match to 6.30 on the first morning. Plastic covers had been placed over the pitch, and the last few paces of the bowlers' run-ups covered, because of the threat of rain. It would have suited Tyson and Statham and, by implication, a fully-fit Bedser, but with Archer and Davidson to complement Bill Johnston and Lindwall, Australia were well-served in the pace department. According to the newspapers, parity was maintained in the slower bracket, with Benaud and Burke lined up against Appleyard and Wardle, although this reasoning did not impress Lindsay Hassett, who thought Morris's decision would expose Australia to England's higher-quality spinners later in the match.

Slightly over 23,000 people witnessed the day's play, which began at 11.30 with Hutton facing Lindwall's field of five slips and two short fine-legs. 'Thus does a keeper, entering the cage, sense the tiger', in Alan Ross's fine phrase. Nearly 49,000 had seen Hutton face Lindwall in the corresponding Sydney game on Brown's 1950–51 tour. Perhaps Sydneysiders were saving their pennies to see Australian tennis whizz-kids Lew Hoad and Ken Rosewall take on the Americans in the Davis Cup final in a few days' time.

Lindwall was generous with runs in his opening overs as Morris kept the field up in the search for inroads rather than economy. At the other end, Archer from short of a length furnished an appropriate foil. During his first three overs, Lindwall, working up speed, provided wide half-volleys for Hutton to steer toward the covers, in the hope he would present a catch to the slips cordon. At ten, Hutton looked ready to walk for a caught behind appeal off Lindwall but, with umpire Wright ruling otherwise, he remained.

Lindwall did gain an early break. He yorked Bailey middle stump with the second ball of his fourth over. The first wicket had taken thirty-seven minutes to fall. Bailey had made no attempt to score, and did not. Lindwall in his next over gave May a torrid time. In the *Sydney Morning Herald*, O'Reilly attributed May's subsequent dismissal to 'some magnificent bowling' by Lindwall, who had run a slower ball tantalisingly away from May's defensive bat before an in-dipper all but yorked him.

Such a sketchy account of this passage of play calls to mind Ken Barrington's replay of the Lindwall–May encounter at The Oval in May 1953. In the second innings of that Surrey–Australians match, Barrington was nonstriker as Lindwall bowled to May what Barrington a decade later still felt inclined 'to call the greatest over I've ever seen bowled . . . To me, a novice, it seemed that Ray bowled just about every type of delivery possible in that over . . . three deliveries did everything but bowl him. In the next over May was out [to Archer for one]. To me it was a lesson in tactics, temperament and Australian attempts to demoralise that I have never forgotten'.

History sometimes repeats itself precisely. In the next over, May played an in-swinging half-volley listlessly from Archer to backward short-leg to be caught by Johnston. England were 2-19 after an hour's play. His job done, Lindwall came off at 12.40, and at lunch England had reached 2-34. Graveney was on seven, and Archer had bowled seven overs for four runs and May's wicket.

Hutton was 19 after ninety minutes. According to a number of journalists, Hutton had done little to inspire confidence in his team-mates, but had depressed those due to follow him, a charge that would be maintained a generation later against his Yorkshire and England successor, Geoffrey Boycott.

For batsmen, mere occupation of the crease must not be the only priority. For bowlers, unsettling batsmen as well as getting them out is the aim. In Lindwall's case, those watching from behind his arm in the MA Noble stand could testify to his constant changes in pace and lift. His spell after lunch provided evidence that, when he lost his real speed, Lindwall's control of length, swing and subtle variation meant he would remain a great bowler. Hutton played two maiden overs from Lindwall in which the bowler adjusted the swing and pace of each delivery as he attacked first one stump then another. Even a batsman of Hutton's calibre was unable to let the ball go. Nor did he receive one that had finished swinging in the air.

The England fifty arrived in three times as many minutes, and

Davidson joined fellow left-arm fast-medium bowler Johnston in the attack. Forty minutes after lunch Hutton glanced a rising ball from Johnston correctly enough toward short fine-leg only for Davidson to dive wide to his right to take a right-handed catch low down. England's score was 3-58, of which Hutton had accumulated 30. For all his restraint and resistance, the home side had taken this first round.

Johnston achieved a second breakthrough less than ten minutes later, when Graveney glided a ball to Les Favell, at third slip, with a stroke one critic reckoned would not have passed muster in an annual office match. As often seemed the case at this stage of his career, twenty-seven-year-old Graveney had appeared inhibited in his stroke-play, and undercommitted to remaining at the crease, during his innings of eighty-eight minutes. Some observers felt Hutton influenced Graveney adversely, so that this grand stroke-player struggled to become a permanent England player before the age of thirty-nine.

With four wickets down, England were all too close to collapse when Colin Cowdrey and Bill Edrich came together. Briefly, the tempo of scoring increased. Cowdrey glided Johnston fine for four, and Edrich pulled an Archer no ball for four more but, after a half-hour's resistance, Edrich gave a gentle gully catch off Archer to be out for ten. When Tyson lost his leg stump to Lindwall, and Evans played inside an Archer half-volley, England's score slumped to 7-88. Archer had three for eight off ten overs.

Wardle was the new man in and England advanced its score by six to 7-94 at tea, by which time Cowdrey had reached 18. Cowdrey had been dropped by Benaud off Lindwall in the gully. His poor stroke was excused by commentators, but his failure to show initiative while accompanied by the England tailenders was viewed less favourably. When he departed, caught behind off Davidson, England's score read 8-99. Appleyard did not last long, being beautifully caught low down at first slip, by Hole, to make the score 9-111. The last wicket partnership, however, added forty-three runs in under half an hour, with the batsmen taking nineteen off an over by Johnston. Wardle cover-drove a four, scored two twos, and acquired two fours through slips, also giving Benaud the chance to drop him running back from slip. A single gave Statham a chance to score two runs of his own. In one over this pair had thus managed more than half of what it had taken England the entire pre-lunch period to acquire. Another measure of Wardle's contribution was that he registered five boundaries, or as many as the other ten batsmen, before being caught at deep mid-on off a skier. A short life, but a merry one.

Contemporary accounts vary in their evaluation of Wardle's personality, though they agree on his playing skills and insight into the game. *News Chronicle* correspondent Crawford White called him the 'Clown Prince' of cricket at the time. A left-arm spinner of great talent in both the orthodox and unorthodox styles, he shone as a batsman with an important innings given the winning margin at the finish.

Morris was praised for his efforts in the field. There was no fuss or bother about his handling of the team, and his decision to send England in to bat appeared to have been vindicated.

The Australian innings should have begun just before five, but a light shower of rain reduced it to twenty minutes. Australia ended the first day at 1-18, with Favell 6 and Bailey still bowling his second over of the innings. Morris spoiled his day by getting out to the third-last ball, caught at leg-slip for 12. From fifty-eight overs and one ball, 172 runs had been scored for the loss of eleven wickets in what would have been a five-hour day, the sessions being scheduled to run 11.30–1.00, 1.40–3.30, and 3.50–5.30.

DAY 2

The second day crowd of nearly 45,000 was the best of the tour. Four years earlier, there had been nearly seven thousand more. The difference could not be blamed on the weather, which was cloudy but fine, or on Bedser and Compton, both on the sidelines for this test, who had gone to the races at Randwick. Nor should the arrival of the Australian fifty in forty-four minutes have discouraged the punters. Tyson's no balls and full tosses forced Hutton to spell him after two very erratic overs for thirteen runs. Slow over rates, however, curtailed scoring.

Statham delivered his best spell, into a light breeze, from the Paddington end. Bailey bowled from the Randwick end from noon to lunch, Favell in his second test nibbling at him outside off stump before being caught ankle-high by second slip. Then Jim Burke, having reached the thirties, was missed in the same place off the same bowler. Bailey's length remained excellent. He also varied his angle of delivery and his margin of swing, rarely bowled outside leg stump, and bowled an occasional faster ball straight at the stumps.

Australia were 2-88 at lunch (Burke 39, Harvey 5) and afterwards Hutton maintained his pace attack. Bailey's post-lunch spell was 6-2-15-1, to give him figures of 3-43 from fourteen overs, while Tyson's figures totalled 2-36, with a spell of 6-0-23-2 after lunch. How were these figures achieved? Burke was caught shoulder-high by second slip off Bailey. Harvey, after almost seventy minutes for 12, with no boundaries, eventually became frustrated and twice played shots past the head of gully, before being caught playing a reflex back-stroke off a ball that reared startlingly. Australia were now 4-104 with South Australian Graeme Hole and vice-captain Benaud at the crease.

Hole, with his circular flourishing backlift, was bowled leg stump for 12 by a ball Tyson brought back off the pitch and Benaud was out for a sketchy 20 to a ball that cut back on him and kept low. Australia were now 6-141, thirteen short of the lead. Benaud had mis-hit Tyson for four over the keeper to go to seven, and two balls later had been badly dropped by Graveney at backward short-leg. Off-spinner Appleyard's first ball to him took the edge, then several spun off the pitch the other way, and another almost carried as a catch to Edrich at backward short-leg. Benaud's diffident approach meant he had not justified his batting spot at number six at a time in his career when he needed to make the most of every opportunity. He did not appear vice-captaincy material.

Archer and Davidson began a crucial stand twenty minutes before tea, and at the break the score was 6-158, Australia having lost four wickets in the session for seventy runs. Archer, having off-driven uppishly to the fence, pulled Appleyard for six from a shorter ball to take his side into the lead. The real value of all-rounders to a side was illustrated as the pair added fifty in even time before Davidson played a Statham delivery onto his leg stump.

Lindwall glanced Appleyard to the fence, but then was out mis-hitting a tired Tyson bouncer to Evans, suggesting that the legendary delivery which was to hit Tyson during the England second innings may have been a reprisal. Hutton took the new ball at 207, giving it to Tyson for the first time in the series. Tyson missed Archer's off stump with one delivery, then induced a mis-timed edge to third slip from the next. Archer's spirited innings of 49, a polished performance in desperate circumstances, was praised by Crawford White in his tour account, *England Keep the Ashes*. It was also the sort of innings which might have prompted Neil Harvey to write a decade later in *My World of Cricket* that he had considered Archer more likely to succeed to the Australian captaincy than either Ian Craig or Benaud. Injury was to end Archer's career prematurely, however, and there would be another four years, twenty-two tests, and turns for Ian Johnson, Lindwall, and Craig before the captaincy passed to Benaud.

Wicketkeeper Gil Langley was last man out, nine minutes from the scheduled close, in Bailey's sixteenth over. In the day's play, England had delivered a mere 414 balls. Australia finished with 228, giving it a lead of seventy-four off virtually the same number of overs as England had faced.

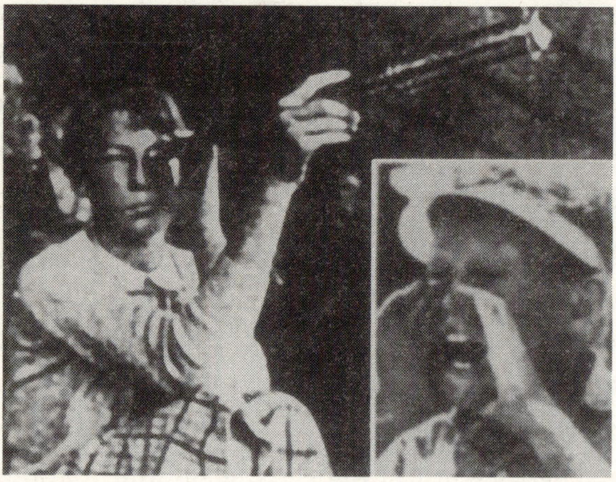

Monday's play attracted a crowd of nearly 32,000, including three spectators featured in the *Sydney Morning Herald*. One was Betty Couchman from Condobolin, who was pictured on the front page of the Monday morning paper using a telescope to pick up flaws in the game, though perhaps the picture was meant to mock serious female interest.

One headline recorded that England hoped to make at least three hundred runs. If this was a serious proposition, the six maidens bowled in the first twelve overs of the day must have made such a total likely to take a long time.

Archer opened with three consecutive maidens, including an over of half-volleys to Bailey. Twelve runs were on the board after fifteen minutes but, after steering Lindwall's eighth ball down the gully, and turning Archer to the fence, Hutton batted as if he was expecting to bat from Monday through Wednesday and into the last day of the test. Bailey, as usual, was immobile. He was struck on the back as he tried to duck an Archer lifter, and remained forty minutes for six, with a single boundary off Lindwall. His departure, caught behind off Archer, brought vice-captain May in to join captain Hutton at 1-18. The time was eight minutes past noon. Hutton glanced Johnston for four, drove him past cover, and turned Archer, uppishly, for four through the short-legs. When drinks were taken after an hour, England had reached 1-32, with Hutton 15 and May 11.

Hutton was out trying to play the third ball of Johnston's second over. Johnston replaced Archer after the Queenslander's opening spell of 6-4-15-1, and conceded eight runs in his first over as a result of obtaining greater outswing than any other bowler. Hutton then attempted to push a slower ball, thought he was checking his shot, but the chance went low to short gully off the middle of his bat.

Graveney succeeded his captain, but left after only six balls, out trying to drive. At least he brought joy to one onlooker. Eleven-year-old Robert Curley of Coogee was the second spectator front-paged as he yelled joyously for the dismissal. A year later, he could well have doubled for English child actor Colin Petersen as the juvenile lead in the Australian movie *Smiley*. The pairing of Peter May with Colin Cowdrey, which commenced eight minutes before lunch, would steadily wipe the smile from his face during the afternoon. England were 3-58 at the break.

Though Lindwall unleashed seven consecutive overs before lunch, and seven thereafter, he was unable to move the ball in the air. In the afternoon session, May snicked a Lindwall delivery just clear of his stumps, and cleared the England deficit with a mis-timed shot. Morris brought Benaud on for his first bowl at 118, after May and Cowdrey had added sixty by determined but undramatic play.

Leg-spinner Benaud delivered seventeen continuous overs from the pavilion end either side of tea, throwing the ball up and bowling at the stumps in a long duel with class batsmen. Just before tea, May almost played on to Davidson, but walked in with 58 of the England total of 3-129, having reached his fifty with eight fours in two hours twenty-two minutes. Cowdrey was on 37.

A schoolteacher from Albert, sixty miles west of Dubbo, became the third spectator whom newspaper coverage allowed to make a small mark on Anglo–Australian test history. Kenneth McKim employed the tea adjournment to inspect the wicket and talk with a member of the ground staff. The papers reported that he asked spectators to sign his diary to verify his feat for all the folks back home. Where are they now, Betty Couchman, Robert Curley and Kenneth McKim, these three faces briefly risen from the throng? How differently have subsequent pitch-invaders been treated!

England reached their 150 and Cowdrey his fifty (six fours) five minutes later. The century partnership was the next milestone reached but then, unaccountably, Cowdrey retreated into Bailey-like introspection before he was caught hitting Benaud's wrong'un to the only deep fielder in the area. May was 81 when the 116-run stand was broken but, with Edrich, added another thirty-three runs in the twenty-five minutes to stumps. Edrich had swung Johnston high to the leg boundary, off-driven him for four, and pulled a short Benaud delivery for his third boundary. Johnston contributed four no balls to the score, just to show he was willing. For his part, May had hit Johnston wide of mid-on then past mid-off for his ninth and tenth boundaries. England were 4-204 overnight, with May 98 and Edrich 16, from the seventy eight-ball overs Australia had delivered in the day. This was a twenty per cent improvement on the England ration.

Over the series as a whole, Australia averaged fourteen overs an hour, more than sixteen balls an hour ahead of England. England scored its runs at a rate of thirty-five per hundred balls bowled, Australia at forty-seven per hundred. Hutton linked pace to parsimony as a strategy, as a tactic linked economy of effort in the field to endurance by the batting side, and put far greater value on winning than entertainment. He was fortunate that in Tyson and Statham he had the bowlers, and in Cowdrey and May the batsmen, to achieve his purpose.

Commendations of May's unfinished innings were lavish. From the Australian side, some journalists believed the real strength and richness of his batting lay in his many on-side placements, while for others his innings was an exhibition of control that laid to rest stories that he did not possess the temperament for test cricket. But one English journalist, Alan Ross, still had reservations, saying that May still needed to throw off the unhappy characteristic of being a second-innings batsman. 'He should by nature be the architect of a match, not its restorer.'

A decade later, the Reverend David Sheppard made some perceptive remarks about May after both their test careers had ended. He commented that when he returned to the England team against Australia for the 1956 series, he found May toughened, his 'intensity of concentration for runs' matched only by Hutton, Ken Barrington, and Australian Bobby Simpson.

Lindwall bowls Bailey for nought

DAY 4

Lindwall bowled an opening over, then drizzle delayed the new ball, no doubt to the frustration of the 20,000 crowd. May pushed his second ball for two through the on-side to reach three figures in twenty minutes over the four hours. This was his third test hundred, exceeding his previous best score against Australia of 44 in the second innings at Brisbane. One newspaper article noted that the hundred made him England's sixth post-war centurion in Ashes matches, after Hutton, Cyril Washbrook, Edrich, Compton and Reg Simpson. Cowdrey and Graveney would become the seventh and eighth later in this series. An immediate question, not posed in the papers, was how many Australians had performed the equivalent feat. The answer was nine. Among the batsmen, Bradman, Hassett, Sid Barnes, Morris, Harvey and Burke (on debut); of the all-rounders, Miller, Lindwall and Colin McCool.

Seventeen minutes were lost to rain before Australia extracted seven more overs from the old ball while May added three runs. England used this period of grace to take its score to 4-222, though Edrich was almost caught and bowled by Davidson in the meantime.

At 12.20, two minutes short of five hours at the wicket, May was out to Lindwall's third delivery with the new ball. His departure, bowled middle and off stumps, began a five wicket flurry. Tyson, with a single to his name, was injured fifteen minutes before lunch after taking his eyes off a short ball from Lindwall. Hit on the back of the head, he had to be helped from the field and, for all anyone could tell at the time, might have taken no further part in the match. His replacement, Evans, was dropped first ball by Hole at first slip. After his rapid run-getting the previous evening, Edrich had reached 29 in ninety minutes when Archer bowled him. Lunch saw England 158 ahead, with the score 6-232.

Evans was seventh out, caught by third slip off Archer shortly after play resumed, then Tyson returned, receiving a consoling arm around the shoulders from Lindwall and no more short deliveries. After he batted for over forty minutes altogether, however, England lost five wickets for forty-six runs to the new ball and were only 176 ahead when the ninth wicket fell at 250. As in the first innings, a spirited last-wicket stand occurred, this time led by Appleyard, who was described as having batted like 'a man who has taken his big scores on big occasions with little effort'. Statham played his part with five boundaries. Both men made their highest scores of the tour in adding forty-six in fifty minutes before Johnston had Statham caught behind at 296.

Australia began its chase less than half an hour to tea, needing just 223. The home side started shakily. Statham almost got Favell with three of his first four deliveries. Favell survived an lbw appeal off his second ball, then was missed fourth or fifth ball at first slip by Edrich off Statham before he had scored. (There is as much uncertainty in the newspaper accounts as in Favell's batting.) He managed his first two runs from a deflection, then glanced the last ball of the opening over for four, before square-cutting the same bowler for another four in his next over. Hutton kept Statham on at the Paddington end into the breeze because he was getting more lift from the still-grassy pitch than any other bowler.

Morris, meanwhile, was batting as flashily as Favell. Tyson beat him twice outside off stump, and most of Statham's third over had the same effect on the Australian captain. He played a pair of risky swishes as his version of attempted square-cuts, then survived an lbw appeal. But to be dismissed by the second last ball before tea, to a shot O'Reilly described as a 'suicidally wild swing toward the leg, a shot borrowed unspoiled from kerosene-tin cricket', was uncharacteristic and perhaps a result of the burden of captaincy. Losing a wicket at the break was bad enough, but Tyson's sixth ball of the final session had Favell offering a head-high chance to first slip: 2-34.

Australia's stumps score, 2-72, represented a recovery and had been achieved off twenty-three overs. Thirty-five runs had been accrued in the eighty minutes after Favell's departure. Such a scoreline might suggest that, while the play had not been exhilarating, the pre-tea alarms had not recurred in the last session. Consider however, how Burke, who acquired 13 in eighty-seven minutes, had fared in that time. Match reports indicate he had almost been hit as he ducked low under a Statham bouncer, and hit on the upper leg and in the groin by a ball coming back in at him off the pitch, both times by the same bowler. He was also struck in the stomach and over the heart by Tyson. The bowler rushed to Burke's assistance, but was booed by the crowd. Along the way, Burke ran three for a shot to square-leg off Tyson, remained scoreless for fifty minutes, scored three off an edge through slips from Appleyard, and found a four by steering Tyson down the gully.

At the other end, Neil Harvey almost edged his first two deliveries from Tyson to the slips. He had managed 26 in seventy-eight minutes after off-driving and sweeping Wardle to the fence from consecutive balls in the last over of the day. These were, untypically, the left-hander's only boundary shots.

DAY 5

A final day crowd of 14,000 (match aggregate 135,000) could have read nothing in the pitch, described as 'corn coloured', and offering no help to the bowlers. Nothing in the match so far would have helped them predict what was about to be enacted.

Tyson opened from the Randwick end with a south-east wind to assist him. Five runs came from his first over. In his second over, Tyson's third ball was a very fast yorker even Burke could not intercept on its way to his off stump. A swinging yorker in the same over removed Hole's middle stump. Fifteen minutes after the start, the scoreboard read Australia 4-77. Harvey remained. May stopped two square-cuts off Statham, but the left-hander put a third past him to the boundary.

Bailey replaced Statham, so Statham could switch to Tyson's end with the wind, after which Hutton brought on off-spinner Appleyard for Statham, with the score at 100. In retrospect, this latter change was one of those insightful tactical moves which win matches. Benaud ended his brief innings when he skied Appleyard's in-dipper to deep square-leg, where Tyson held the catch. Australia were 5-106. Fifteen minutes remained till lunch.

Denis Compton featured heavily in advertising but missed the Sydney Test through injury.

Harvey endured, straight-driving Tyson for four, and fought his way through to lunch on 51. The score was 5-118 with Archer on five. Forty-six runs had been added in the ninety-minute morning session.

When play resumed at 1.40, Tyson bowled with the breeze. In Swanton's phrase, Statham laboured 'up the cellar steps' into it for eighty-three minutes unchanged, in the decisive gamble of the match. As the dice fell, the odds started to stack up in England's favour, Australia parting with four wickets in fifty minutes for twenty-seven runs.

Archer was dismissed, cutting, and lost his off stump at 6-122 before Davidson was caught two-handed by Evans, diving to his left in front of second slip. Though Evans almost lost the ball as he hit the ground, he regained it. Lindwall took eight off the rest of the Statham over, but received a breakback first ball from Tyson, and was beaten by sheer pace and bowled second ball. Langley then had his off stump snapped by Statham.

At 2.30, Australia were 9-145 and Harvey had reached 64. Six runs later, he hooked Tyson over the head of Bailey, who shortly thereafter relieved Statham after a six-over spell in which he had claimed two wickets for seventeen runs. Johnston led his usual charmed life. He nearly lost his off stump first ball, was almost lbw to his second from Statham, but lasted thirty-seven minutes. He thus had time to score two boundaries, the second from the penultimate ball of his innings, before Evans caught him off the exhausted Tyson to give England victory by thirty-eight runs.

Harvey was undefeated on 92, having scored nine fours in his four-hour-nineteen-minute marathon. He scored twenty-eight of the last-wicket stand of thirty-nine, and exactly half of Australia's final 184.

The last dismissal occurred just after three o'clock, England winning with a day in hand. Tyson's final spell of 7.4-1-41-3 sent his figures to 6-85, but more significant was the thought by Alan Ross that, in this one match, Tyson had 'reimposed the menace of speed on Australian batsmen', as succeeding matches were to show.

Certainly veteran Australian radio commentator Alan McGilvray repeats the Cardus story that Hutton had vowed he would defeat Australia with speed. Cardus rated Hutton's plan for Sydney and thereafter 'a firm-mindedness and shrewdness never excelled by any other captain'. Reports generally agree that Hutton led England with patience, skill and admirable control, attacking whenever possible, and making the most of periods of defence. Despite what some see as a blind spot about unorthodox spin of the Wardle variety, it is agreed that Hutton was clearsighted enough about the potential of pace on this occasion.

Bill O'Reilly, in his summation, revisited his old theme about Bedser's omission unthinkingly. Thus he commented that 'England must not act on a hunch again about Bedser. What a comfort he would have been to English hopes today when the runs were mounting up and the two fast men were bowling their hearts out'. The question of whom Bedser might have replaced – Appleyard or Wardle, scarcely Bailey – went unasked. Bailey seemed to have 'performed the duties which Bedser had so often done since the war on good wickets. He moved the ball consistently and sufficiently from a good length' to confine stroke-players to nervous defensive measures. It all sounds as though Bedser was redundant. Without detracting from Bedser's test record in his days of bowling greatness, old sweats like O'Reilly appeared to be hankering after their own glory days.

In the immediate aftermath of Sydney, the Typhoon that was Tyson chilled many Australian cricketers' traditionally hot Christmas dinners and did not finally clear the Australian coastline until early March 1955. By that time, Australia had lost the series 1–3. Thereafter, although Tyson returned to Australia as a player for the 1958–59 tour, his greater impact on the country was as a permanent resident from the early 1960s onwards.

For his part, Hutton went home to rewards and retirement. Exhausted by the England captaincy, he left the game before he was forty. His retirement allowed the captaincy to return for the 1955 season to the amateur Peter May. Umpire Frank Chester believed that, if his leadership developed as his batting had once he won his battle of nerves, May would gain a place in the gallery of great England captains. Whether or not May justified such expectations, with him and fellow Oxbridge amateur Colin Cowdrey the captaincy would remain until 1961. Another professional would not captain England until well after the amateur–professional distinction had been officially abandoned. When this happened, Yorkshiremen Brian Close and Ray Illingworth followed in the footsteps of their fellow Tyke.

•LORD'S 1961•

WILLIAM THE CONQUEROR

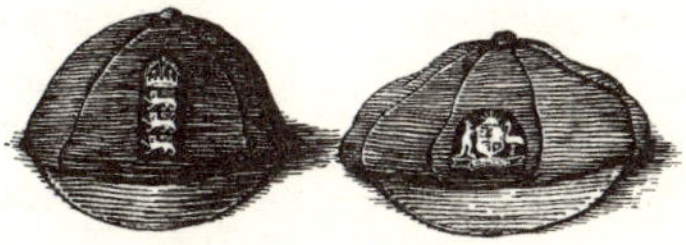

This match is often written up as the Battle of the Ridge, but we explore a number of other angles. Among these are Neil Harvey's one chance at test captaincy, the emergence of new Australian test heroes in Bill Lawry and Graham McKenzie, and the passing of the baton of premier batsman from amateurs Peter May, Colin Cowdrey and Ted Dexter to the professional Ken Barrington. Heaviest accent is laid on selection, where Australia picks the better-balanced team for the conditions and Cowdrey's management of the resources at his disposal proves poor. England fights back at the finish, but Peter Burge's enterprising second-innings thirty recalls a similar match-winning effort by Lindsay Hassett in the 1938 Leeds test.

ENGLAND v AUSTRALIA 1961 (2nd Test)

Played at Lord's, London, on 22, 23, 24, 26 June.
Toss: England. Result: AUSTRALIA won by five wickets.

ENGLAND

G Pullar	b Davidson	11	c Grout b Misson	42
R Subba Row	lbw b Mackay	48	c Grout b Davidson	8
ER Dexter	c McKenzie b Misson	27	b McKenzie	17
MC Cowdrey*	c Grout b McKenzie	16	c Mackay b Misson	7
PBH May	c Grout b Davidson	17	c Grout b McKenzie	22
KF Barrington	c Mackay b Davidson	4	lbw b Davidson	66
R Illingworth	b Misson	13	c Harvey b Simpson	0
JT Murray†	lbw b Mackay	18	c Grout b McKenzie	25
GAR Lock	c Grout b Davidson	5	b McKenzie	1
FS Trueman	b Davidson	25	c Grout b McKenzie	0
JB Statham	not out	11	not out	2
Extras	(LB 9, W 2)	11	(B 1, LB 10, W 1)	12
Total		**206**		**202**

AUSTRALIA

WM Lawry	c Murray b Dexter	130	c Murray b Statham	1
CC McDonald	b Statham	4	c Illingworth b Trueman	14
RB Simpson	c Illingworth b Trueman	0	(6) c Illingworth b Statham	15
RN Harvey*	c Barrington b Trueman	27	(3) c Murray b Trueman	4
NC O'Neill	b Dexter	1	(4) b Statham	0
PJP Burge	c Murray b Statham	46	(5) not out	37
AK Davidson	lbw b Trueman	6	not out	0
KD Mackay	c Barrington b Illingworth	54		
ATW Grout†	lbw b Dexter	0		
GD McKenzie	b Trueman	34		
FM Misson	not out	25		
Extras	(B 1, LB 12)	13		
Total		**340**	(5 wickets)	**71**

AUSTRALIA	O	M	R	W	O	M	R	W
Davidson	24.3	6	42	5	24	8	50	2
McKenzie	26	7	81	1	29	13	37	5
Misson	16	4	48	2	17	2	66	2
Mackay	12	3	24	2	8	6	5	0
Simpson					19	10	32	1
ENGLAND								
Statham	44	10	89	2	10.5	3	31	3
Trueman	34	3	118	4	10	0	40	2
Dexter	24	7	56	3				
Lock	26	13	48	0				
Illingworth	11.3	5	16	1				

FALL OF WICKETS

	E	A	E	A
Wkt	1st	1st	2nd	2nd
1st	26	5	33	15
2nd	87	6	63	15
3rd	87	81	67	19
4th	111	88	80	19
5th	115	183	127	58
6th	127	194	144	
7th	156	238	191	
8th	164	238	199	
9th	167	291	199	
10th	206	340	202	

Umpires: CS Elliott and WE Philipson.

Bill Lawry

Former England off-spinner Jim Laker wrote of this series that England were 'a team of individuals battling their own way through problems and difficulties without any definite team plan of campaign'. The same tendency had been all too evident during the disastrous 1958–59 tour of Australia. New players like Geoff Pullar and Ken Barrington seemed, according to Laker, 'obsessed with the fact that failure would mean a swift return to county cricket' and so took few chances with their batting.

For Barrington, the no-risk policy and his anxious disposition would bring nearly 7000 test runs and twenty centuries, a heart attack that ended his playing career in 1968, and a premature death in 1980, aged fifty. After seventeen tests since 1955, Barrington's career was well under way. By comparison, Australian opener Bill

Lawry, plumber, pigeon-fancier and reputed Phantom fan, was in only the second of his sixty-seven tests. Lawry would make his maiden test hundred in his second test, at Lord's, where England has beaten Australia only once this century. Barrington would make nine test hundreds before his first at home three years later.

The Australian batting order for this test, the second of the series, seemed obvious. Lawry was thought a lucky selection for the tour, but the selectors were not plumbing the depths in piping him abroad. His eight-hour 266 at Sydney in the preceding season was only his second three figure score since his Victorian debut in the 1955–56 season, but a thousand runs in seventeen completed innings put him high in the national averages. He quickly made his mark in the early weeks of the England tour with hundreds at Lord's and The Oval.

Fellow opener Colin McDonald had made two English tours (1953, 1956), and Bob Simpson stiffened the middle order. Neil Harvey was a frequent tourist (1948, 1953, 1956) and a world-class player. Norm O'Neill, after exceeding five hundred runs against the West Indies during the 1960–61 series, was thought to be on the way to becoming one. Peter Burge was on his second England tour and about to re-establish his test career, while Brian Booth would get his chance later in the tour.

The Australian attack picked itself on form. Of the quicker bowlers, Alan Davidson, despite a strained back and an asthma attack suffered at Canterbury two days before the test, had promised the team he would rise to the occasion – and did. Richie Benaud, in *Willow Patterns*, could not recall a more penetrative opening bowler, who moved the ball as late as anyone and whose bumper lifted to shoulder height from frighteningly near the opposite batting crease. Frank Misson, following five wickets against Kent, remained in the side from the First Test at Edgbarton. Ron Gaunt had been sidelined by injury and remained out of the side for the moment. More importantly, Graham McKenzie replaced injured Richie Benaud on the strength of seven wickets against Leicestershire, despite taking 1-133 against Kent in the match prior to the test.

Ray Lindwall, a commentator on this series, thought the Lord's test the best match for Australia's leg-spinning captain to miss, especially since leg-spinning all-rounder Simpson had recovered his 'loop' at Leicester. According to Laker, the Australian camp felt that 'if any of the reserve Australian spinners had shown any form at all then they would certainly have been included in the side'. This was a curious statement. Victorian left-handers, unorthodox Lindsay Kline and the uncapped finger-spinner Ian Quick had taken eighteen and twenty-two wickets at moderate cost in eight and nine games respectively.

In Benaud's enforced absence, Harvey had lead the Australians to a win over Leicestershire and a draw with Kent since the First Test. For this, his seventieth test, Harvey secured the captaincy by default. Five years and twenty or so tests before, he had believed, with some justification, that he might succeed to the role in his own right. At that time, both Harvey, then with four thousand runs and sixteen test hundreds behind him, and Benaud, were rumoured to be the subject of Board of Control concerns that they were not fit candidates. The captaincy, for which Queensland all-rounder Ron Archer had seemed a strong candidate until he injured himself in Pakistan after the 1956 Ashes tour, then settled briefly on the youthful shoulders of New South Welshman Ian Craig.

In 1956–57, after missing the opening two Sheffield Shield games, Harvey replaced Sam Loxton as Victorian captain. He averaged over ninety in five games as captain, scoring four hundreds. When Craig gained the captaincy for a New Zealand tour in February–March 1957, vice-captain Harvey sublimated his suspicions by opening the batting and scoring 209 against NSW on Australia Day. When the roles remained unreversed for the South African tour of 1957–58, Harvey secured employment in Sydney in June 1958, only to find Benaud replacing Craig, unavailable because of hepatitis, for the opening Shield game of the 1958–59 season. Harvey captained an Australian Eleven against England in Sydney a fortnight before the Brisbane test that year, but Benaud succeeded Craig as national captain, and Harvey continued as the vice-captain.

In *Captain's Story*, Bob Simpson remarked that, before 1958, many people had doubted Benaud's temperament for the role. Fellow players, who reportedly had found the intense all-rounder aloof and unapproachable, noticed a complete change once he secured the captaincy. For his part, Bill Lawry wrote in *Run Digger* that he could never understand how the selectors could have overlooked fellow Victorian Neil Harvey in favour of Craig.

Craig, recovered from illness for the 1960–61 season, made 197 in New South Wales's final Sheffield Shield match to take his season's record to 627 runs at an average of 57 just before the touring party was announced. He was in the running for his third England tour, although he turned twenty-six only ten days before the Lord's test and was just eight months older than Ashes newcomer Simpson. Craig had been Australia's golden boy, the equivalent of England's amateur captains. He could, in theory, have captained Australia from 1957 until 1976–77, when Simpson emerged from retirement during the crisis of World Series cricket to resume the national captaincy. Australia played 138 tests from 1957–58 to the Centenary Test in Melbourne in 1977, when Craig was approaching forty-two. Good health and form, and greater financial rewards than his pharmacy career might have provided, could have seen him set Allan Border a steeper set of targets than he eventually surpassed.

Back in the real world, the twenty-four-year-old Lawry kept Craig from making the tour, and captain Benaud's reaction to missing out on leading Australia at Lord's seems to have gone unrecorded.

The England side, as usual, were playing musical chairs. Batsman Peter May and bowler Tony Lock replaced batsman Mike Smith and bowler David Allen.

Fierce media pressure on Peter May helped speed the day when his London business commitments and Surrey homelife pulled him out of big cricket. But in 1961 illness also prevented him from playing regularly. After reaching 150 in Surrey's match at Taunton on the opening day of the Birmingham test, May missed two games with a muscle strain. He was a calculated risk for this match. England colleague Reverend David Sheppard later commented that May left test cricket with 'the music playing rather softly in the background', perhaps because he had turned down the volume of runs voluntarily.

As for Sheppard himself, his work at the Mayflower Youth Centre meant he could play no first-class innings in 1961, and would not be in the running for an England cap again until 1962. Even so, he gained an optimistic mention in the 1962 *Wisden* editorial on the series. An even more ingenuous *Wisden* suggestion was that Roy Marshall, capped four times by the West Indies in Australia during 1951–52, was about to become qualified for England after many seasons with Hampshire. Of more likely possibles, professional Tom Graveney had been ruled officially unavailable because he 'needed' to qualify for Worcestershire following his loss of the Gloucestershire captaincy and subsequent wish to change counties.

With regard to the attack, England maintained the faith in old fast-bowling warriors, Yorkshire's Fred Trueman and Lancashire's Brian Statham. In his 1961 tour account, Ray Lindwall favoured the Essex all-rounder Barry Knight but other hopefuls David Larter (Northampton) and Harold Rhodes (Derbyshire) had taken only 2-246 for MCC against the Australians at Lord's in May, thus ruling themselves out.

Rhodes also represented a different sort of difficulty, having been regularly called for throwing. This was the summer of the 'throwing truce' and two Australians had not made the Australian touring side because of doubts about their actions. Western Australia's Keith Slater was disbarred as a quick but not as a slow bowler, and Victorian Ian Meckiff, who had played two tests against the West Indies, was also overlooked. Laker cruelly quipped that Meckiff's future 'lay in

American baseball and not in first-class cricket', a judgement partly and sadly borne out at Brisbane thirty months on.

The England selectors comprised three former amateurs – 'Gubby' Allen, Wilf Wooller, and Doug Insole – and ex-Yorkshire professional Herbert Sutcliffe. They picked a traditional, balanced attack after apparently misreading the pitch. Their decision virtually decided the match.

Let a professional participant tell it like he thought it was. Ken Barrington wrote that 'the entire feeling of playing in a test at Lord's is different to that of anywhere else. The tension is almost terrifying, almost afire with intense, pent up excitement and expectancy'. But he continued: 'What a tragedy, then, that the playing conditions at Lord's in recent years have not been better. The Australian match was the fourth test I had played at HQ and each had followed a similar pattern: the wicket proved fiery on the first day, then improved.'

Barrington first played at Lord's in 1955. In that test, England were dismissed for 133 on the first day, and thereafter Statham accounted for the South Africans in a spell of twenty-nine overs unchanged. Barrington didn't play in 1956, when Keith Miller took ten of the thirty-three wickets which fell to the quick bowlers, nor in 1957 when Bailey's fast-medium aggregated 43-14-98-11. In 1958, the England spinners ruled supreme, with Laker and Lock filching figures of 49-29-66-14 against the Kiwis.

Barrington returned for the 1959 test, when 226 was the highest of three completed innings. In this game, the England spinners took nine wickets, the fast men ten, and the Indian seamers ten in an England eight-wicket win. The 1960 pitch saw the pace bowlers take all twenty-eight wickets in the match, Statham returning 41-11-97-11.

In 1961, the collective efforts of the seamers in bowling 279 of the match total of 335 overs netted them thirty-three of the thirty-five wickets to fall. Barrington, unsurprisingly, believed England erred in omitting an extra seamer. He said that he would have 'loved' to have seen thirty-eight-year-old Trevor Bailey in the side for his bowling. The *Wisden* editorial similarly regretted Bailey's absence, feeling he might have made all the difference on the ridge. Two years later, Bailey was widely touted for The Oval test against Frank Worrell's West Indian side. While one Barnacle doesn't make a bouillabaisse, an extra quicker bowler might have had Australia in a stew.

Prematch opinion was divided. South African journalist Charles Fortune thought it a 'pretty good track', which would become a slow turner. Laker's eyes led him to assert that 'the groundsman appeared to have lowered the blades on his mower, and less grassier pitches had been the result'. He went on to report that he had 'never seen a wicket quite like it before. There were an unusual number of bare patches interposed among the grassier patches, which naturally held more moisture'.

For this reason he was sure the ball would turn as the game progressed, a confident opinion from one used to making the most of turning surfaces. In the meantime, any ball pitching on a bare patch would come through at normal pace and height, but balls striking grassier parts, containing more moisture, would lift and fly. He predicted that, as the grassier patches dried out, the ball would behave more rationally, with the danger remaining occasional balls coming off what Laker called 'this small ridge'.

Alan Davidson commented in his autobiography, *Fifteen Paces*, that a ridge, three metres in front of the Nursery end batting crease, was almost imperceptible to the eye, though it soon enough became 'evident to the bodies of batsmen' who had to cope with the flying ball.

The Times headlined its 22 June preview 'Australia without their main inspiration'. Sharing the general English misconception about the Lord's wicket, their unnamed correspondent ventured to predict that on the Monday, when the ball began to turn, the Australians would wish they had Benaud, or left-hander Johnny Martin, who was playing for Colne in the Lancashire league, a poor reflection on Kline and Quick. Considering the England batsmen would find themselves 'freed from the worry of Benaud's bowling', and since Davidson had been 'lacking in his usual zest', the correspondent exceeded even the inclinations of his kind with two of the most optimistic expectations ever committed to hard copy: 'England should get all the runs they want. If ever there was a time to be a batsman against Australia this must be it.' By Tuesday's *Times*, the same correspondent was reporting, without comment, that a quartet described without irony as 'the game's greatest batsmen' – Cowdrey and May for England, Harvey and O'Neill for Australia – had managed only ninety-four runs during eight visits to the Lord's creases.

A similarly bland and ultimately unperceptive comment recorded that the wicket looked different from those prepared in recent years. 'It has far less grass for one thing and its bounce should be more predictable.'

||| DAY 1

England took two spinners – Tony Lock and Ray Illingworth – into the game, but the 30,000 crowd saw no spin all day. They sat five and six deep on the grass, despite a cloudy, slightly humid day, and many will have realised this was a difficult toss for Cowdrey to win. After eight successive successes in that department, Neil Harvey might have expected the fall of the coin to favour him. It did not. Cowdrey chose to bat.

Readers of *The Times* in the crowd could have appreciated from the outset the enviable understatement that 'anyone who has watched England in most of their Test matches since the war knows that it is never possible to await their innings with unfettered confidence'.

Their fears were also borne out as Davidson, opening from the Pavilion end, 'came into his second over like an ageing lion who suddenly had rediscovered the secret of youth'. In the fine words of South African cricket writer Charles Fortune: 'For weeks he had bowled as one kept going only by momentum gathered in years gone by. He had become no more than a commuter moving to and fro along familiar tracks with no liking for the business. Here suddenly all lethargy left the man . . . Now into his work went every fibre of the massive frame.'

Johnny Moyes described Davidson's opening spell in Melbourne eighteen months later in similar style: 'Davidson came down from the pavilion end like a man in a hurry. His arm came over quickly and he bowled with a speed I had not seen from him since the Melbourne Test four years earlier . . .' Just as Davidson broke down in this later series at Adelaide, so in 1961 he scarcely recovered for the remainder of the season, and experienced difficulty in stooping to field the ball as late as the Fifth Test.

In both cases, the imagery conveys the reason why. In this case, left-hander Raman Subba Row was beaten three times in an over, before scoring a run through gully from a shot aimed at mid-wicket. That is, playing across the line of the fast left-hander's in-swing, Subba Row succeeded only in getting the ball away in a direction one hundred and eighty degrees different from his intention.

His opening partner, Lancashire left-hander Geoff Pullar, was dropped at five off the splice by Burge. The bulky Queenslander got both hands to the ball as he ran to point from gully, but his momentum made the chance miscarry. Davidson was again the cause of the batsman's discomfort. Against the odds, England had registered twenty-three in the first half hour. Pullar added six in the next two overs before losing middle and off stumps through the bat-pad gap with his score at eleven. He had been late on the shot, as he had been at Birmingham.

Misson replaced McKenzie and was on-driven by Subba Row for four. Twice hit in the ribs by Davidson, Ted Dexter then drove Davidson to the Pavilion steps. The left-hander was rested five minutes after the hour, having bowled nine overs for eighteen runs. In that time, England had entered the forties for the loss of only Pullar's wicket, and brought up the fifty ten minutes later.

Life was not proving easy for England, or for Frank Misson. Lawry at short-leg dropped Dexter, barely into double figures, off a Misson chest-high delivery, and Subba Row on 33 was reprieved wide on the leg side by wicketkeeper Wally Grout – who was sporting a black eye from a knock at practice – again off Misson. Subba Row then took consecutive fours from the same bowler to bring up the fifty partnership in a minute over the hour.

With just over five minutes to lunch, England were an adequate 1-87. But then Ken Mackay claimed Subba Row lbw for 48, attempting to turn a low delivery to leg, and Dexter, 27, playing back, 'stabbed' or 'spooned' (according to different expert onlookers) an easy catch to mid-wicket. May and Cowdrey remained scoreless through lunch and the Queen's presentation to the teams.

To many optimistic onlookers, it must have seemed time for May and Cowdrey to repeat their Edgbaston effort of four years earlier, when they had added 411 together against the West Indies. This time Davidson hit Cowdrey on the thumb, helping to keep him strokeless for twenty minutes. May managed a four off McKenzie in the next over to move to 17 but, playing back, got a lifter from Davidson which he edged to wicketkeeper Grout. Lindwall, an expert at inducing them in his day, judged it a 'poor shot'. England were now 4-111. Barrington, after a single scoring shot from a long-hop, was caught by a juggling second slip attempting to cut. His dismissal gave Davidson three wickets in fifteen overs at a cost of less than ten apiece: 5-115.

Cowdrey now came alive momentarily, taking three fours around the boundary off McKenzie, after previously reaching only four in the three-quarters of an hour since lunch. English supporters must have hoped for a close resemblance between the wickets at Lord's and at Canterbury, where Cowdrey had been in excellent touch immediately before the test in scoring twin centuries against the Australians. But Cowdrey's resistance was short-lived. He was caught off a combination of glove and handle for 16 as a lifting delivery from McKenzie cut back in at him. It was the young Western Australian's first test wicket. England were 6-127.

John Murray lasted an hour till he swept recklessly at Mackay, and Illingworth lasted ten minutes longer than had Murray before letting himself be bowled behind his legs. Having lost 3-47 in the hour after lunch, to reduce themselves to 6-134, England at tea were 8-167, with Lock and Trueman to resume. Lock did not last long, but Trueman and Statham added thirty-nine for the last wicket, the former getting out to the new ball at 5.23. Recalling *The Times*'s pre-match comment, England's 206 was exceedingly modest.

When Lawry opened for Australia with McDonald at 5.32, Statham bowled to the ridge from the Pavilion end. Trueman hit McDonald on the shoulder, then kept one low to him, but it was Statham who bowled McDonald for four as the opener played back, giving the Red Rose stalwart his two hundredth test wicket in his second over. As the third opener in the side, Simpson was promoted by Harvey from number six in the order, but the newcomer was caught off the splice in the gully after an edged shot, earlier in the Trueman over, had failed to carry to the slips. Australia were struggling at two for six. England's score looked less modest.

Lawry was joined by his captain, and reached 32 out of 2-42 overnight. Cowdrey had set an umbrella field, and twenty runs had come from shots to third man or fine-leg, keeping the last hour of the opening day up to par in terms of the scoring rate, when spectators might have imagined a run drought.

DAY 2

A crowd of more than 30,000 enjoyed the sun as Lawry started his working day by hooking Trueman for four and taking the next ball in the ribs. Harvey warmed up by playing and missing three times in Statham's second over, perhaps in anticipation of the near-shooter he received in Statham's fourth over. Lawry was 43 in an Australia total of 56 when the pair raised their half-century partnership. Harvey celebrated with a four over the slips off his handle from Statham, whose three-quarters-of-an-hour spell went unrewarded.

Harvey was eventually caught shoulder-high at first slip, but not before being hit on the body several times by Trueman after driving that bowler for four and evading a bouncer, all in the one over. Starting the day at six, Harvey had spent ninety-six minutes over 27 and bore the bruises for several days to remind him of his role in seeing Australia to 3-81.

Lawry at 45 cocked Statham over Cowdrey's head at second slip for a boundary, then mis-hooked Dexter into open country to reach his second fifty in his first two test innings. This landmark arrived shortly after O'Neill's arrival. Dexter moved the ball up the hill to bowl O'Neill for a single and make the score 4-88. This dismissal at the Pavilion end was the highlight of Dexter's ten-over spell for nineteen runs.

The Australians encountered severe difficulties. Around 12.45, a ball glanced off Burge's gloves but fell short of the short-leg fielder. Lawry was hit in the stomach by Trueman, then fell flat on his back avoiding a Statham bouncer. Half an hour before lunch, Cowdrey brought Lock on from the Nursery end to try pitching in the rough to Lawry, and switched Statham to bowl at the Pavilion end. Despite this manoeuvre, Lawry reached 64 at the long break, with Burge on 14 and the total 4-111. Six of the last seven overs before lunch were maidens.

After lunch the pitch eased. Around 2.15, Burge took two off Statham, then late-cut Trueman for four and gloved one over the slips for four. Lawry, meanwhile, revealed a reluctance to score which, although untypical during this tour, would become familiar to crowds over the next decade. While Lock contained him, Lawry pulled and square-slashed Dexter, on to replace Trueman, for two boundaries. Burge played a late-cut for four then, late on his hook against a Statham bouncer from the Pavilion end, was caught off the edge by Murray for 46. Australia were 5-183, with Lawry 99. Burge and

Lawry had scored ninety-five together at an hourly rate of thirty, and Lock had allowed scoring shots in only two of his twelve overs. Considering that his last fourteen overs yielded only one further maiden, and he conceded forty-eight runs overall, one wonders about the respect paid him at this stage of the match.

Lawry went to his hundred with a sharp single round the corner, making three figures out of 184 at 3.54, after four hours and forty-four minutes. He was 102 at tea out of Australia's 5-191. Four runs later, he became the first Australian to top one thousand runs for the tour. Davidson was three, and would sooner have been bowling than batting. Leaving lbw to the new ball at 6-194, he brought his preference closer to performance.

Ken Mackay was comprehensively beaten second ball by Statham, who then hit the left-hander on the foot, necessitating his use of Simpson as a runner. It must have been a painful blow because it was his first use of a runner in fifteen years of first-class cricket. Bringing up the Australian two hundred with a four through point, Mackay seemed troubled by the England pace attack but comfortable against Lock and Dexter. His play against Lock contrasted with his 1956 difficulties against spin on this ground.

Hitherto undiscomfited, Lawry was finally dismissed – for 130 at 5.39 in Dexter's first over after replacing Trueman. The score was 7-238 and he had batted for 369 minutes with eighteen fours. His parting shot was described as an uncharacteristic high, wide slash. More characteristically, *The Times* remarked that, 'when, on a fiery, ill-natured wicket, a man can shield and outshine batsmen far more gifted, he relies on temperament and courage'. His innings made victory for his side possible.

Lawry's departure was followed immediately by Grout's. Australia were only thirty-two runs on, with two wickets in hand and last innings in prospect. This seems the point in the match where England first began seriously to lose it, given they could not have done much about the first-day pitch.

England's characterisation as a team lacking a definite team plan for the test has already been mentioned, but *The Times* missed the point, as much as Cowdrey missed the plot, in commending him for handling 'things with much skill and good nature as he felt the game slipping from his grasp'. Good nature is no substitute for keeping a grasp on the game, and is perhaps immaterial if it means, for instance, allowing Illingworth and Lock to bowl a final hour during which fifty runs were scored in better than even time. The outcome was that Australia were allowed to close the day at 8-286, with Mackay 32 and McKenzie 29.

||| DAY 3

McKenzie turned twenty on the Saturday and a crowd again in excess of 30,000 meant the gates were closed for the first time since 1957. In hot sunshine, after cloud, the pitch seemed more amenable than on the first two days, allowing Australia to bring up its three hundred in 448 minutes and McKenzie to raise the fifty partnership in even time. He took his personal score to 34 before Trueman removed his off stump. This innings represented one highlight in a fine all-round debut, the most significant at test level by a Western Australian-born player to that date.

Considering this was his first test, McKenzie may have thought of other Sandgropers whose debut matches had remained their solitary marks on the sands of test cricket: such cricketers were Ken Meuleman (1945–46), John Rutherford (1956–57), Ron Gaunt (1957–58, though he added two further tests while playing for Victoria), Keith Slater (1958–59) and Des Hoare (1960–61). McKenzie became a major role model for the stream of West Australian test players of the next three decades.

Having treated McKenzie as a first-game weak reed, Cowdrey proceeded to concede singles to Mackay so his bowlers could concentrate on Misson. He also contrived to treat the New South

Welshman as a number eleven. Superficially, this seemed reasonable, since Misson appeared on the scorecard in that position. The tactic overlooked, however, the fact that Misson had opened for Glebe in Sydney grade cricket, and scored 43, 20 and 50 in successive Sheffield Shield innings in December 1960. Cowdrey should have known this, and taken it into account.

The Times noted that Misson, not beaten once in his seventy-seven minute stay, 'resisted . . . with such insolent unconcern that Mackay was the more fallible partner'. Conversely, Cowdrey removed his slips for the 'Slasher', 'one of the game's renowned snickers of the ball', to concentrate entirely upon removing Misson. This was not the last time that tactical considerations went awry in Cowdrey's captaincy career.

Illingworth eventually straightened a ball out of the left-hander's rough to have Mackay caught by third slip, after the batsman had completed his fifty with eight fours. Australia had lasted nearly an hour and a half, to extend its lead from eighty to 134. Its five hundred minute innings left sixteen hours in the match.

For the England second innings, Harvey avoided the umbrella field used by Cowdrey and, again in contrast to England, allowed nearly 150 overs of pace before employing the spin of Simpson.

Seven overs had been enough at lunch to see England advance to thirty-one without loss with Pullar 24 to Subba Row's seven. Lunch consumed, Subba Row added one before Grout swallowed an edge to a wide ball. Reports indicate the ball was now squatting rather than lifting. Dexter, for instance, got a shooter from Davidson during his first spell, but was reported to have looked as though he was expecting a lifting delivery every ball, and playing one-handed air shots into the bargain. Clearly the changed conditions required a change from first innings techniques. The change was not forthcoming.

Dexter recorded boundaries with an on-drive and a cut off Davidson, and fifty was raised in even time and without further loss. England looked to be making ground, until McKenzie, bowling at Harvey's instigation onto the ridge to maximise the available lift, stamped his mark on test cricket – and Ted Dexter. First he hit Dexter over the heart, then bowled him off his body next ball as Dexter missed a pull. The batsman had moved too far across outside his off stump to be able to kick the dropping ball away: 2-63.

Four runs on, Pullar was caught off a wide ball at the wicket, flashing at Misson. Cowdrey, hit early on the hip by McKenzie, was later hit by Misson. He played a one-handed flip which brought him a four to fine-leg but almost brought his dismissal to a catch by Lawry, who lost sight of the ball in the crowd. Within five minutes, he had presented an easy catch to cover point, playing back to a half-volley. *The Times* explained that 'the stroke reflected his state of mind and the pressure he was under. It was almost a half-volley, which he began to drive before changing his mind. By the time he stopped the stroke he was half-committed and the ball just carried to Mackay'. Perhaps the writer was being charitable.

Cowdrey's dismissal meant he had made only fifty runs in his first four innings of the series. For a player of his undoubted class, he looked strangely out of sorts. England needed runs as well as leadership from its captain. Instead it was 4-80.

Two Surrey players, May and Barrington, were together now with England fifty-four behind. They had reduced these to sixteen when they went in to tea at 4-118. Soon afterwards, though, May ended his hundred-minute stay by slashing a wide ball from McKenzie toward first slip where he was caught one-handed by keeper Grout at 5-127. With only five wickets remaining, seven runs were still needed to make Australia bat again.

Simpson was brought on against the England number seven, Illingworth, and immediately troubled him with a delivery that jumped and hit him on the shoulder. The Yorkshire all-rounder was then caught firm-footed off a similarly lifting delivery, by Harvey at short-leg. It was an excellent example of Harvey's imaginative captaincy.

McKenzie hit Barrington on the hand toward the end of his twenty-over spell, in which he conceded thirty-three runs for two wickets, and was replaced by Misson, whose mixture of full tosses, long-hops, and wide deliveries brought two boundaries to Barrington. Having made seventy-three in his first three innings of the series, it must have been on the professional's mind that another failure could see him omitted from the side.

As it was, Barrington at least helped England ensure Australia had a target to chase. An hour later, England were 6-178, with Barrington 59 and Murray 14. Nearly eighty overs had been bowled in the day, and the home side were forty-four ahead, no doubt nursing the anxiety that, in the seven most recent encounters between the sides, they had passed three hundred only once.

The Times, nevertheless, believed 'a closing score of perhaps 3-200 should not have been beyond them . . . but their batting, for the umpteenth time in recent years, has been wretchedly irresolute'. Others wondered how, 'against bowling of so poor a quality, England should twice be dismissed so cheaply'. EW Swanton, as usual, had an answer, suggesting England had batted 'surely rather limply'. Plain-speaking folk thought England were simply too defensive.

Dexter's role at number three was also queried, a thought echoed from the 1958–59 tour when May and Cowdrey entered too low in the order. One suggested option was to deploy Dexter at five, with Cowdrey first drop, followed by May, with Barrington at six. Another was for Cowdrey to open, as in 1956, instead of letting Davidson bowl to two left-handers.

DAY 4

Whatever the strategic niceties, 20,000 people braved the dull, cloudy, and sultry conditions to see the play on Monday.

Both batsmen were untroubled in adding a boundary in the first two overs, Murray driving Simpson past mid-off, Barrington forcing

Ken Barrington

Misson to mid-wicket. This was but the calm before the storm. Davidson took the new ball after twenty minutes, with the score 190. He operated from the Nursery end for the first time, bowling a full length and swinging the ball, while the less experienced but more energetic McKenzie dug it in.

Barrington added seven to his overnight score before holding his bat aloft to be leg before to an in-swinger in Davidson's second over. His 66 included eleven fours in three hours twenty minutes. He was twice dismissed in the match by Davidson and later wrote of the left-hander: 'What shook me was the number of times I played and missed at balls leaving me outside the off stump. So after much thought I evolved my new stance in an effort to counter him, trying it out for the first time in the second innings of the MCC match.' In this May 1961 game, Barrington scored 55 caught and bowled by Davidson, and 35 leg before to McKenzie. Barrington went on to explain that he opened up his old stance considerably by bringing his left shoulder round so that he looked at Davidson two-eyed and full-chested, facing his line of flight as he delivered left-arm over the wicket.

This stance was widely criticised, and Barrington noted that commentator Jim Swanton lamented that it was 'far from beautiful, and restricted his off-side play'. While acknowledging Swanton was 'right technically' about his new stance, Barrington asserted its virtues against nearly all types of bowling, in that it made him the hardest man to dismiss in test cricket in the 1960s. Whatever the long-term merits of this technical disquisition, Barrington was on this occasion out to the new ball after adding nearly fifty with Murray.

Within half an hour, England were all out with a lead of just sixty-eight. McKenzie took three for three in twelve balls. Lock, after half an hour of ineptitude, lost his off stump; and keeper Grout helped send Trueman and Murray back, each courtesy of a 'brilliant diving catch one handed and far away on the off-side' in front of Simpson at first slip. When he caught Murray for 25, Grout secured his hundredth test dismissal. It was Murray's hundredth minute at the crease. McKenzie's outstanding second innings figures read 29-13-37-5, and the young Western Australian led the side off the Lord's arena.

When McDonald and Lawry reappeared at 12.45, the proceedings seemed but a formality. Someone had neglected to issue black tie and tails to Statham, however, or to Trueman who, from the Nursery end, bowled faster than before.

McDonald was soon out to Trueman, caught one-handed low and wide in the gully in the fourth over at 1-15. McDonald's 14 had included a five for overthrows that could have run him out had the stumps been covered. With the score unchanged, Lawry gloved Statham to Murray. In measured tones of reproof, *The Times*'s correspondent concluded 'both these were the shots of batsmen anticipating the joys of a victory which was soon to be amazingly in doubt'.

Four runs later, Statham knocked O'Neill's off stump some distance. Harvey told the incoming batsman, Burge, to keep playing his shots, but did not linger to see from the opposite end the result of his instruction. Trueman got him to edge to Murray another fast delivery with his arms well away from the body. At 4-19, Australia's position suddenly seemed precarious.

Simpson, reverting to number six in the order, edged Trueman for a fortuitous four past his leg stump. Burge dabbed a boundary over the slips to send him on his way to one of the minor, matchwinning scores that are so often overlooked among the list of soft centuries stockpiled on lifeless wickets.

Burge played many typically powerful shots, particularly the pull and the hook, though he gave Lock an almost-crucial chance to run in from leg-slip to short square-leg and dive for a catch from a mis-hook off Statham's last ball before lunch. Burge took two, but the dramas were not yet over. Subba Row nearly tripped Simpson in the course of the second run.

These near misses epitomised the fact that the ball was finally running the Bananabender Burge's way. His career had begun in 1954–55, and given him eighteen baggy green caps over ten series, but he had never won a secure place in the side. With a big hundred in The Oval test, Burge earned himself another twenty-three tests, including four hundreds against England, after this innings.

Thus 4-35 at lunch could easily enough have been 5-33, and about this time, no doubt, *Wisden* editor Norman Preston was preparing the notes on the basis of which later editorialised that: 'Australia won because their bowlers performed so much better . . . than did Statham and Trueman.' This seems a harsh judgement in the face of their combined figures of 98.5-16-278-11.

Trueman, thirty in the February, had taken 176 wickets in forty-two tests before this game, and would take another 131. Statham, thirty-two five days before the test began, had claimed 199 wickets in fifty-six matches. He might have been closer to the end of his test career than his partner, but 'George' was still one of the most potent spearheads England could have mustered.

Elsewhere in that edition, Preston correctly identified a persistent England tendency to 'steadfastly decline to hit the ball', and indicted Cowdrey for the way in which he had surrendered the initiative to the Australian attack. More accurately, he should have praised Burge for the way in which, by the time the match ended at 2.50, he had made thirty-seven of the last fifty-two in an hour. In the process he lost Simpson, caught in the gully off a final lifting delivery, before finishing with a leg-glanced four and a single off Trueman and two successive pulled fours off Statham to win the match by five wickets.

The Times summed up by arguing that the match 'rewarded the more tenacious side with victory' – a fair enough conclusion – but counter-argued that England should have won the match had they been allowed to play 'according to their technical ability'. This seems precisely the point: Lawry first tasted champagne because Harvey and his side did not allow the home side to play up to its ability for those June days.

In the immediate aftermath, Walter Robins, chairman of the Lord's Ground Committee of the day, lent his name to an enquiry that solemnly reported a two inch fall from the Pavilion end to the Nursery end, with 'slight variations against the normal of this fall'. Further, it was reported that one of the high points appeared about twenty-three feet from the Nursery-end stumps so that the ball lifted off an upward slope. Laker commented drily that a survey of all first-class wickets in England would have found many more ridges than people had ever dreamed existed.

One person who did not seem concerned was Bill Lawry, who went on to a series total of 420 runs at 52.50, spending 1111 minutes at the crease and facing 1017 deliveries. Well might Bill Bowes call him another 'William the Conqueror'.

Television came to cricket during the 1960s.

•SYDNEY 1971•

PLAYING IT BY THE BOOK

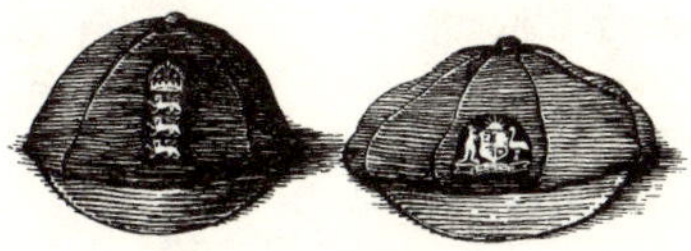

The final test of the 1970–71 series is an important match not only in the context of that Ashes series but in test cricket as a whole. Ray Illingworth's appointment as captain represents a changing of the guard in English cricket and for most of the series he is opposed by a man of similar mould, Bill Lawry. Ian Chappell's accession to the Australian captaincy is not painless, but it represents the beginning of a new era in Australian cricket. John Snow is the most powerful personality in the series, and the pivotal figure in this game, but observing it all at close range is Dennis Lillee, a fast bowler in only his second test. He will go on to be Australia's main strike bowler over the next thirteen years. The game remains dramatic because of the variety of perspectives presented in participants' memoirs. While there is hooliganism among the spectators, some critics feel the poor behaviour begins on the field. Illingworth has often been seen as something of a shop steward in the Yorkshire dressing room, and undoubtedly Australia's new leader learned something from this approach.

AUSTRALIA v ENGLAND 1971 (7th Test)

Played at Sydney Cricket Ground on 12, 13, 14, 16, 17 February.
Toss: Australia. Result: ENGLAND won by 62 runs.

ENGLAND

JH Edrich	c G Chappell b Dell	30	c I Chappell b O'Keeffe	57
BW Luckhurst	c Redpath b Walters	0	c Lillee b O'Keeffe	59
KWR Fletcher	c Stackpole b O'Keeffe	33	c Stackpole b Eastwood	20
JH Hampshire	c Marsh b Lillee	10	c I Chappell b O'Keeffe	24
BL D'Oliveira	b Dell	1	c I Chappell b Lillee	47
R Illingworth*	b Jenner	42	lbw b Lillee	29
APE Knott†	c Stackpole b O'Keeffe	27	b Dell	15
JA Snow	b Jenner	7	c Stackpole b Dell	20
P Lever	c Jenner b O'Keeffe	4	c Redpath b Jenner	17
DL Underwood	not out	8	c Marsh b Dell	0
RGD Willis	b Jenner	11	not out	2
Extras	(B 4, LB 4, W 1, NB 2)	11	(B 3, LB 3, NB 6)	12
Total		**184**		**302**

AUSTRALIA

KH Eastwood	c Knott b Lever	5	b Snow	0
KR Stackpole	b Snow	6	b Illingworth	67
RW Marsh†	c Willis b Lever	4	(7) b Underwood	16
IM Chappell*	b Willis	25	(3) c Knott b Lever	6
IR Redpath	c and b Underwood	59	(4) c Hampshire b Illingworth	14
KD Walters	st Knott b Underwood	42	(5) c D'Oliveira b Willis	1
GS Chappell	b Willis	65	(6) st Knott b Illingworth	30
KJ O'Keeffe	c Knott b Illingworth	3	c sub (K Shuttleworth) b D'Oliveira	12
TJ Jenner	b Lever	30	c Fletcher b Underwood	4
DK Lillee	c Knott b Willis	6	c Hampshire b D'Oliveira	0
AR Dell	not out	3	not out	3
Extras	(LB 5, W 1, NB 10)	16	(B 2, NB 5)	7
Total		**264**		**160**

AUSTRALIA	**O**	**M**	**R**	**W**	**O**	**M**	**R**	**W**
Lillee	13	5	32	1	14	0	43	2
Dell	16	8	32	2	26.7	3	65	3
Walters	4	0	10	1	5	0	18	0
G Chappell	3	0	9	0				
Jenner	16	3	42	3	21	5	39	1
O'Keeffe	24	8	48	3	26	8	96	3
Eastwood					5	0	21	1
Stackpole					3	1	8	0
ENGLAND								
Snow	18	2	68	1	2	1	7	1
Lever	14.6	3	43	3	12	2	23	1
D'Oliveira	12	2	24	0	5	1	15	2
Willis	12	1	58	3	9	1	32	1
Underwood	16	3	39	2	13.6	5	28	2
Illingworth	11	3	16	1	20	7	39	3
Fletcher					1	0	9	0

FALL OF WICKETS

	E	A	E	A
Wkt	1st	1st	2nd	2nd
1st	5	11	94	0
2nd	60	13	130	22
3rd	68	32	158	71
4th	69	66	165	82
5th	98	147	234	96
6th	145	162	251	131
7th	156	178	276	142
8th	165	235	298	154
9th	165	239	299	154
10th	184	264	302	160

Umpires: LP Rowan and TF Brooks.

John Snow and Ray Illingworth in dispute with umpire Lou Rowan.

(Sydney Morning Herald)

Sydney 1971 was for Ray Illingworth the best of tests. For Ian Chappell it must have seemed the worst of tests. For Lou Rowan it was the dickens of a test with which to end his international umpiring career. For Dick Whitington, cricket writer and former Australian Victory Test and South Australian player, it was 'the kind of test that occurred at Melbourne in 1932–33, at Leeds in 1938', high praise indeed. This chapter is not a tale of two cities, but a tale of one test as seen by three of its protagonists.

The Dickens text goes on about it being the age of wisdom and the age of foolishness, an epoch of belief and of incredulity. This was still the age of *Wisden*, and the incredulity was expressed at umpiring decisions. Dickens might have ended with a reworking of his classic closing comment: in short, the 1970–71 series was so like more recent ones of equally low repute, that some of its noisiest (but nameless) authorities insisted on the captaincy of Lawry and Illingworth, and Snow's bowling, being received, for good or evil, in the superlative degree of comparison only. That is, instead of these being the good old days which, two decades on, nostalgia may well make them, that summer was hailed as epitomising the bad new days.

Dickens's supposed revision might conclude that, both in England and Australia, it was clearer than crystal to those at Lord's and in Australia's northern state, that things in general might be unsettled for ever by uncouth behaviour. Thus Queensland detective Lou Rowan opened his autobiography with the words, 'For a few minutes . . . the whole future of cricket between Australia and England were in jeopardy.'

It is clear, in his estimation, why this should have been so. Rowan's earlier dealing with MCC officials such as Gubby Allen and Billy Griffith had helped the Queensland test umpire form some clear opinions. One was that he felt comfortable with 'the many titled gentlemen so closely connected with cricket in England, great players and personalities' like amateur captains Colin Cowdrey and Mike Smith. Another was that the England captaincy 'would best be left in the hands of amateur rather than professional players'. A third was that men like Mike Smith possessed 'the ability to handle even the most difficult professionals'. A final opinion, that this later category would include Snow and Illingworth, is implicit in his book.

Another Australian, former international Bill O'Reilly, was equally to regret that 'the job of handling Snow had not been given much more preliminary thought before the team left home' to save him from 'squandering his energy on a larrikin-type bowling'. Did he mean Snow could have dismissed the Australians even more expeditiously?

Illingworth and Snow in their books make it clear they knew what they were about. Thus the former was prepared to complain on the Wednesday before the test about the state of the nets provided for the tourists, a complaint published in the local press. England opening bowler Bob Willis confirmed that Illingworth had been similarly concerned before the tour about facilities and treatment off the field after touring with amateurs whose extra privileges were unwarranted. On this basis, the England captain gained the confidence of the majority of his team and kept, for the time being, the confidence of the selectors.

Australian broadcaster Alan McGilvray found 'a fire' in Illingworth, 'the intensity of hard battle', which made him a leader who demanded his team followed him. He was a leader for whom results didn't just happen, but were obtained through 'unrelenting effort'. Younger and perhaps more impressionable, Willis felt the team would win simply because his captain gave the impression of having everything under control.

Not so the Australian captain with whom the selectors had started the summer. He was in a different, more difficult position. In one of the cruellest ends to a test career, Bill Lawry learned of his dismissal as both captain and player on a mid-day news broadcast over the radio. Although it was later unreliably rumoured the selectors had tried to notify him, later England captain Mike Brearley rated the lack of prior discussion, subsequent explanations, or easy exits as 'one of the most insensitive and improper selection procedures' of his experience. Lawry was not even consulted about playing under his successor in the deciding test. The manner of his removal struck a chord with Ian Chappell that resonated through the rest of the seventies, in many respects a discordant decade for Australian cricket.

Lawry's predecessor as Australian captain, Bob Simpson, had predicted in 1968 that the responsibility of captaincy would make him an even greater player. Richie Benaud also believed the captaincy would be the making of Lawry, describing him as both a shrewd tactician and good judge of his players. In addition Benaud rated him an outstanding batsman and, at the time of the 1968 tour to England, the best captain in the country. Benaud felt Lawry would not leave the game as early as Simpson or he himself had. In the end, Lawry retired at approximately the same age as Benaud.

While he was scoring slowly at this time – Lawry himself later recognised he probably gave bowlers too much respect – he had averaged forty after batting over the equivalent of four entire days in the series. Brearley quotes him as saying that if spectators wanted to see park cricket, they should go to the park. A decade later, he was to be commended by his former opposite number, Ray Illingworth, as 'more willing to give up his wife than his wicket'.

At the time it was not enough, even though, only three tests earlier at Sydney, he had played a lone hand against John Snow to carry his bat through an Australian innings of 116 for 60. He was also one of only eleven players to reach 5000 test runs. The selectors apparently agreed with Ray Robinson that, in the previous test at Adelaide, 'Australian morale had sunk below seagull level', for which Lawry was held partly responsible. Sir Donald Bradman's last act as an Australian selector was therefore to open the way to a new era. Perhaps the greatest tragedy for Lawry was that his last test was Dennis Lillee's first.

South Australia's Ian Chappell got the job. According to one source, Chappell had ring-led a player revolt on the 1969 tour to South Africa. This group refused to play an unscheduled fifth test unless additional payment was forthcoming. Differences of opinion within the tour party meant there was no game, Chappell treating the issue as a matter of principle in a manner that foreshadowed the introduction of World Series Cricket.

Such disputes would have struck sympathetic echoes in the England camp. Snow similarly complained about the England management's failure to consult the touring party over adding an extra test to the 1970–71 tour. There was almost a strike to ensure that, as professionals, the players received 'a chance to be considered and consulted'. Such examples would not have sat well with conservatives on either side of the Ashes fence.

Australia made four changes for the Sydney match. In place of Lawry, thirty-five-year-old Victorian opener Ken Eastwood was the most surprising. Eastwood had spent much of his career living in Lawry's shadow. Another man to whom Australia might have turned was thirty-six-year-old Queenslander Sam Trimble, who had made 177 for his state against the tourists in November. But Trimble, who remains probably the unluckiest Australian never to play test cricket, missed out again.

The rest of the batting – Keith Stackpole, Ian Chappell, Ian Redpath, Doug Walters and Greg Chappell – had a familiar look, although several players had struggled against Snow. Another Victorian batsman, Paul Sheahan, filled the twelfth man role. An outstanding cover fielder, he had been tagged as a future Australian captain, but had not played a single first-class innings in seven weeks.

The bowling looked to have more bite than before. Out had gone New South Wales fold-finger-spinner Johnny Gleeson, South Australian off-spinner Ashley Mallett, and unorthodox Victorian opening bowler Alan 'Froggy' Thomson, who had disappointed in four matches. In for his first test came lumbering fast left-hander Tony Dell from Queensland, to partner Western Australian Lillee in his second test. Leg-spinners Terry Jenner, from South Australia, and Kerry O'Keeffe, from New South Wales, reappeared after making their debuts earlier in the series.

The attack was short on experience, with the four main bowlers having played just three tests and taken six wickets between them. Some thought Graham McKenzie might have been recalled to open the attack with Lillee, but the selectors decided he had already caused the England team sufficient disservice by breaking the arm of their leading run-scorer, Geoffrey Boycott, in a one-day match played on the sort of damp Sydney wicket expected for the test.

Umpiring and the bouncer problem were also issues in this match. The bouncer element related to the key player in the England team, John Snow. Snow began the Australian summer with ninety-nine test wickets at 27.51 in twenty-five tests. He wanted to eclipse Maurice Tate's 1924–25 series record of thirty-eight wickets. Halfway through the series he had twenty-two, but four wickets in the Melbourne test and three in Adelaide meant he needed ten in Sydney to break Tate's record. After his previous appearance there, when he took 8-63, it seemed a good bet. An analysis of his dismissals so far made interesting reading: Stackpole six times, Ian Chappell five times, Lawry four times, Redpath and Gleeson three times each, Marsh twice, Doug Walters only once, plus Sheahan, Greg Chappell, Mallett, Jenner, Connolly, and Alan Thomson. Most of Snow's 'rabbits' were still in the side for Sydney, not that it mattered, as it turned out.

Snow perhaps went too far in his war of words with the cricket authorities, believing Rowan had stayed one tour too many. Rowan believed his long-time umpiring partner, Colin Egar, had retired one tour too soon to his dry-cleaning business. Rowan was also certain that continuation of his partnership with Egar would have ensured 'the cricketing world would not have been embarrassed by the petulant childish actions of John Snow and Ray Illingworth'. He added, 'We would have demonstrated to those two long before they began to allow themselves too much rope, that we both held strong views on the proper conduct of cricket as a sport and as a spectacle.'

Few people understood the personalities of the protagonists, but this did not stop veteran journalists going over the top with their similes. Thus Ray Robinson described Snow as 'like a swordfish among salmon . . . a piranha among perch'. Dick Whitington thought him 'one of the most faithful and effective servants Nemesis ever employed . . . Never did he lose that aura of menace.' When he loped in off a 'sinisterly deceptive approach to bowl, he wore malevolence like Mandrake wore a cloak', a reference to the Lee Falk magician who had inhabited the comic-book consciousness of Australians for nearly four decades by that time.

Snow's literary tendencies also came in for a mixed reception. Whitington this time suspected that 'Alfred Hitchcock might have liked to have used [Snow's poems] as plots for his horror films', whereas Robinson thought 'some of his poetry takes a little longer to sink in than his bouncer . . . he has a healthy touch of brimstone in his bloodstream'. Rowan used 'verse-writing' as a a sneer term when commenting on Snow in *An Umpire's Story*.

Bouncers were the major controversy. Snow commented that 'some umpires . . . cannot seem to distinguish between a cricket ball bouncer and the dance hall variety'. The applicability of the remark to Rowan seems inescapable. Having been cautioned in the Second Test in Perth, Snow bowled a real bouncer to Redpath, and told Rowan, 'That's [what I call] a real bouncer!' Robinson added that, when Illingworth told Rowan that Snow's shorter balls were not bouncers, the umpire said, 'Somebody's bowling them from this end and it's not me,' echoing Bill Woodfull's famous comment to Pelham Warner at Adelaide during the Bodyline series of 1932–33.

A reading of Rowan's book makes this kind of witticism sound believable. While Snow thought the local batsmen simply not good enough in Perth to play chest-high balls, he suspected that Rowan confused their technical difficulties with intimidatory bowling.

DAY 1

The crowd had reached just half its eventual 10,445 when the match began on time at eleven o'clock despite early-morning rain. Ian Chappell made an aggressive start to his captaincy by inviting England to bat on a well-grassed wicket. Aggression seemed far from the minds of the England openers, John Edrich and Brian Luckhurst, for whom the pitch posed problems, but not so many that it should have rendered them strokeless.

Dennis Lillee, in his second test, opened the bowling to Edrich. With his then ungainly run, he reminded Ray Robinson 'of a thirst-crazed buffalo scenting a waterhole'. Lillee, actually born in the Chinese Year of the Buffalo (1949), wasted the new ball striving for pace. Mindful that their side needed only a draw to regain the Ashes, the openers neither capitalised on Lillee's inaccuracy nor condemned themselves to quick dismissal.

Tony Dell, the six-foot-four-and-a-half inches, sixteen-stone Hampshire-born left-hander, became Australia's first post-war migrant to make the national side in his adoptive country, although Indian-born Rex Sellers had played one test in India in 1964. Making the team after a mere eight first-class matches, and having captured twenty wickets at thirty-three, he obviously gained his place on the basis of judgements like those of Barry Richards, who dubbed him the quickest bowler in the country.

The left-hander began with six successive maiden overs but did not bowl well initially. Overcome by nerves, his first over consisted of two balls down the leg side to Edrich, the third halfway down the wicket, the fourth and fifth down leg side again, the sixth short but straight, the seventh and eighth to the off and leg sides respectively.

Looking for a wicket after half an hour in which only five runs had been scored, Chappell introduced medium-pacer Walters into the attack. The renowned partnership-breaker immediately had an effect on the game. From Walters' third ball Chappell himself dropped Luckhurst at slip, and two balls later the opener departed for nought, caught at short-leg. Edrich and Keith Fletcher were then associated in a long, slow stand that was undisturbed at lunch, although Fletcher almost managed to have himself run out by Greg Chappell.

Such a dismissal would have lent weight to Snow's dismissal of 'The Gnome' as a player of 'great natural ability and power' who had not produced 'the weight of runs expected'. Snow had greater regard for other, less talented players he characterised as 'the workers'. In Illingworth's team, he identified Edrich, Boycott, Basil D'Oliveira, and Alan Knott as players who seldom let England down. The match can be read in these terms.

Jenner came into the attack with his leg-spin at 1-40, as England took almost two hours for its first fifty. Thirty minutes after lunch, the pugnacious Edrich was caught at third slip to give Dell the first of his six test wickets and reduce England to 2-60. Dell was so far probably the pick of the Australian attack. His in-swinger and lift caused most concern. Nevertheless the England batsmen shouldn't have needed fifty balls before taking their first run off him. Fletcher, twice hit on the left arm and chest by Dell, was soon afterwards caught at leg gully to give O'Keeffe the first of his fifty-three test wickets. A run later D'Oliveira, after being hit on the body by Dell, was bowled through the gate. England were in trouble at 4-69.

Illingworth joined John Hampshire at the wickets, and the two Yorkshiremen aroused recollections of their Lord's exploits of eighteen months earlier, when Illingworth, batting at eight, had joined Hampshire with England 6-189 in the face of a West Indian total of 380. Hampshire had become the first England player to score a century on debut at Lord's and Illingworth, with Snow's help, had gone on to his own maiden test hundred. While their reunion here was worth less than half their Lord's association, it helped pave the way for Knott and Illingworth to doggedly add forty-seven in seventy minutes. Shortly after tea wicketkeeper Knott was caught at short square-leg, where Stackpole's agility belied his bulk.

In the hour after tea the Australian spinners bowled eighteen eight-ball overs. They were operating when the new ball became due after sixty-five overs, with the score at 6-145. Former captain Lawry said that it would be taken, but Chappell, after discussion with vice-captain Redpath, kept his spinners on for the further eleven overs it took to separate Snow and Illingworth and finish the innings.

Jenner bowled both partners in the seventh-wicket stand and the number eleven, while O'Keeffe chipped in to have Peter Lever caught by fellow spinner Jenner at silly mid-on. O'Keeffe and Jenner between them bowled forty overs to claim six wickets for ninety runs. Ian Chappell's intelligent field placings for his young leg-spinners won him the acclaim of veteran journalist Bill O'Reilly as 'another Benaud', with the result that Australia had just over half an hour's batting time chasing England's 184.

Whether it was Chappell's tactical insight, or the bowlers the selectors had given him, or the state of the pitch, the Australians required about twenty overs less to dismiss England than in any previous innings in the series.

Educated opinion was that the Australian bowling had been wayward and short. Trevor Bailey, passing through Sydney, said that even at forty-seven he would have liked a bowl on this wicket. He thought a good county attack would have had England out for 150, a remark reminiscent of comments made in the previous decade about what Sydney grade sides might have done to counties such as Bailey's own Essex. Less contentiously, Ian Chappell was quoted in the *Sydney Morning Herald* on the second morning of the match as saying there was nothing wrong with the wicket, and predicting an Australian lead.

This was brave talk after Australia had faced six overs on the first evening, which they were unable to negotiate safely. The crewcutted Eastwood began confidently enough against a hostile Snow, but, in attempting a leg glance off Lever, was caught low down the leg side by Knott. Playing for Tasmania during the 1969–70 season, Knott had dismissed the Victorian left-hander in the same way, suggesting that locally-acquired knowledge was Eastwood's undoing.

Australia, 1-11 after seventeen minutes, then had to face what Ray Robinson considered Snow's best over of the series. Two leg-cutters were succeeded by an off-cutter that took a thick inside edge from a foot outside the off stump. Knott took a spectacular diving catch to his left, only to find Stackpole's off-bail had gone.

Australia entered the weekend at 2-13, twelve wickets having fallen in the day for 191 runs. Nightwatchman Rod Marsh had made two in thirteen minutes and the lager-loving left-hander had the chance to win a keg of beer offered by an anonymous Mt Isa publican if he made a second-day hundred to compensate for the century some felt he had been denied in the Fifth Test in Melbourne. Lawry's declaration on that occasion had left Marsh with 92 not out.

DAY 2

If there had been on-field drama for the first day, there was much more on the second.

Ian Chappell took a three, a two and another three from D'Oliveira's first over from the Paddington end. Snow bowled four bouncers in his second over, and, in his third, Chappell deflected a no-ball bouncer off his glove to Knott, prompting Snow to query umpire Rowan over his foot-fault.

Marsh then played from Lever what was to all intents and purposes, except those of backward square-leg Willis, a leg glance. Willis dived full stretch to his right to take a superb catch to give Lever two wickets for eight runs. New batsman Redpath then cover-drove Lever's first ball, edged the second ball just in front of D'Oliveira at second slip, and sliced yet another ball in the same over just past his leg stump to show that good luck, as well as bad, still had its part to play on the cricket field.

During the remainder of the morning, Australia reached fifty in the eighteenth over after one hundred minutes. Willis then reasserted his presence by beating Ian Chappell twice in an over before bowling him for a patient 25 at 4-66. Lever gave Walters three consecutive bouncers, all directed over the stumps, to enliven the ten minutes before lunch, which Australia took at 4-84.

For three overs following the break, Snow pitched the ball short to Walters, who pluckily survived. Walters, like Redpath, enjoyed his share of luck. He was missed by slip-fielder Fletcher off Derek Underwood, then dropped by Underwood at third man off Willis. Streaky batting it may have been, however Walters and Redpath not only survived, but took eighteen from Snow's three overs to reach a fifty partnership.

In his book, Snow commented that Illingworth quickly guessed his bowlers' moods and problems. Fast bowlers often can't strike their rhythm right away and their bowling suffers. On this occasion, Illingworth spelled the Sussex speedster, not bringing him back until the new ball became due at what would turn out to be a crucial moment in the match.

The runs continued to come in better than even time after lunch when Walters, on 41, snicked Underwood onto his pad and into the off-side, for Knott to flick the ball back between his pads into the stumps. Walters appeared to be well out of his crease and his bat aloft, but Rowan refused the appeal. This 'escape' was not costly for England because, when Walters had helped Redpath add eighty-one in 103 minutes, he was decisively stumped by Knott off Underwood to give the Kent left-hander 1-28 in his thirteenth over.

With Australia 5-147, Illingworth brought himself on and, amid Sydney's contribution to minimalist music – a tin-can chorus – he and Underwood restricted Redpath and Chappell to fifteen runs in the next forty-five minutes. Redpath reached the first fifty of the match before returning a catch to Underwood. The sixth wicket was down for 162.

O'Keeffe was caught behind off Illingworth to make Australia 7-178 and on the point of collapse. Greg Chappell was joined by fellow South Australian Terry Jenner, for whom Illingworth immediately brought back Snow after two-and-a-half hours out of the attack. Aware of the newcomer's frailities in his first test at Brisbane with the bat (c Cowdrey b Snow 0, c Boycott b Shuttleworth 2), Illingworth moved to silly mid-wicket after the first ball.

Illingworth's captaincy qualities were most evident in such circumstances. He knew which bowler would get most out of the wicket and bring the worst out of each batsman. He also knew where to place fielders for likely catches without forgetting economy. Snow also commented that 'because of Ray's tactical flair and experience I always felt that I was bowling exactly when I should have been . . . He harboured and nurtured his bowlers like no other captain I have served.' Even Rowan acknowledged Illingworth's resourcefulness in handling his bowling, though deploring other aspects of the Illingworth armory without recognising that they formed a complete package.

The main conflict followed. Some thought Snow and Illingworth came out of the incident very well, but many did not share this view. For Jim Swanton, what happened scarred the memory of his final Australian tour. At a Lord's dinner in 1971, he told several members of the England team that he did not like the way the series had been won.

What sickened Swanton happened when Snow took the new ball. According to Alan Knott, Snow had not bowled a bouncer all day. According to Knott's wicket-to-wicket view of events, Snow's first ball of the fateful over was fended off Jenner's ribs around the corner for a single. Three balls to Greg Chappell followed before Jenner reached the business end again. The fifth ball of the over was approximately, according to Snow, left armpit height, but Jenner had to avert his head to avoid it. The sixth ball was pitched outside the line of the leg stump. Jenner ducked and simultaneously leaned backward into it, but escaped contact. The score was 7-195.

Illingworth rearranged the field, moving Willis from mid-off to mid-on. He located Underwood at long-leg, left Hampshire in a backward short-leg position, and placed himself at forward short-leg. Robinson called this configuration a four-man leg-trap, and believed that Jenner 'recognised the field adjustment as preparation for catching a mis-hit off a bouncer to come'.

Had Jenner been as bad a batsman as some claim, one wonders whether he would have been able to draw this conclusion from Illingworth's elaborate preparations. In fact, Jenner was an accomplished batsman and was regarded as something of an all-rounder in the Sheffield Shield. In 1973–74, he achieved the first match double of a hundred runs and ten wickets for South Australia since before the

The incident that sparked the walkoff: Terry Jenner felled by a Snow bouncer.

(*Melbourne* Herald)

first world war when he scored 59 and 47, and claimed match figures of 11-170 against Western Australia in Adelaide.

With his seventh ball, which Snow claimed was again rib-height, he hit Jenner on the left side of the head.

Having seen Jenner escorted from the ground, and allowing Lillee to join the younger Chappell, umpire Rowan intervened. After twice speaking to Snow regarding fair and unfair play, Rowan told the bowler to ease up on on the short deliveries. Rowan signalled one finger to umpire Tom Brooks to indicate the mandatory first warning had been given, but Brooks apparently wanted nothing to do with it. Rowan's own remarks indicate that Brooks, standing in his first series, differed from the senior umpire in his reading of the matches in which they umpired together.

Snow objected. Illingworth intervened, retaliating with some finger wagging of his own. Snow completed his over, with Rowan turning down the bowler's appeal for a catch behind the wicket against Lillee. Snow snatched his hat from Rowan and returned to his fielding position on the fine-leg boundary beneath the Paddington Hill. It was argued in the press that Snow's normal position was two to three metres inside the fence, but that he deliberately taunted the crowd – a charge he later denied – by moving so close to the fence that it was possible to lay hands on him. Snow claimed he shook hands with younger spectators. The action of moving close to the crowd, however, triggered pandemonium and hundreds of drink cans were thrown onto the playing surface. Illingworth told his strike bowler to stay away while the gutters were cleared, but Snow returned to his long-leg position rather than to third man as Illingworth suggested. Most published accounts, significantly perhaps, do not refer to this act of insubordination.

Illingworth led his side from the field without any word either to the batsmen or the umpires. England were off the field for seven minutes, during which time, Rowan explained in his book, he told Illingworth that if England did not return to the field, they would forfeit the match. Illingworth responded that he would return as soon as the ground was fit for play, asking Alan Barnes, secretary to the Australian Board of Control, to announce this over the public address system. He also asked Barnes to point out that he would remove his team again, should the disturbance be repeated.

Some former players suggested Illingworth had lost control of the situation, though this seems harsh. It was the view of the *Sydney Morning Herald*'s Bill O'Reilly, and certainly among sections of the English press. Jack Fingleton told *Sunday Times* readers that the players' nerves were wearing thin, and that Snow had been warned in both Perth and Melbourne for intimidatory bowling, on both occasions dissenting with the support of his captain. Another former player, Denis Compton, wrote in the *Sunday Express* that Illingworth's action, which he labelled 'hasty, unnecessary and tactically unwise', was the worst mistake of his cricketing career.

Non-players were less critical. Michael Melford in the *Sunday Telegraph*, for instance, noted the beer can incident occurred in one small section of a large ground. He thought nothing would have happened but for Snow's unwitting encouragement in approaching the boundary fence, adding that, had the amount of drink cans justified the retreat, cricket could not be played in some parts of the world at all.

Newspaper interviews reported that Illingworth was concerned with the safety factor, agreeing with Snow that removing the target removes the point in throwing anything. Illingworth also remained unrepentant about exacerbating the situation by fielding his fast bowler on the fence. He said he would not allow the crowd to determine his field placings. Ian Chappell thought Illingworth's reaction 'rather hasty and unjustified' though he admitted that, had he been the fielding captain in an equivalent situation overseas, he might have done the same. Richie Benaud later wrote he would have acted as Illingworth did.

Upon England's return to the field, Snow fielded in front of the

Members' stand. He was replaced in his former fielding position by Lever. Snow bowled one more over after resumption before being replaced by Willis. There were no more bouncers that day, though Willis was to hit Lillee in the stomach with a short ball. Lillee was sufficiently undisturbed to remain with Greg Chappell while the pair added a further forty runs before the close. It had been thought that the Australians' resistance might falter after the interruption, but it was in fact they who gained the psychological edge.

Nine people were arrested after the disturbance, and charged with unseemly conduct or language, or offensive behaviour. A total of $700 in fines was exacted upon thirteen young men, a mix of labourers, a welder, a fireman, a clerk, a student, and a glazier who, true to his trade, threw two stubbies on the field. More than a dozen people had been injured on the Paddington Hill, with fifteen people involved in a beer can fight that an unnamed former test player called 'the worst display of hooliganism I've ever seen at an Australian cricket match'.

Such shenanigans notwithstanding, Australia overnight enjoyed the fifty-one run lead its total of 7-235 had earned it. Australia had faced seventy-seven eight-ball overs in total, seventy-one in the day or twenty-eight more balls than dictated by the ninety six-ball over minimum limit which prevailed in the 1990s.

Snow and England manager David Clark visited Jenner before leaving the ground at the end of the day. Over the next few days, a hundred letters were reportedly written to Illingworth regretting and exonerating the walk-off.

||| DAY 3

A wind-change on the third morning found Snow bowling from umpire Brooks's end for three overs. Rowan believed that the switch was a ploy. Snow pitched the ball up – to applause from a crowd of 30,030 – and conceded eleven runs. After nearly an hour at the wicket, Lillee edged the first ball from Willis to Knott for a record twenty-second catch in an Anglo–Australian test series, and in his second over Willis bowled Greg Chappell behind his legs for 62. Jenner returned to face thirty-two more balls and to score another twenty-two runs. Lever was brought back to end the innings at 264, bowling Jenner off his thigh for 30. His dismissal gave Australia a final lead of eighty.

For their second attempt, England had the batting task in front of them for the last time in the series. They showed considerably more enterprise this time. Luckhurst took a boundary from his first ball to escape a pair, and made thirty-eight of England's first fifty. He reached his own half-century in seventy minutes, with square and cover-drives for four off the same O'Keeffe over. It was ironic that the fastest fifty of the series should come from the man who had made a duck in thirty-seven minutes in the first innings.

As a result, England opened with ninety-four in near even time before they lost a wicket. Ian Chappell dropped Luckhurst from a low slip catch off O'Keeffe when the batsman was on 55 but, after adding only four runs, he was out. This time he was caught by Lillee, attempting to sweep O'Keeffe's leg-break.

Fletcher then joined Edrich. An inspired bowling change saw Chappell bring on Eastwood to take the second wicket just before tea with his occasional left-arm wrist-spin. His only first-class over for the season had been hit for sixteen by John Benaud, but Chappell had had trouble with his wrong'un in the nets, and figured he might be deceptive. As it turned out, Eastwood had Fletcher caught for 20 from an overpitched ball in his second over: 2-130.

Edrich reached his fifty shortly after tea with a back-foot cover-drive off Jenner for four, only to edge O'Keeffe in his second over of the last session low to Ian Chappell, who took a juggling catch. Soon after, the same fielder made a galvanic running dive a pitch length back from his first slip position to give O'Keeffe Hampshire's wicket. England had slumped to 4-165.

Illingworth joined D'Oliveira, and was almost run out by an Ian Chappell return after edging Jenner through slips for his first two runs. Once, when O'Keeffe was running in to bowl to D'Oliveira, Illingworth baulked again – but this time because of fielders moving with the bowler. Thereafter umpire Brooks blocked the bowler in his run-up if there was threat of any repetition, and motioned fielders back from the pitch if shadows intruded.

Dell was less accommodating, collecting Illingworth amidships two or three times, then almost crippling him with a loose delivery that hit the England captain on his left knee and left him limping for the remainder of the match. At the close, England had reached 4-229, with D'Oliveira 37 and Illingworth 25. The lead was 149, with the rest day to follow.

||| DAY 4

Ian Chappell was optimistic in the weekend press about being set around 280 to win the match, draw the series, and retain the Ashes. A crowd of 18,000 came to see whether there were indeed still plenty of runs in the pitch, and who would get them. The start of the fourth day must have left Australia pleased with its work as Lillee and Dell excised the England lower order, except for Lever, who fell to Jenner.

Six runs after the resumption, Illingworth was out for 29 to Lillee. It was the only one of ten lbw or bat-pad appeals upheld in the England innings, the only leg before victim in the match, and the third and final dismissal in this manner for Australia in the series. On this point, Rowan said the claim that he allowed twelve lbw decisions each season, with it a matter of luck who obtained them, was 'good for a laugh now and then', though it is unclear who would have found it humorous.

D'Oliveira was dismissed for 47 in Lillee's fifth over, caught off a low snick from an out-swinger: 6-251. Despite modest contributions from Knott 15, Snow 20 and Lever 17, so that England reached 7-298, the last three wickets fell for four runs. England's final dismissal for 302 meant that Australia were left 223 to win, the identical total it had faced against Hutton's team four tours earlier.

Australia began badly, losing a wicket before registering a run. Eastwood was yorked sixth ball by Snow, who twice in his second over nearly sent back Stackpole. This was almost his last on-field contribution for, in the next over from Lever, Snow at fine-leg not only missed catching Stackpole from a high hook which hit the top of the fence and fell in the boundary gutter, but badly injured his bowling hand fending off the pickets. It was a sickening moment for bowler and England, but a promise of respite for Australia. The promise was short-lived. In the next Lever over, Ian Chappell was caught behind from an out-swinger, and didn't wait for Rowan to signal. The score was 2-22.

Stackpole, now the hope of the side, hit a six off Underwood and then Redpath added forty-nine with his state partner before Illingworth took to the bowling crease and drifted a ball to him. The catch was taken by Hampshire at leg-slip: 3-71.

Stackpole went to his fifty in 105 minutes and increasingly matters seemed to rest with him, for Walters was caught deep in the gully slashing at Willis. The last of the unfortunates to wear the tag of a 'young Bradman', Walters had begun his test career five years before with hundreds in his first two matches against England, but this time departed for a single with Australia a rocky 4-82. The score became 5-96 after half an hour of precise Illingworth off-spin. Stackpole swept, only to be bowled off his pads for what would prove to be the highest score of the match. His 67 took 159 minutes, and included two sixes and six fours.

The score could have become 5-103 twenty minutes before stumps when Marsh, on four, was stranded well out of his crease, but Knott missed a stumping chance off Illingworth, reputedly Knott's first miss since Brisbane.

For his next over Illingworth went over the wicket to Greg Chappell, who remained on 19 (eighty-eight minutes) overnight.

Marsh, who had reached 12 after his escape, had been in for fifty-four minutes, the pair having added twenty-seven runs. Australia had batted altogether for 215 minutes and forty-one overs for its total of 5-123, and Ian Chappell was anticipating a very reasonable fifth day track as Australia aimed for the remaining even hundred runs.

The England slow bowlers' figures at this stage make interesting reading: Illingworth 11-5-21-2, Underwood 5-1-16-0. On the last day, Underwood would deliver a spell of 8.6-4-12-2 while Illingworth would return figures of 9-2-18-1. Bill O'Reilly, who was never short of a word when it came to discussing spin bowling, judged that the England bowler presenting the difficulties was Illingworth who, throughout the series had 'shown so little confidence in his own ability to strike a penetrating bowling blow that he has hitherto done little more than pay courtesy calls to the bowling crease. With his slow off-spinners, which take considerable turn, interspersed with some highly knowledgeable changing of pace, he has succeeded in breaking the back of our batting hopes'.

DAY 5

It was twelve years and twelve days since Richie Benaud's Australian side had lifted the Ashes from Peter May. Not many more than 8000 Sydneysiders came to see if the morning's play might represent a historic turning of the tide. Illingworth opened with his spinners. If one counts D'Oliveira among their number, they would take five wickets for thirty-seven on this last morning, and the surrender was almost anti-climactic.

Marsh, whose 16 in seventy-nine minutes was out of character, was first to go, bowled by Underwood with a ball that kept low as he tried to pull. The score was then 6-131. Greg Chappell, on 30, was next to leave as he played inside the line of what wicketkeeper Knott identified as a straight ball from Illingworth. The bowler himself thought Chappell had missed an out-floater, which Swanton believed was his arm ball. The resultant stumping was Knott's twenty-fourth dismissal of the series, and Australia were now 7-142. After all this exertion for one wicket, albeit the crucial one on the final day, Illingworth rested with figures of 3-39, representing eighteen scoring scores in twenty overs, ten of them singles.

England had reached the tail by now, and when O'Keeffe, who had defended grimly while adding 12, clipped a leg-side half-volley to Ken Shuttleworth (substituting for Snow) at square-leg, the Australians were on the ropes at 8-154. Lillee continued the procession, caught first ball at second slip, leaving it to Dell to avert an unexpected D'Oliveira hat-trick.

Underwood was recalled to get Jenner, whose four in forty-six minutes contrasted with his breezier first innings batting. At 12.35, he was caught at silly mid-off by Fletcher to end the series. Willis recorded that Marsh was the first Australian into the England team's dressing room at the end of the game. There he might have seen Illingworth, who had failed to secure a stump or souvenir bail as he was chaired from the ground, being presented by Fletcher with the match ball. Fletcher had pocketed it. English journalist Frank Keating has recently recalled this incident as a hopeful sign for the future co-operation of England manager (Fletcher) and chairman of selectors (Illingworth).

EM Wellings, in the 1972 *Wisden*, wrote of Illingworth's bowling that 'some said he should have bowled more. Although his bowling was unsuited to the conditions, he averaged twenty-two eight-ball overs per test'. His series figures were 132-43-349-10 and, in his later coaching manual on *Spin Bowling* (1979), Illingworth revealed he had been troubled with pulled hamstrings until England physiotherapist Bernard Thomas exercised him out of his difficulties. Wellings in his *Wisden* report backed a winner with the following words: 'Illingworth did a magnificent job. Under severe provocation he remained cool off the field and courteously approachable by friend and foe alike.' A masterly piece of omission about on-the-field approachability!

One of northern cricketers' sternest critics, EW Swanton, did not omit to write that, 'whatever qualifications had to be made as regards attitude and behaviour, no one could withhold admiration for Illingworth's keen tactical grasp and for the wholehearted team effort'.

Snow went back to his county side and a sacking for alleged 'lack of effort'. His most cogent comment was that 'the so-called "quality" papers took the county line with reference to my past misdemeanours . . . the "popular" papers offered sympathy', which just about sums up the response to Sydney.

This chapter opened by reworking Dickens's famously ambivalent introduction to *A Tale of Two Cities* into a tale of one test; it closes by noting that England had beaten Australia by 229 runs in the earlier Sydney test of the season to record a convincing 2–0 margin. Ray Illingworth became only the fourth England captain to regain the Ashes from Australia in Australia, and the first since Douglas Jardine in 1932–33.

Ian Chappell after he took over the Australian captaincy from Bill Lawry.

Both he and Ian Chappell spoke out after the series against the concept of 'The Ashes', as Ted Dexter and Richie Benaud had done after the drawn 1962–63 series. On each occasion, the captains agreed that test series between the two countries would be improved were they not weighed down by tradition but were decided in their own right. Nothing was done about the idea on either occasion, and nothing has been done since.

The figure of Ian Chappell might appear relatively absent from this account, given the pivotal role he would play in shaping world cricket during the decade ahead. Already an established test campaigner with the bat, his tactical abilities in this match have been noted, but he was at the start of a learning curve so far as captaincy was concerned. He was undoubtedly under no illusions about the security of his position, given the treatment meted out to his predecessor. He became a hard campaigner, and the circumstances of his accession might explain one of the reasons for his resolve. His brother Greg, Rod Marsh, and Dennis Lillee were all given a baptism of fire in their first series, and together they formed the nucleus of the next few years of Australian cricketing supremacy.

•MELBOURNE 1977•

CENTENARY

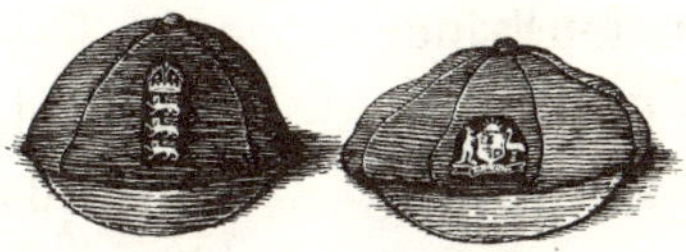

The Centenary Test at Melbourne in 1977 is a great celebration of test cricket, and also presages the new commercial spirit of the game. The weight of history seems to affect batsmen more than bowlers, especially during the first half of the match. Lillee asserts himself as the dominant figure, although Randall's marathon innings of 174 puts spirit back into English stocks. Rod Marsh, David Hookes, and Rick McCosker all show heroism in different forms. Marsh, as well as his masterly wicketkeeping and century, also shows that disputing an umpire's decision can sometimes be morally positive. In the cellars, Kerry Packer's agents strike their deals.

AUSTRALIA v ENGLAND 1977 (Centenary Test)

Played at Melbourne Cricket Ground on 12, 13, 14, 16, 17 March.
Toss: England. Result: AUSTRALIA won by 45 runs.

AUSTRALIA

IC Davis	lbw b Lever	5	c Knott b Greig	68
RB McCosker	b Willis	4	(10) c Greig b Old	25
GJ Cosier	c Fletcher b Lever	10	(4) c Knott b Lever	4
GS Chappell*	b Underwood	40	(3) b Old	2
DW Hookes	c Greig b Old	17	(6) c Fletcher b Underwood	56
KD Walters	c Greig b Willis	4	(5) c Knott b Greig	66
RW Marsh†	c Knott b Old	28	not out	110
GJ Gilmour	c Greig b Old	4	b Lever	16
KJ O'Keeffe	c Brearley b Underwood	0	(2) c Willis b Old	14
DK Lillee	not out	10	(9) c Amiss b Old	25
MHN Walker	b Underwood	2	not out	8
Extras	(B 4, LB 2, NB 8)	14	(LB 10, NB 15)	25
Total		**138**	(9 wickets declared)	**419**

ENGLAND

RA Woolmer	c Chappell b Lillee	9	lbw b Walker	12
JM Brearley	c Hookes b Lillee	12	lbw b Lillee	43
DL Underwood	c Chappell b Walker	7	(10) b Lillee	7
DW Randall	c Marsh b Lillee	4	(3) c Cosier b O'Keeffe	174
DL Amiss	c O'Keeffe b Walker	4	(4) b Chappell	64
KWR Fletcher	c Marsh b Walker	4	(5) c Marsh b Lillee	1
AW Greig*	b Walker	18	(6) c Cosier b O'Keeffe	41
APE Knott†	lbw b Lillee	15	(7) lbw b Lillee	42
CM Old	c Marsh b Lillee	3	(8) c Chappell b Lillee	2
JK Lever	c Marsh b Lillee	11	(9) lbw b O'Keeffe	4
RGD Willis	not out	1	not out	5
Extras	(B 2, LB 2, W 1, NB 2)	7	(B 8, LB 4, W 3, NB 7)	22
Total		**95**		**417**

ENGLAND	**O**	**M**	**R**	**W**	**O**	**M**	**R**	**W**
Lever	12	1	36	2	21	1	95	2
Willis	8	0	33	2	22	0	91	0
Old	12	4	39	3	27.6	2	104	4
Underwood	11.6	2	16	3	12	2	38	1
Greig					14	3	66	2
AUSTRALIA								
Lillee	13.3	2	26	6	34.4	7	139	5
Walker	15	3	54	4	22	4	83	1
O'Keeffe	1	0	4	0	33	6	108	3
Gilmour	5	3	4	0	4	0	29	0
Chappell					16	7	29	1
Walters					3	2	7	0

FALL OF WICKETS

	A	**E**	**A**	**E**
Wkt	**1st**	**1st**	**2nd**	**2nd**
1st	11	19	33	28
2nd	13	30	40	113
3rd	23	34	53	279
4th	45	40	132	290
5th	51	40	187	346
6th	102	61	244	369
7th	114	65	277	380
8th	117	78	353	385
9th	136	86	407	410
10th	138	95		417

Umpires: TF Brooks and MG O'Connell.

Rick McCosker

Derek Randall

The Melbourne Centenary Test in March 1977 was surrounded by more hype than any match that had preceded it, but lived up to all the expectations. The minds of the many were focused on the feast before them: they owed it largely to one man. The game was the brainchild of Hans Ebeling, whose solitary test appearance at The Oval on the 1934 tour of England had featured the wickets of Hammond, Allen and Verity and an innings of 41. For the Australian seasons immediately prior to and succeeding that tour, he had captained Victoria to successive Sheffield Shield wins. Turning down the South African trip of 1935–36, his cricketing career had outlived a clash with Bradman over allegations at Adelaide that Ernie McCormick, in taking 9-40 for Victoria, had been bowling bodyline at The Don.

By the 1970s, the former swing bowler had become Vice President of the Melbourne Cricket Club. He found it necessary to gain the support of major cricket bodies to stage the special match: first the Victorian Cricket Association, then the Australian Cricket Board, and finally the English Test and County Cricket Board. Then came the idea, and the logistical nightmare, of bringing all living past England and Australian test players together, which involved gaining the support of QANTAS to fly out the players from England, and Trans Australian Airlines to fly the Australian players to Melbourne. Altogether, of the 244 internationals and eligible to attend, 218 came.

To bring the likes of Jack Ryder, Bob Wyatt and Gubby Allen, the ailing Percy Fender, Harold Larwood and Bill Voce, Sir Donald Bradman and Bill O'Reilly, Sir Leonard Hutton and Cyril Washbrook, Neil Harvey and Denis Compton, Keith Miller and Ray Lindwall, Trevor Bailey and Freddie Brown, Alec Bedser and Godfrey Evans, Peter May and Colin Cowdrey, Richie Benaud and Alan Davidson, under the roof of the Melbourne Hilton near the MCG at one time was a triumph of goodwill. The oldest living test player, ninety-one-year-old EJ 'Tiger' Smith was unable to attend owing to doctor's orders. Similar considerations kept Herbert Sutcliffe and Frank Woolley away. When the Centenary Test organisers asked Jack Fingleton to intercede on their behalf, he was able to persuade the previously-reluctant Larwood to attend.

Another major sponsor was the Benson and Hedges tobacco company, which sparked some controversy in the lead-up to the match. The Victorian Premier's Department contributed $10,000 towards the running of the match. This grant brought opposition from the Victorian Department of Youth, Sport and Recreation, and in particular incensed its Minister, former well-known Australian Rules footballer Brian Dixon, who believed sport and smoking should not be associated. Benson and Hedges offered large cash awards. The winning team was to receive $9000, the losers $4500 and the Man of the Match $1500. Cash contributions continue to clash with duty-of-care considerations in Australian sport.

Sponsorship aside, the Victorian Cricket Association remained the major organising body, and David Richards, the VCA secretary – and now secretary of the International Cricket Council – held weekly press briefings for three weeks to promote the event. This was a media exercise, not an area where cricket in either England or Australia had previously demonstrated great expertise. An early promotion was run by the *Age* newspaper in which readers had to name their best post-war Australian team. To win, they had to match the choice made by former Australian captain Ian Johnson in batting order. Only one entrant of thousands succeeded – probably not surprisingly, given that Johnson's former Victorian teammate, and Australia's leading run-scorer during the period, Neil Harvey, was named twelfth man. The eleven was: Simpson, Morris, Bradman (captain), Hassett, Greg Chappell, Miller, Benaud, Tallon, Lindwall, Lillee, and Johnston.

When, in February 1977, the *Australian* newspaper ran a computer Centenary Test competition, readers selected an all-time Australian team to bat as follows: Trumper, Morris, Bradman, Harvey, Greg Chappell, Miller, Benaud, Lindwall, Oldfield, Lillee, and O'Reilly, with Davidson as twelfth man. The England combination was chosen by *Sun* readers, and adjudicated by writers Jim Swanton, John Arlott, and David Frith. The team batted Hobbs, Grace, Hammond, Compton, Woolley, Ames, Rhodes, Barnes, Larwood, Tate, Laker, with current England captain Tony Greig as twelfth man. The computer simulation was published over the five days immediately preceding the start of the Centenary Test itself. The result of the match was at once immaterial and predictable, but the interest generated was enormous.

In a second promotion, the Victorian Education Department ran an essay competition in conjunction with the match, the essay topic being 'The importance of test cricket to the Australian way of life'. Prizes for the best essays included tickets to the match, cricket books, and equipment worth $750 to the schools of two winners. At the time, the judges' view of the Australian way of life was probably somewhat less pluralistic and rather more traditional than the views of many school children, themselves the product of the post-war immigration boom, television and alternative lifestyles.

With the momentum of the publicity machine building, hotel rooms filling, and special package tours being advertised heavily by Australia's internal airlines and QANTAS, organisers began to anticipate record crowds.

The minds of the many may have been focused on the feast before them, but the minds of a few, among them a significant number of participants in the Centenary Test, were focused on other prospects being paraded before them by agents of the entrepreneur Kerry Packer.

Tony Greig led an England team that had survived a busy tour of India where it won a five match series 3–1. The Australian team had experienced a similarly busy season, but with much tighter results. It hosted and drew 1–1 a three test tour with Pakistan, followed by two tests in New Zealand where it had a 1–0 margin. While the batting, led by Greg Chappell, Doug Walters and Rick McCosker, was generally solid, the bowling lacked Jeff Thomson after he broke down with a shoulder injury in the first test of the summer. Thereafter, it was the sustained hostility of Dennis Lillee that carried the Australian attack. In the five matches Lillee captured thirty-six wickets, including ten wickets in both the Melbourne test against Pakistan and the Auckland test against New Zealand. The Western Australian was at this point of his career 'in his pomp', as John Arlott had written of Yorkshire fast bowler Fred Trueman.

It is strange, therefore, that Yorkshire opening batsman Geoff Boycott, playing for Waverley in Sydney grade cricket during his continuing absence from the England side, should have chosen such a moment to claim in his *Sydney Telegraph* column that Lillee had not learnt a thing in his six years of test cricket. Boycott apparently objected to Lillee's poor sportsmanship when an appeal against Glenn Turner was turned down on the fourth evening of the Christchurch test. The bowler's response – eleven wickets in the next game – and his 160 test wickets nevertheless impressed Harold Larwood. In the same week, Larwood described Lillee as 'a very great fast bowler. Without doubt, one of the greatest of all time'. Among Boycott's critics in Australia were many who argued he should let his bat do the talking at test level.

England's bowling was stronger than its batting, which had little to recommend it. Dennis Amiss had huge psychological hurdles to overcome against Lillee's pace, after being dismissed by Lillee for three successive ducks at the end of the 1974–75 series. Keith Fletcher had also struggled against Australian speed. As openers, Mike Brearley had not yet cemented his test place, and Bob Woolmer appeared something of a stop-gap, as did Derek Randall in the middle order. The latter was described by Robin Marlar in the *Sunday Times* as 'an over-promoted bundle of fun, a welcome addition, but not a huge contributor', except in the field. Greig and wicketkeeper Alan Knott remained, as they had been on Mike Denness's ill-fated 1974–75 tour, the most likely run-getters in the side.

In the pace department, old-stagers Bob Willis and Chris Old returned to prove whether they were still capable of bowling with a lot of fizz. By way of contrast, and despite an inordinately lengthy run, left-armer John Lever had proved a revelation in India with twenty-six wickets at fourteen in five tests. Left-arm orthodox spinner Derek Underwood was in peak form after twenty-nine wickets at seventeen in the Indian series. 'Deadly' remained the meanest bowler in the game, and Greig's competitiveness meant his off-spin would take wickets.

Australia's team appeared better balanced. Among the batsmen, Greg Chappell and Doug Walters loomed as matchwinners, a point underlined by Walters's career high of 250 in the recent drawn Christchurch test. And the home team had found a 'wonder boy'. Twenty-year-old South Australian left-hander David Hookes had won his first test place by making five centuries in six innings: 163

(his first first-class hundred) and nine against Victoria; 185 and 105 against Queensland; and 135 and 156 against New South Wales. In so doing, he became only the second player in first-class cricket history to score twin centuries in successive games.

On the bowling ledger, medium-pacer Max Walker and leg-spinner Kerry O'Keeffe could be expected to provide steady support for Lillee, as well as make useful runs, but there was concern about the bowling form and fitness of left-handed all-rounder Gary Gilmour. Chappell and Walters could provide medium-pace support, but Lillee was the one that mattered.

DAY 1

The match, when it finally began, had an air of anti-climax. The sky was overcast and, despite the profusion of advertising material, the crowd of 61,316 – healthy by most standards – disappointed the organisers, who had believed their own press releases. Also absent at the outset was the atmosphere associated with the first match of an Ashes series. This was a special encounter, a celebration of an ongoing tradition, but neither an opening match nor the start of the season. Normally the international Australian cricket season is well over by March.

England won the toss of a specially-minted gold coin and Greig put Australia into bat, perhaps fearing the effect of moisture in the pitch. Before the game got under way, former captains paraded on the ground. With one exception, all were wearing suits and ties. The exception, to no one's surprise, was Ian Chappell. Chappell was described overseas as having given world cricket the 'ugly Australians' in the 1970s and his rebellious spirit was yet to be quelled – as coming events would soon enough demonstrate. In a column headed '100 years war' in the Melbourne *Age* the day before the game, Chappell leavened a piece about nationalism and Ashes battles with a little republicanism:

Perhaps it goes all the way back to Australians disliking the fact that our heritage is British and for so many years this controlled our destiny, but the Englishman finds it hard to accept the fact that Australia has grown up and with it has grown away from much of the early control.

When play began, the Australian cricket administrators' nightmares must all have seemed to come at once as Australia crumbled against England's far-from-hostile attack. Ian Davis and Rick McCosker began slowly against Lever and Willis, and had put only eleven runs on the board in just under half an hour when Davis pushed across a ball from Lever that moved back to him. A half-hearted appeal was enough to gain the verdict from umpire Tom Brooks.

Gary Cosier then joined McCosker, but the New South Wales opener did not last long. In attempting to hook Willis, McCosker deflected the ball on to his face, from where it fell on his stumps. While the English players clustered around McCosker and Willis called urgently for a doctor, several minutes elapsed before he was helped from the field. Not only had McCosker's jaw been broken, he was also out – bowled. The score was 2-13, not at all what had been expected.

Greg Chappell came to the crease but the procession continued. Cosier batted breezily and hit two boundaries in reaching double figures but got no further when caught by Fletcher playing a weak hook shot off Lever at 3-23. This was an awkward time for Hookes to commence his test career, but he refused to be shackled in half an hour at the wicket, and looked solid in defence before being caught by Greig off Old for 17 when forty-five were on the board. Walters came and went, falling to a typical slash over slips. When at lunch the Australian's sorry card read 5-57, some optimistic England supporters may have begun to entertain hopes of reversing England's recent Ashes humiliations.

The strangest innings of the first day, and the oddest of his career, was that played by the Australian captain. Greg Chappell was the premier batsman appearing in the match. He could hold his head high with any among the exalted company of cricketers from the past looking on. Thus he should have been the least likely to have been overawed by the occasion. Normally the batsman to whom his country looked to stamp his authority on games, Chappell instead crept to nine in nearly an hour and a half before the long break. His unduly defensive play probably infected the rest of his team with uncharacteristic caution.

Even after the other main batsmen had departed, spectators might have expected that Chappell would lead a rearguard action. Marsh, Gilmour and O'Keeffe were all capable batsmen, and Lillee and Walker no novices. Marsh did attempt to raise the tempo of the scoring after lunch with two straight boundaries. He dominated a half-century stand with Chappell, but this was only because of his captain's inexplicable inactivity. Marsh's 28 in an hour and a half was slow by his standards and, when he was caught behind by Knott attempting to cut Old, the total was 6-102.

Gary Gilmour and Kerry O'Keeffe batted at eight and nine. Gilmour, the hard-hitting left-handed Newcastle all-rounder, 'the new Alan Davidson' to many, had made his maiden test century two matches previously, but his richly-promising test career ended in this game. He hung around nearly half an hour for four before edging an Old out-swinger to the slips to make the score 7-114. His performance in this match was far below the twenty-six-year-old's previous exploits. O'Keeffe, another talented but ultimately unfulfilled all-rounder, left three runs later without scoring. The tall right-hander's test career was almost over by this time, too. For all his determination and obduracy with the bat, neither this nor his gully fielding stood him in good stead when, as a leg-spin bowler, he lost the ability to turn the ball from leg.

These two are perhaps symptomatic of Australian cricket at this time. Following the retirement of high-class all-rounders Benaud and Davidson during 1963–64, O'Keeffe and Gilmour were touted as their natural heirs in the 1970s – but Gilmour's career was cut short by injury before it reached full stature, and O'Keeffe was no Benaud. Both went to Packer, then out to pasture. England had been even less well served by genuine all-rounders for even longer until the advent of Greig. Ian Botham was about to emerge, of course, though the Whitbread scholar's club form during the 1976–77 season of Melbourne grade cricket gave little hint of his talent.

Lillee joined Chappell, but still the captain failed to seize the initiative, so that at tea the total was 8-126. Australia's innings continued for three-quarters of an hour after the break. Chappell's slow hand ended when he hit out at Underwood and was bowled for 40 made in three minutes under four hours. Walker fell to the same bowler at 138.

The Australians had given a dismal display of batting on what appeared to be a good wicket and England's star seemed to be in the ascendant. Despite a spirited attack by Lillee in the final hour of the day, the only wicket to fall was that of Woolmer, who split a finger while batting. At stumps England's score was 1-29 with Brearley and nightwatchman Underwood to resume on the morrow with a deficit of 109 to overcome.

Ralph Steadman on Dennis Lillee

DAY 2

The second day saw ball dominate bat in even more astonishing fashion than on the first. Again, there were more than 60,000 spectators in the ground, and they became much more raucous, chanting LILLEE, LILLEE to stir the efforts of their fast bowler and then later singing 'Waltzing Matilda' to accompany the hapless footwork of the England players. In just under two-and-a-half hours Lillee and Walker took nine wickets for sixty-six runs as England were dismissed for ninety-five, an unexpected deficit of forty-three.

Brearley fell in Lillee's first over, steering a catch to third slip from a ball that lifted outside the off stump. Then Walker in his first over had Underwood freakishly caught at first slip by Greg Chappell. The ball rolled down his right arm as he fell to the ground, but he grabbed it first with his left hand to make the total 3-34.

The Australians were visibly invigorated by the cheering, jeering crowd in the outer. Walker, at fine-leg, was raising his fans in 'Bay 13' to a frenzy. In the members' stand, one South Australian supreme court judge turned to another. 'Was Rome like this?' he asked.

Randall and Amiss were at the wicket, but neither they nor Fletcher in the middle order was able to stem the tide. All were dismissed for the paltry score of four, all in the slips cordon, although they lasted for differing periods. Randall and Amiss both left at 40 and it began to seem all too like the tests of two years previously, when Greig and Knott alone looked like providing any resistance.

The England captain showed more enterprise than his Australian counterpart or any of his teammates. In partnership with Fletcher, Greig drove both Lillee and Walker to the boundary but, after reaching 18 in just twenty-six minutes, chanced his arm once too often. With the total on 61, Walker produced a perfect in-swinger that flicked Greig's right pad before careering into his stumps.

Fletcher was joined by Knott. The Essex enigma, with a test average of almost forty, yet again failed to live up to his reputation in matches against Australia to become Walker's fourth victim. Gilmour relieved Lillee but, after several wild deliveries, Lillee returned to mop up Old – always uncomfortable against real pace, and, unlike some, prepared to show it – with a fearsome bouncer that Old touched to the wicketkeeper. England's lunch score read 8-83.

Half an hour after the break came the end. Knott's resistance ended when Lillee trapped him leg before wicket, and Marsh set an Australian wicketkeeping record when his 188th dismissal – Lever off Lillee – passed the mark made by Wally Grout. Marsh took four catches as England slumped, and his catch ended the innings. Lillee took 6-26, his best test figures. Walker finished with 4-54, Gilmour and O'Keeffe contributing six overs for eight runs. Though Walker may have seemed tangle-footed in his delivery stride, his tireless enthusiasm and ability to shock batsmen with his in-swinger and leg-cutter made him a better prospect than anything Gilmour's more sporadic brilliance offered his side.

In Australia's second innings, the absence of McCosker prompted Chappell to instruct O'Keeffe to open with Davis. The move worked well enough, as the makeshift pair added thirty-three in fifty minutes before O'Keeffe was caught off Old for 25. This brought Chappell to the crease. He did not occupy it for long, losing his stumps to Old for only two so that the Australians went to tea at 2-49. Resuming after the break, Cosier's stay was similarly brief before he essayed another wild hook off Lever and Knott took the catch.

At 3-53 the Australian situation looked perilous, but Davis and Walters played soundly until the close, by which time the score had reached 3-104, an overall lead of 147.

At the end of the second day's play, the captains attributed the poor batting to the enormous build-up the game had received. Rod Marsh and Dennis Lillee concurred. When, on the first two days, twenty-three wickets had fallen for 337 runs, the only reason Tony Greig could think of was the occasion itself. Greig went on to give the example of Greg Chappell's second innings dismissal, saying that previously he had never seen Chappell miss a straight ball and be bowled. 'The guy was just so tense'. Greig said. As Marsh put it, in one of his two memorable quotes from this game:

> Every time you walk into the Hilton Hotel there are about four hundred cricketers who could probably all play the game better than you. It makes you feel inadequate.

But was such an explanation sufficient? This feeling of the pressure of the past was no doubt allied to the weight of a secret Packer-dominated future. But a supplementary question might also be asked. Why should batsmen alone suffer nerves? Had bowlers similarly suffered, and lost length and direction, surely there would have been easy runs available or at least enough loose deliveries to offset temporary lapses in technique and concentration?

David Hookes and Alan Knott

||| DAY 3

The balance of the game began to change on the third day. The bat got on top of the ball as only five wickets fell for the addition of 283 runs from a pathetically slow fifty-seven overs. Davis and Walters consolidated their overnight stand for the first three-quarters of an hour, Davis in particular playing a number of elegant drives before Greig had him caught behind for 68. Despite having made his only test hundred in Adelaide against Pakistan, this innings, which took a minute under four hours, was probably his best. Davis was another who never played test cricket post-Packer. By the time he left, the score had reached 4-132.

Hookes joined Walters and the pair were still together at lunch with the total 4-186. Walters was out four minutes after play resumed when, like Davis, he was caught behind off Greig. *Wisden*'s waspish comment was that he had joyfully ridden 'his fortune in the manner that has charmed so many admirers of the cavalier approach to batsmanship'. In fact, his 66 had been a subdued innings that occupied just over three-and-a-half hours. It was suited to the tempo of the match, if not the mood of the occasion.

When Marsh joined Hookes, some historic fireworks finally began to explode. Australia's captain was reported to have identified this over as 'the real turning point' of the test. Greig went around the wicket to Hookes in his thirteenth over. Hookes played the first two balls defensively, then hit five consecutive fours, lofting the third ball of Greig's high over mid-off, swinging the fourth – a short ball – fine down the leg side, gracefully cover-driving the fifth past Randall before that electric performer could move, sending the sixth with an elegant stroke through mid-wicket to bring up his fifty, and bisecting the covers again with the seventh. Though the last ball was again played to cover, this time Amiss was in the way to temporarily dam the 'fount of youth' from which *Wisden* thought he had drawn his increasing confidence.

The crowd of 55,000 went wild. Former test players reportedly had tears in their eyes as the game came unmistakeably alive, and Sir Donald Bradman commented that Hookes's innings reminded him of the absent Frank Woolley, an unusual comparison for the Australian maestro to make. Woolley had scorned mere scorelines throughout his career in pursuit of the interests of his team and muse. True to the premature typecasting, Hookes would take the same style into the nineties, without ever accumulating an equivalent number of runs at test level as the older and greater left-hander achieved. He performed well for Packer, but was never consistent enough to keep a secure place in test cricket thereafter. Even on this day, the drama faded too early: Hookes fell the next ball he faced to a tumbling bat-pad catch off Underwood for 56. His innings remains one of the great miniatures in test cricket history.

Perhaps Hookes's knock gave Rod Marsh the inspiration to regain his status as a test-quality batsman. The Australian wicketkeeper was already having a good game, with four catches and twenty-eight runs in the first innings, and he proceeded to hit the ball cleanly for the rest of the afternoon. With Hookes he added fifty-seven runs, with Gilmour thirty-three before the seventh wicket fell at 277, and with Lillee seventy-six runs in eighty-seven minutes for the eighth wicket. He then enjoyed an unbeaten stand of thirty-four with the injured McCosker.

Australia's heroes thus came in different guises. Davis had been the early backbone of the innings, and Hookes provided the panache in a brilliant cameo, Marsh put some punch into the later stages of the innings, and Rick McCosker offered true grit. He entered the arena at two minutes past five with his head covered in bandages, his jaw wired together and held in place in a sling. He was unable to speak or hear, and needed Kerry O'Keeffe, who had deputised for him at the top of the order, to act as a runner.

The Englishmen might have thought they were opposing the Elephant Man – although the film was not released for another three years – but he showed little concern for their bouncers, and at stumps had nudged his way to 17.

With Marsh on 95, the score stood at 8-387. Australia led by over four hundred and appeared to have the game in its keeping. Many of the large English press contingent had filed stories contrasting Australia's heroes with the English mugs. The *Yorkshire Post* reported

Greg Chappell as saying the task was already too great for England, with the changing fortunes of the contest having swung almost irreversibly toward Australia. The only optimist appeared to be Tony Greig, who said England had 'by no means written it off yet. This test has swung back and forth and maybe it will go our way again'.

Nicholson in the Melbourne Age

DAY 4

It did not seem that way at the start of the fourth day when Marsh cruised to his third test century, the first ever by an Australian wicketkeeper against England. Only McCosker's wicket fell in the hour's play before Chappell declared the innings closed at 9-419. England were set 463 for victory, a figure never before remotely approached to win a test. Yet it seemed by the end of play that there might to be some wag left in the Lion's oft-twisted tail.

Brearley and Woolmer made a sound enough opening but, when Woolmer fell lbw to Walker for 12, their partnership had registered only 28. The nervously energetic Randall then joined the determined Brearley, with Randall certainly, and Brearley probably, fighting for their futures as test batsmen. In India Randall's top score in four tests was 37 with an average of 12.28, not much of a recommendation for success. Randall's recollection of his innings in his autobiography, *The Sun Has Got His Hat On*, is modest, noting that he began this innings sketchily, playing and missing a good deal, especially at Lillee.

Nevertheless, it was obvious that Greig's men were not going to give in without a fight. With the batsmen remaining in occupation at the tea interval, Brearley had been at the crease nearly three hours before he was dismissed lbw by Lillee for 43 with the score at 2-113. He was replaced by Amiss.

The big test for the English players, particularly Dennis Amiss, was to attempt to counteract the Lillee jitters. For once, shoddy Australian fielding gave them the chance. When bad light ended play eighteen minutes early on the fourth evening, Amiss with 34 and Randall 87 were still *in situ* at 2-191, needing 272 runs to win.

Both had savoured their share of fortune. Two opportunities were missed off Lillee: Randall at 42 had been dropped from a hot chance to O'Keeffe in the gully, and Hookes at third slip let a snick pass by him when Amiss was on eight. Amiss also had further lives when short-leg Cosier missed two possible catches from O'Keeffe. This was not quite the Amiss of the Melbourne test of Christmas 1974, when for once he had taken the fight to the Australian attack. On most occasions in that series, his first error had been fatal, often enough occurring in the first over he faced from Dennis Lillee. Here Amiss rode his fortune and gave some evidence of his careworn class.

The views of the captains at the end of the day predictably differed: Chappell felt history favoured his side, while Greig thought the game remained in the balance.

DAY 5

Overnight opinion was that much would depend on the first session of play. If that was the case, England had emerged as favourites by the time the cucumber sandwiches were consumed. Seventy-six runs were added in the pre-lunch period, Randall had raised his first test century, and he and Amiss were still in possession at 2-267. One hundred and ninety-six runs in the afternoon session, including the mandatory fifteen eight-ball overs in the last hour, seemed achievable.

England hopes received their first dent shortly after resumption, however, when Amiss was bowled by a ball that kept low at 3-279. Chappell's only wicket of the match opened the way to the fragile Keith Fletcher, who had been guarded for so long by Randall and Amiss. The latter's 64 took ten minutes under four hours and guaranteed him a start in the forthcoming series in England but, more immediately and importantly, his partnership of 166 with Randall had revived his team's prospects.

Fletcher, like Amiss, had several points to prove against both Australia and Lillee but, unlike his predecessor, was not up to the task. He scored a single before fending a rising Lillee delivery to Marsh, and departed at 4-290. Randall noted that Lillee bowled magnificently throughout this match, and he witnessed at first hand why 'everybody in the game rated him the best around. He was quick, intelligent and skilful, able to make the ball move late and at great pace'.

By this crucial point, Lillee, forced to operate as a stock bowler owing to the deterioration of Gilmour, was for the most part bowling off a short run to conserve energy. This seemed in many ways the more heroic side of the Lillee persona: the bowler of Sydney, January 1973, where he rose above injury, and Adelaide, December 1976, where he covered for Jeff Thomson's injury. In these games against Pakistan he subordinated his instincts to attack to team plans, rising above histrionics to an even higher level of gritty heroics than all-out assault and crowd encouragement could ever assure, while performing a role not fully reflected in his match figures.

Fletcher had surrendered a good deal of England's hard-won initiative by his tame departure. Greig now joined Randall but, when the score had reached 4-320 and honours were again appearing even, Randall flashed outside off stump against Chappell, and Marsh appeared to hold a tumbling chance. After a rowdy appeal, umpire Tom Brooks signalled Randall out, but Marsh then ran forward to indicate he had not taken the ball cleanly. Fortunately for the Australians, Marsh's sporting generosity did not prove too costly as, after adding a further thirteen runs, Randall was caught by a diving Cosier off O'Keeffe at 5-346.

Randall's 174 was a monumental innings in his first test against Australia. It occupied seven-and-a-half hours and included twenty-one boundaries, many of his off-side drives, according to Jack Fingleton, reviving memories of May and Compton at their best. More importantly, however, England had discovered a new hero, a man prepared to stand up to Lillee and swap blows with him. Randall had the cheek of an Artful Dodger and a repertoire of responses to Lillee's bouncer. Evading one bouncer before lunch on the final day, he ducked and completed a backward double somersault. After receiving a glancing blow from another bouncer, he retained enough presence of mind to draw himself to his full height, doff his cap to the bowler, and offer him a polite bow. The bowler seemed barely amused at the levity, which Randall recognised 'did not particularly endear me to him'.

He was not afraid to hook other short-pitched deliveries to the square-leg fence with speed and power that some old-timers found reminiscent of Bradman. It was the sort of match that encouraged over-the-top comparisons and comments.

Randall had shown character and two more men of character – Greig and Knott – had succeeded him at the wicket. They remained there at tea with England 5-354, needing just 109 to win, but with a tail to follow. So much depended on England's two most dependable batsmen. Greig played a double-edged game, interspersing long periods of defence with seven spanking boundaries. When at 369 he was surprised by O'Keeffe's bounce and gave Cosier a simple catch at short-leg, his side was undeniably in trouble.

Knott, as usual, was willing to challenge the Australians, but the English tail let him down. Hard-hitting Old had three first-class centuries for Yorkshire to his name, but hung out his bat to the first ball he received from Lillee to be caught at slip. Old left at 7-382, and three runs later Lever was lbw playing back to O'Keeffe. Underwood supplied some resistance, as he and Knott added twenty-five at a run a minute, before Lillee yorked him for seven. At the start of the final fifteen overs England needed fifty-one runs with one wicket remaining.

Lillee ended the game halfway through the second over when he caught Knott's pad with an off-cutter and his lbw appeal was upheld. Knott had made 42 and England's gallant second innings reached 417, so that by an uncanny coincidence Australia's winning margin of forty-five was the same as it had been in the first of all test matches.

Lillee took 5-139 in the second innings to give him 11-165 for the match, and his was the decisive performance, although Randall won the Man of the Match award. It has often been remarked that, when Queen Elizabeth II, who was in Australia to mark the diamond jubilee of her reign, met the players mid-afternoon on the final day, Lillee had the temerity to ask for her autograph but was refused. Given his standing on this and many other occasions, he should have offered her his.

In the immediate aftermath of the match Lillee reported himself unavailable to tour England owing to a back injury. He was replaced by Jeff Thomson, who returned after wrecking his shoulder in a collision with Alan Turner in an earlier test that summer. Lillee would not play for Australia again until December 1979. He joined World Series Cricket where he continued to perform mighty deeds, but missed twenty-nine test matches as a result.

Randall's innings established his credibility as a test player. He began the 1977 Ashes series in good touch with 53 in the First (Jubilee) Test at Lord's and 79 in the Second at Manchester but, after Geoff Boycott ran him out for a duck in front of Randall's home crowd at Nottingham, he lost his way a little. He was still a valuable contributor to a series which England won 3–0 and a reasonably regular player in to the early 1980s, playing forty-seven tests and scoring seven centuries.

The longer term aftermath of the match was the revelation of the signings to World Series Cricket. Rod Marsh's second significant quote was to the effect that the attendants who moved the Melbourne sightscreens during the Centenary Test were being paid as much as the players for considerably less physical endeavour. As Gideon Haigh reported in *The Cricket War* it was this state of financial affairs that paved the way for media magnate Packer to place a yellow brick road of attractive contractual arrangements before teams drawn from the Australian and international scene. Marsh was last to sign on with Packer's agent JP Sport, after his plan for improving the player provident fund was rejected. At the end of the Centenary Test JP Sport's Austin Robertson was a mysterious figure in the dressing rooms, handing out signing-on cheques like theatre tickets. The Australian Cricket Board learned how to promote test cricket too late and ignored players' interests too long.

·LEEDS 1981·

500:1 TO 6:4

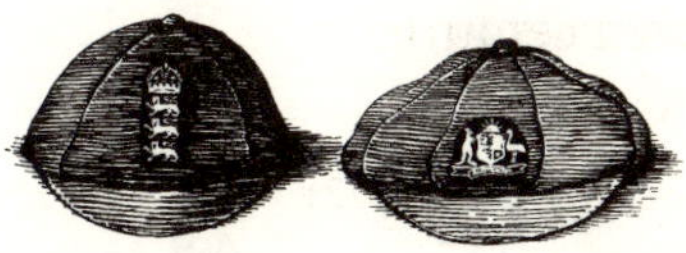

The Leeds test of 1981 is about comebacks. As in 1894, and for only the second time in test history, England won after following on, the odds on the victory in this instance reducing from 500:1 to 6:4. But the comebacks are personal, too. First there is the return of the prodigal, Ian Botham, whose enormous gifts seemed lost under the pressures of captaincy and then wonderfully restored immediately that burden was removed. Equally, the fast bowling aggression of Bob Willis, which had been lost following injury and loss of confidence, is rediscovered. These are the decisive individual performances in the match, but they probably would not have been sparked except for the comeback as captain of Mike Brearley, whose flair and management skills enable him to draw the best from his charges when it matters. Australia, by contrast, is a divided team. In the absence of Greg Chappell, Kim Hughes proves unable to command sufficient respect as a leader and is left to rue the fact that he is learning on the job.

ENGLAND v AUSTRALIA 1981 (3rd Test)

Played at Headingley, Leeds, on 16, 17, 18, 20, 21 July.
Toss: Australia. Result: ENGLAND won by 18 runs.

AUSTRALIA

J Dyson	b Dilley	102	c Taylor b Willis	34
GM Wood	lbw b Botham	34	c Taylor b Botham	10
TM Chappell	c Taylor b Willey	27	c Taylor b Willis	8
KJ Hughes*	c and b Botham	89	c Botham b Willis	0
RJ Bright	b Dilley	7	(8) b Willis	19
GN Yallop	c Taylor b Botham	58	(5) c Gatting b Willis	0
AR Border	lbw b Botham	8	(6) b Old	0
RW Marsh†	b Botham	28	(7) c Dilley b Willis	4
GF Lawson	c Taylor b Botham	13	c Taylor b Willis	1
DK Lillee	not out	3	c Gatting b Willis	17
TM Alderman	not out	0	not out	0
Extras	(B 4, LB 13, W 3, NB 12)	32	(LB 3, W 1, NB 14)	18
Total		**401**		**111**

ENGLAND

GA Gooch	lbw b Alderman	2	c Alderman b Lillee	0
G Boycott	b Lawson	12	lbw b Alderman	46
JM Brearley*	c Marsh b Alderman	10	c Alderman b Lillee	14
DI Gower	c Marsh b Lawson	24	c Border b Alderman	9
MW Gatting	lbw b Lillee	15	lbw b Alderman	1
P Willey	b Lawson	8	c Dyson b Lillee	33
IT Botham	c Marsh b Lillee	50	not out	149
RW Taylor†	c Marsh b Lillee	5	c Bright b Alderman	1
GR Dilley	c and b Lillee	13	b Alderman	56
CM Old	c Border b Alderman	0	b Lawson	29
RGD Willis	not out	1	c Border b Alderman	2
Extras	(B 6, LB 11, W 6, NB 11)	34	(B 5, LB 3, W 3, NB 5)	16
Total		**174**		**356**

ENGLAND	O	M	R	W	O	M	R	W
Willis	30	8	72	0	15.1	3	43	8
Old	43	14	91	0	9	1	21	1
Dilley	27	4	78	2	2	0	11	0
Botham	39.2	11	95	6	7	3	14	1
Willey	13	2	31	1	3	1	4	0
Boycott	3	2	2	0				
AUSTRALIA								
Lillee	18.5	7	49	4	25	6	94	3
Alderman	19	4	59	3	35.3	6	135	6
Lawson	13	3	32	3	23	4	96	1
Bright					4	0	15	0

FALL OF WICKETS

	A	E	E	A
Wkt	1st	1st	2nd	2nd
1st	55	12	0	13
2nd	149	40	18	56
3rd	196	42	37	58
4th	220	84	41	58
5th	332	87	105	65
6th	354	112	133	68
7th	357	148	135	74
8th	396	166	252	75
9th	401	167	319	110
10th		174	356	111

Umpires: DGL Evans and BJ Meyer.

Mike Brearley and Ian Botham

Greg Chappell's withdrawal from the 1981 tour to England became one of the most talked-about English tour decisions since Clarrie Grimmett's enforced omission in 1938, although some critics agreed players were entitled to temporarily halt their careers to spend time with their families before resuming the round of tests and tours.

Chappell's relinquishment of the captaincy after thirty-three tests was one thing, but returning it to vice-captain Kim Hughes was another. Hughes had earned his chance as a batsman, having dominated the rain-ruined Lord's Centenary Test of 1980 with sensational innings of 117 and 84, but other players could press captaincy claims. Rodney Marsh had stronger credentials as a senior test player and proven state captain, but had little support from the Australian selectors. According to broadcaster Alan McGilvray, Marsh was tarred with the brush of Ian Chappell, 'the brush of revolution and extremism'. The selectors could apparently accept Greg Chappell's dignified manner more readily than Marsh's knockabout demeanour.

Chappell's 1981 abdication was the subject of a damaging allegation. Australia's *Cricketer* magazine editor Ken Piesse claimed that it forced the selectors to send to England one of Australia's most inexperienced and unproven batting line-ups since 1968.

In fact, of the four preceding touring parties to England only Ian Chappell's 1975 side was collectively more experienced – by eleven tests – than the Hughes combination. In terms of individual inexperience, the 1977 tourists had included six players with only one test between them, as against the three newcomers Hughes took with him. In terms of front-line batsmen alone, Hughes's line-up was more experienced than both 1968 and 1972 and as experienced as 1977. Finally, in terms of batsmen with at least twenty test appearances, Hughes was equipped with the greatest number possessing that minimum qualification. Such fault as there may have been in his team did not result from any selectorial punt on untried batting talent.

Among the experienced batsmen previously mentioned but unavailable to Hughes was, of course, Greg Chappell. He had toured in 1972, 1975 and 1977. This time, a third brother, Trevor, lent the Chappell name, if not quite the same charisma as Ian and Greg, to the Hughes enterprise.

On the bowling front, New South Wales quick bowler Len Pascoe, aged thirty-one, withdrew from the 1981 tour because of a knee injury, and Jeff Thomson, also thirty-one, was written off for lacking the fitness or variety to last, a libel belied until 1985. Victorian Merv Hughes at twenty was tipped as one among a number of colts with promise, while others to warrant mention included Carl Rackemann, Mike Whitney, Shaun Graf, and Rod McCurdy.

The spearhead of the attack would inevitably be Dennis Lillee, nearing thirty-two. He'd last been seen in England in 1975. Piesse commented that Chappell had bowled him in five- and six-over spells in the 1980–81 summer, and that similar treatment in following seasons could mean Lillee remaining a dangerous bowler at thirty-five.

Twenty-five-year-old Alderman opened his international career with an unbroken spell of 24-7-68-4 at Trent Bridge, and the demands of the summer saw Lillee similarly extended despite an early-season infection. Other fast bowling contenders for a lengthy test bowl during the tour were Geoff Lawson and Rodney Hogg, but both suffered back injuries at crucial times. Lawson, however, had a moment of glory at Lord's when he took 7-81 in the first innings of the drawn match.

The tour was managed by Peter Philpott, less than a year after he had survived a four-hour open-heart operation. This cannot have been an easy tour to either manage or captain.

The England selectors, whose background for once bore the pedigree of professional cricket, also had difficulties with the captaincy. The committee was chaired by Alec Bedser, whose fellow selectors Brian Close and Charles Elliott had been against making Ian Botham captain of England. Two series losses against the West Indies had not helped Botham's cause. Bedser and John Edrich, replacing the recently-deceased Ken Barrington, wanted to give Botham a chance against the sort of 'manageable opposition' which Australia might be imagined to represent. This was a view that Barrington would supposedly have shared.

In *The Cricketer*, Christopher Martin-Jenkins thought, with a fine Tolkienesque flourish, that the captaincy 'had weighed more heavily than Frodo's Ring' on Botham. Beforehand, he'd made 1336 runs, with six hundreds, at 40.48 and taken 139 wickets at 18.52 runs apiece, including fourteen times five wickets in an innings, three times ten wickets in a match, in his twenty-five tests. During his twelve tests as captain in 1980 and 1981, he would make 276 runs at thirteen and take thirty-five wickets at thirty-three apiece. The alternatives were Cambridge graduate Mike Brearley and Keith Fletcher.

After an England loss at Trent Bridge and a drawn Lord's test, Botham's confidence had reached rock-bottom, not helped by the selectors' refusal to appoint him for more than a match at a time. A pair at Lord's prompted his resignation, which was gratefully received. As far as his replacements were concerned, Brearley reckoned the range of alternatives included Roger Knight of Surrey and John Barclay of Sussex, both gentlemen and scholars, though never test captaincy material. At this stage of their careers, future test captains Graham Gooch, David Gower, and Bob Willis were not considered.

Willis about this time wrote that, despite what he described as 'some unconvincing performances', Keith Fletcher could show an excellent test record. There seemed little doubt, according to Willis, that Fletcher would have proved a better proposition during the late seventies than others whom the then thirty-one-year-old fast bowler dismissed as the 'younger brigade'. In fact, in 1981 Fletcher hadn't played a test at home in six years, and not at all for England since the Centenary Test in 1977. His fifty-two tests had netted him just under three thousand runs at forty. His seven test hundreds had included a soft century against a crippled Australian attack, minus Lillee and Thomson, at the end of the 1974–75 tour, when the then England captain, Mike Denness, had prospered similarly. Fletcher's subsequent seven test sub-contintental comeback in 1981–82 led to a 1–0 loss to Gavaskar's India and a win over Sri Lanka. As a tour, it was not a success. As a captain, he was not what had been expected.

Recalling Brearley turned out the better bet, after all. He was given three tests, with an option on a fourth in the Sixth Test at The Oval match, and began his brief tenure prepared to let his former star all-rounder stand down should Botham so prefer.

While Brearley's playing career had not been marked by any batting bonanza, he was acknowledged for his player-management skills, and for his captaincy. Brearley, who had an eventual win–loss ratio of eighteen wins to four losses in his thirty-one tests, began the Headingley match sharing the record number of England wins against

Australia with WG Grace. He was faced with the task of becoming the first England captain to recover from one-down in an Ashes rubber since 1888. Then Grace – eight wins in thirteen matches, four losses – had replaced fellow amateur AG Steel, who had won three of his four tests as captain against Australia before being sacked following his first defeat.

Brearley replaced Bob Woolmer for Headingley, and earned himself a sleepless first night over his self-induced lack of spin. Having omitted his Middlesex teammate, off-spinner John Emburey, in order to include Yorkshire captain and seam bowler Chris Old, he then discovered on the first day that part-time off-spinner Peter Willey, despite an injured index finger, could still turn and bounce the ball off his second finger. The downside was that Willey had been more accurate than the seam bowlers at Brearley's disposal.

These included Bob Willis, who had suffered from a virus at Lord's and was reported as deeply depressed about not being an original inclusion in the Headingley twelve. In the end the selectors checked with him again before the match. Even though he missed Warwickshire's Saturday match, he played on the Sunday and had a net on the Monday prior to the test, eventually displacing Mike Hendrick.

Australia opted to play left-arm orthodox spinner Ray Bright rather than Hogg, and were thus unchanged from Lord's, giving them an attack of Lillee, Alderman, Lawson and Bright.

Headingley's three most recent tests in 1978, 1979 and 1980 had seen nearly sixty per cent of the possible playing time lost to bad weather but, despite the first rain in Leeds for three weeks just before the start, there was a net loss in 1981 of only just over three hours. An attendance of 52,500 – twenty thousand up on the West Indian test crowd of 1980 – watched the ground's first four-innings, finished match since 1976. It was all recorded on the Yorkshire County Club's new electronic scoreboard.

||| DAY 1

Hughes began the match by winning the toss, but took Marsh and Lillee out to re-inspect the wicket before deciding to bat. He had already taken veteran Australian broadcaster Alan McGilvray out to look at the pitch before breakfast that day, and had been advised against batting last. In the conditions, McGilvray's advice was sensible, and batting a sensible enough move by Hughes. *Wisden* lent a Brontean tone to those conditions by describing how the 'familiar slategray clouds engulfed the chimneys which stretch away from the Kirkstall Lane end' of the ground. The game was to be played against a background of race riots which swept English cities (including Leeds) during the summer.

Despite the rain, Headingley provided a drier-looking than usual pitch and a fast outfield. The first day started with a cool breeze coming from opposite the pavilion. Willis opened from the Main stand end with the wind slightly behind him. Australia's opening batsmen were Western Australian left-hander Graham Wood, and New South Wales right-hander John Dyson.

Seam and swing merchants Chris Old and Ian Botham would have been happy enough to bowl from the other end, but there was time for only one over before the sides were off, back on for a half hour, off again, then returning only for thirty-five minutes before lunch. There were seventy minutes of play in the middle session.

Brearley began with two short-legs for the ball that Willis was trying to bring back into Dyson's ribs. Dyson edged both bowlers past leg stump before short-leg Mike Gatting claimed a catch off the glove from Willis – a claim that was disallowed. Dyson drove an overpitched delivery from Graham Dilley for four, after the blond Kent paceman had replaced Willis. The England captain, seemingly eager to be in the action on his return to the test side, moved himself from mid-off to slip, then from slip to silly mid-off in case Dyson, lunging forward, offered a bat-pad chance.

Brearley remembered Wood thick-edging Willis between third slip and gully for four, then easing a wide half-volley the other side of gully for four again, which forced him to remove leg-slip. His account of the match, in *Phoenix from the Ashes*, is technical and intelligent.

Just before the end of the abbreviated, sixty-five minute morning session, Wood was lbw to an in-swinger from Botham's third ball of the match, leaving Australia at lunch 1-60, with Dyson 20 and Trevor Chappell yet to score.

The Cricketer described the afternoon session as 'colourless', and establishment journalist John Woodcock was quoted by Brearley about the lack of typical Anglo–Australian 'cut-and-thrust' in the non-events of the first day. The middle session was one of those where time drops slowly, but the England field dropped its chances quickly. Gower at third slip dropped Chappell (then three), coming forward to Botham, off an inside edge. Then Botham missed Chappell on seven as the batsman was brought forward by Willis with the score at 90, the ball hitting the fielder in the chest. Botham went to the gully, where he dropped Dyson after the opener slashed at a short delivery from Dilley.

Tea was taken after forty-two overs, at 1-97, but England remained unrefreshed. Dyson had contributed a dour 43 in 161 minutes, Chappell 11 at a rate of a run every eight minutes. Tea over and done with, Dyson (then 57) was dropped, again by Botham, again in the gully, where he had been interchanged with Gatting. Despite his wicket, Botham's three dropped catches left him on the debit side of the ledger at this point in the match. It was to take forty-five overs, during which the pair had added ninety-four, and 160 minutes, before anyone could be persuaded to catch Chappell.

He was finally caught behind off a back-foot forcing shot, attempting to cut a near long-hop outside his off stump. Hughes replaced him, with seventy-five minutes left, and went on to play an innings described by Brearley as full of character and courage. Forty minutes from the close, occasional right-arm medium-pacer Geoff Boycott was brought on for three overs to swing the ball at Hughes in the strengthening breeze. In the last twenty minutes, Dilley was given a go down-hill and down-wind.

Despite Brearley's efforts to permutate his attack into a winning combination, Dyson registered the first Australian century at Leeds since 1964, the first three-figure score of the 1981 series, and his own maiden test hundred (fourteen boundaries, 294 minutes) in his twenty-second test innings. He had not reached fifty since making fifty-three in Perth in 1977.

Dyson's forcing off-side shots were a revelation to Brearley but, hitting across a swinging ball of full length from Dilley fifteen minutes before the close, he terminated his five hours of glory. With scores of 1 and 13 (Edgbaston), and 0 and 5 (Old Trafford) in the next two tests, he lost his place by the last test at The Oval.

Around this time, Brearley reportedly observed to umpire David Evans, standing in his first test, that 'if all went well, you could bowl a side out for ninety on this pitch'. Considering Australia closed the first day after five hours at 3-203 with Hughes on 24 and nightwatchman Bright one, this unusual statement perhaps reflected just how well Brearley thought his seamers had bowled on a track that should have helped them a lot.

Rod Marsh visited the England dressing-room after play, and reports of his conversation indicate the amount of second-guessing going on between the two sides. The Australian wicketkeeper apparently wanted to establish the exact reason for the composition of England's final eleven that morning. Brearley reported Marsh as wondering whether spinner Emburey's omission – leaving England with an all-pace attack, except for part-timer Willey – was a gambit to ensure that Hughes would insert England once he won the toss. Such a move would have denied Australia the use of what Marsh may well have reckoned a good batting track. Marsh's question implies either the Australians were reading more into Brearley's tactics than was warranted, or that the senior players were divided among themselves regarding their own captain's acumen.

Botham, whose figures of 13-4-33-1 had been obtained by bowling in short spells, thought that, with the exception of Old, the bowlers became carried away with the bounce and would have done better to pitch the ball up and rely on seam and swing. Eighty-two overs should have been sufficient to rectify this kind of abandon. Interestingly, Brearley thought Botham had been too sparing in his use of the bouncer.

||| DAY 2

With fifty minutes lost to rain, England bowled over seventy overs, and Australia two, in the day. England began with Old bowling uphill and Dilley from the outer end for four overs. The new ball became available after three overs but Dilley sprayed it all over the place and was replaced by Botham, bearing Brearley's express instructions not to float the ball up like a middle-aged swing bowler. Brearley specifically encouraged Botham to straighten out his approach and run through the crease rather than pantomime being the 'Sidestep Queen'.

Brearley's psychological ploy, combined with the warmer weather, apparently revived the all-rounder's rhythm and sharpness. Dilley must have recovered some of his sharpness too for, having hit Bright painfully, he then bowled the nightwatchman. At 4-220, former Australian captain Graham Yallop came to the crease.

With just over half an hour lost before lunch, the score was advanced to 4-250 in 478 minutes off 102 overs, with Hughes 46 and Yallop 11. Old had bowled thirty-one of those, for fifty-two runs, as three years earlier on the same ground he had bowled forty-one overs at a run an over against Pakistan.

Hughes and Yallop gradually accelerated before tea, helped by England maintaining three slips and a gully throughout. As Brearley observed (without the emphasis), the quicker bowlers *looked* likely to break through every over.

Botham now began to reassert his all-round authority, first imprinting himself on the match and series by bowling a 22.2-over spell either side of tea in which he took 5-48. He had told Brearley he would take five if he were given a longer spell than the three- and four-over spells he had been allowed on the Thursday. When he came on, at 3.30, eighty runs had come from thirty overs. That is, the score was 4-283 and Hughes, on 66, was dropped off Botham by Gooch at first slip, after the ball carried slowly. Gooch had declined both offers he'd received at first slip in two-and-a-half tests, and thereafter fielded elsewhere. In the next over, Brearley at third slip took a low, wide chance, but on the bounce, from Yallop off Old. Still no wicket.

Seventy-five minutes were lost between lunch and tea when the score had advanced to 4-309. By now Hughes was 81, and Yallop 34. The pair added 112 in 160 minutes until, half an hour after tea, Hughes was first hit painfully, then patted the next ball back to Botham off the leading edge in attempting an on-drive. He had survived four-and-a-half hours spread over five separate sessions for his 89. Australia were 5-332. Allan Border lasted barely five minutes, driving Willis for four before going lbw to Botham playing to the off-side of a swinging delivery. In the next Botham over, Yallop was bowled for 58 off a bottom edge, cutting. With the score 7-357, there was an hour to go on the second day.

Lawson was caught off his bat-handle from what Brearley considered a belated bouncer, and Marsh was yorked, both Botham victims. The latter wicket completed Botham's fifteenth five-wickets-in-an-innings haul, and his first for fourteen tests as the Australian score deteriorated from 4-332 to the declaration total of 9-401. Hughes thought the score worth a thousand runs in good conditions.

By the close, England had made seven runs without the loss of anything except confidence. An Alderman delivery had pitched middle and off to Gooch and missed the outside edge before almost decapitating first slip, and Lillee had made Boycott play five balls at shoulder height. Gooch was on two and Boycott nought at stumps.

For all the ball's behaviour, the odds at this stage, given the rain and slow scoring, were on a draw.

||| DAY 3

In honour of Lillee's thirty-second birthday, the Australian attack bowled faster, straighter, and to a fuller length than England had managed, but Brearley thought Lillee's line was not what it had been in the Centenary Test four years before.

Gooch began his day by departing lbw, having aimed across the line of Alderman's first ball as it moved in on him from outside leg stump. This was his second lbw dismissal of the series, but his only such dismissal at the hand of Alderman. Eight years later he was to experience more pronounced difficulties. Brearley came in at number three, and narrowly got away another Alderman in-swinger from an inside edge to square-leg, but after an hour edged the same bowler to Marsh. England 2-40.

One ball to Boycott just before Brearley left had been a shooter just outside off stump, while the next had hit his gloves from the same length. Five minutes after Brearley's dismissal, Boycott lost his leg stump going too far across the wicket to Lawson: 3-42. Bowling from the edge of the crease, Lawson had brought the ball in short of a length and low from far outside off stump as the batsman tried to avoid being late in line.

Lunch found England 3-78, with David Gower 24 and Mike Gatting nine. Now it was the Australian's turn to succumb to a fit of the fielding fumbles, although their errors were less costly than had been the case for England. Gower was missed by Dyson at fourth slip, but the next ball leapt from a good length, to provide keeper Marsh with an overhead catch off Lawson. Gower had not scored since lunch. Gatting was then dropped off Lillee by Wood at first slip, before being lbw to one coming back at him. He had added six runs to be out for 15.

Botham came in at 5-87 and immediately revealed an aggressive intent. He was almost caught off a skied shot over extra cover, and missed a big hit on the off-side. Brearley, from the balcony, encouraged him to hit harder. Bob Willis recalled that, against the Indians on the same ground in 1979, Botham had kept 'smashing the ball into the crowd, looking up and grinning' at Brearley, 'who gave him the block-it sign, knowing full well he would take no notice and give us the inevitable rude gesture'. In 1981, Botham reached his fifty (eight fours) off fifty-four balls. It was his first half-century in his last twenty test innings and was made out of seventy-eight runs scored during his seventy-five-minute stay.

Brearley's reaction reveals in a minute way just what a perceptive captain he was, able to fire up his abundantly-talented all-rounder at the right moment. It is equally revealing, as Don Mosey observed wryly, that Brearley at that moment was sitting next to selector Brian Close. Botham's former mentor and county captain, in the Hutton-Illingworth tradition, might well have wanted England to graft their way out of trouble while keeping an eye out for rainclouds. But his only comment, according to Brearley, was that Botham had lost concentration. Clearly, Brearley was able to suit his psychological approach both to his players and the situations in which they found themselves.

When Botham did fall, it was to the old firm of Lillee and Marsh, and in doing so helped Marsh (in his seventy-first test) overtake Alan Knott's record (achieved in ninety-three tests) of 263 dismissals. Seventy-four of Marsh's victims had come off Lillee.

England reached 174, with minor contributions from the tail, including 13 from Dilley at number nine. Brearley thought such a score about par for the pitch (about double his first day estimation), and reckoned it would have been less had Lillee been at his best. He remained concerned that short balls outside off stump could break back and at the same time not climb above stump height, a dangerous mixture and no moment for ducking.

Tea was taken between the England innings, as Hughes chose to enforce the follow-on. The thought of Sunday's rest day may have influenced him to spell his attack. McGilvray took an opposite view: he wrote later that Brearley had benefited from a poor decision that might allow the England bowlers last use of a deteriorating wicket. Brearley himself commented that captains may hesitate before enforcing the follow-on, but they should do it anyway, an epigram to rank with WG Grace's remark about deciding whether or not to bat when winning the toss, and doing so anyway.

The England second innings had scarcely begun when bad light forced the players off. After an hour's delay, there was time for three more overs, during which Brearley drove a Lillee half-volley to the boundary after surviving two fast leg-cutters.

Umpires David Evans and Barrie Meyer then decided to abandon play five minutes early because of the light. They were subsequently showered with cushions and abuse, as Umpires Don Oslear and Ken Palmer had been on the Friday at Lord's. In any event, within minutes of their decision, the sun was shining again. The Australians were understandably angry at not getting a further go at the England batting.

England had lost one wicket for six runs at the close, Gooch having been caught at third slip from a leg-cutter, thus being dismissed twice in the day and facing only four balls. On the Monday Botham borrowed his bat, figuring it might still have some runs in it.

By this time, Brearley was thinking England's 'initial selection more defensible' than he had after Thursday's play and that, on Saturday through Monday, Hughes might well have been glad of the fourth seamer, especially given his tendency to bowl his quicker men out.

||| DAY 4

Christopher Martin-Jenkins was to remark in the September *Cricketer* that on this day 'the speed with which the match . . . was turned upside down made it unique'.

Three England wickets were lost in the first sixty-five minutes. Brearley, reaching forward, was caught at slip off a delivery he thought good enough to have got Boycott. Gower, scoreless for over half an hour, made nine in an over from Lillee, only to be caught at second slip off the first ball of Alderman's next over as it left him off the pitch. It also left him three short of being the first Leicestershire player to make two thousand test runs. Gatting was reckoned unlucky with a leg stump lbw decision to a delivery that came in at him. Given his tendency to put the front foot down too early and too far across to bring his bat down the line of the ball, and the frequency of lbw decisions in his career, the odds remained with the umpire being right even as they lengthened against England. The sorry scoreline read 4-41.

The odds were scarcely surprising. Going into this match, England had not won since February 1980 (at Bombay) nor had they beaten Australia in seven tries since February 1979. And in over nine hundred previous tests, there had been only one victory by a side following-on. The odds on this being their lucky day looked unlikely.

Willey came in for fifty-five minutes to hit six off-side fours, though he had contributed barely a dozen to the lunchtime scoreline of 4-78, of which Boycott had made an unbeaten 35 in 143 minutes. It was, from an English perspective, a brilliant defensive innings.

Willey glanced and then cut Lillee over slip for two boundaries in an over, and then cut Lawson in his next over, punishing any errors of length until, two overs later, Lillee brought a short ball in to cramp him for space. Willey was caught off the top edge, cutting, at short third man with 122 runs still needed to avoid what increasingly looked like an inevitable Australian innings victory. Lillee had now replaced Hugh Trumble with 141 as the leading Ashes wicket-taker, and he simultaneously overtook Bishen Bedi on 266 to become fourth on the list of test cricket's all-time wicket-takers. This was a match of records.

Boycott was sixth out after three-and-a-half hours, just as he was beginning to play his off-side shots. Some may have thought him a mite unlucky with a leg stump lbw decision to Alderman as he stepped forward to a full ball, but umpire Meyer was not among them: 6-135.

About this time, Brearley changed first into a striped shirt then back into a cream cricket one. He, along with the rest of the England party, would have checked out from their hotel that morning, except that he was scheduled to appear for Middlesex at Old Trafford on the Wednesday after the test's scheduled close.

That event seemed imminent as wicketkeeper Bob Taylor was caught off his glove at short-leg to make England 7-135, 92 behind, with half an hour to tea. Ian Botham had been in for forty-five minutes when Graham Dilley joined him, requiring the bowlers to change their line between the Somerset right-hander and the Kent left-hander. Dilley proceeded to make all but five of the next twenty-seven runs. In the pair's first half-hour together, Dilley scored 25, his tea-time score, to Botham's 16, temporarily upstaging Botham.

Botham was dropped in the gully by Bright, from an attempted cover-drive, with the score not yet 150. Although it could not have been imagined then it was a fumble with dire consequences. Botham, however, shrugged off such minor misdemeanours as he went to tea with the score on 7-176. He had scored 39 in eighty-six minutes, 'playing for a not out', as he joked to Brearley. The team innings had lasted twelve minutes over four hours when Ladbrokes extended the odds on an England win to 500:1. Botham was soon to change all that, and make Australia's wicketkeeper and finest fast bowler wealthier men as Marsh and Lillee made small wagers on their opponents.

Dilley reached his first test fifty in the late session, registering nine boundaries in the eighty-minute, 117-run stand he shared with Botham. Botham makes the point that he had outscored Dilley by just one run in this stand. His partner was dismissed for 56 by a straight ball that Alderman bowled from around the wicket, with the partnership seven runs short of the England record against Australia set by

Patsy Hendren and Harold Larwood at Brisbane in 1928. Alderman had been despatched for sixteen in an over as the innings defeat was averted but, with Dilley's dismissal at 8-252, England were still in deep strife with an effective score of 8-25.

Old had been encouraged by Willey before leaving the dressing room to tough it out against a tiring pace attack, something he was often unwilling to do. On this occasion, he stayed with Botham to add sixty-seven in fifty-five minutes, before being yorked by Lawson for 24, but not before Botham had reached his seventh test hundred by edging Lawson for four through slips.

Botham moved from 39 to 103 (one six, fourteen fours, two singles) with sixty-four runs in seventeen strokes. His astonishing century came in two-and-a-half hours, from eighty-seven balls, one ball faster than the hundred he would make in the fifth test at Old Trafford. In the two-hour session he added 106 out of the 175 runs that came from twenty-seven overs. During this period, nineteen boundaries and a straight six were struck and Alderman was kept on till he was exhausted.

Apart from being dropped at 109 by Marsh off a mis-hook, Botham (like Dilley) was fortunate in having a very fast outfield to give full value to shots. Tactically, they were fortunate that Hughes had removed the infield too soon, though Botham's rampage upset normal considerations. In Brearley's view the Australians persisted too long in bowling just outside the off stump; and not introducing tight left-arm spinner Bright until late in the day. Then, with a defensive field after England had gone ahead at 8-309, he almost took Botham's off stump. Like so much in life, it was a matter of almost but not enough.

England closed a momentous day at 9-351, scored in 385 minutes. Botham was on 145, with twenty-six fours and a six, and Willis one, from the five balls he had been required to face in twenty minutes in the middle. Botham farmed the strike marvellously as the pair added thirty-one runs together. Australia were now 124 behind, and Leeds hotels reported having to cope with a flood of rebookings. Brearley reported that the Australian dressing-room was silent when he visited it.

DAY 5

The following morning, Hughes took the new ball, put eight fielders back, and conceded only a single cover-driven boundary to Botham before Willis, having lasted nine balls, was caught low at second slip after a mere ten minutes and not much further mayhem. The last wicket had realised thirty-seven runs in half an hour. Willis said later that Botham's 'truly great crusading innings . . . gave us the lift we sorely needed – and a win that left foolish critics dumbfounded'. It was perhaps a forgivable overstatement from a man who has been reliably reported to have never watched a replay of the rest of the fifth day.

England were back in the field and the hunt, but Australia still needed only 130 to win, and had most of a day to do it in. With the weather sunny and the new ball swinging minimally, Wood put the first two Botham balls, a long-hop and a half-volley, away through the leg side for fours. It looked like it was going to be easy, but, unlike Hammond at Leeds in 1938, Brearley never thought of attrition. He returned to first slip, placed Gooch at second, Botham at third, and left Gatting at short-leg. He realised he could only win with attack, and was cool enough to gamble on it.

In the third over of the innings, Botham's second, Wood was caught behind off-driving another half-volley, and hitting the ground at the same time. A wicket was down with only thirteen on the board.

Dilley, carrying a minor thigh-strain, conceded eleven in two overs after opening with Botham before Brearley replaced him with Willis. Willis then endured five overs uphill into the breeze before seeking to switch ends. Old bowled another over from the Kirkstall Lane end, and Brearley brought Willey on from the Main stand end for a three-over spell to explore the pitch's responsiveness to off-spin.

With Willey and the pitch failing between them to make the ball talk at all, Old took the Main stand end for what would prove a typically economical nine overs into the breeze. At the same time, Bob Willis switched to the Kirkstall Lane end at 1-48 and was told by Brearley to let it rip as the clouds started to gather. He began steaming in for what was to become a historic spell in which at one point he took six for eight in thirty-two balls. Overall, his full spell of 8-43 would not end until seventy minutes after lunch.

Christopher Martin-Jenkins has written of Willis locking himself into a 'cocoon of concentration' and a number of world-class athletes have described how they have felt 'in the zone' at times of peak sporting performance. Willis on this occasion wore a hypnotic stare, eyes glazed, furiously intent. Tall and hawkish with a weird straight-ahead run, he truly bowled like a man possessed. The turn-around in the game's fortunes began ordinarily enough. Twenty minutes before the luncheon adjournment, with Willis bowling his sixth over, Trevor Chappell fell, caught off a combination of glove and bat-handle at 2-56, protecting his face from a bouncer. In his only three tests, Chappell at number three scored 13 and 6 (Trent Bridge), 1 and 3 (Lord's), and 27 and 8 (Headingley). Border went on to score 2 and 40 at Edgbaston at number three before Kim Hughes moved up the order to score 4 and 43 (Old Trafford) and 31 and 6 (The Oval). It remained a problem for the Australians throughout the series.

Old twice rapped John Dyson on the knuckles as the opener pushed forward. To the first ball of the last over before lunch, the eighth by Willis, Hughes got up on his toes, a position he'd been forced into many times in the first innings. This time he edged a lifter low to the left of third slip, where he was caught two-handed by Botham: 3-58. Brearley claimed this was first intimation of a victory.

Three balls later, he would have become even more animated as Yallop, coming forward, fended a kicking delivery from Willis off to short square-leg for a low catch. Lunch at 4-58 with Dyson 29 not out in ninety-nine minutes was an unreal meal for viewers in Australia

Bob Willis

dashing to kitchens for evening refreshment, as well as for those in England. The rushing sound in the heavens was the odds dropping to 6:4 from 500:1. Anyone who had got their money on earlier might have begun to think about buying a new wallet or three.

Thirteen minutes after lunch, Dyson, who had hooked Willis in his ninth over for four, looked on yet again as Old forced Border to play on. The ball hit the left-hander's leg stump from an inside edge as he misjudged its length: 5-65. In the next Willis over, his tenth, it finally became Dyson's turn. Too early in attempting a hook off Willis, he was caught by Bob Taylor, who thereby equalled John Murray's world record number of catches (1270) by a wicketkeeper. More crucially, Australia were 6-68.

Willis in his eleventh over twice rapped Marsh on the thigh, before a top edge swirled to Dilley for a difficult chest-high catch at deep fine-leg just inside the line. Of all the wickets for which viewers had to wait, this was probably the most tantalising. Would the fielder judge the fall of the ball and the position of the boundary rope? He did: the last of the top order was gone.

Willis at this point told Brearley that umpire Evans had cautioned him against bouncing Lawson. Brearley told Willis in response to keep the ball rib-height for the moment, reviving memories of the Snow–Rowan demarcation dispute on what really does constitute a bouncer to a tailender. The first ball of Willis's twelfth over was enough to pass muster with Evans as Lawson touched a lively delivery to Taylor, enabling him to claim the world record. Australia were 8-75, having lost seven wickets for nineteen runs inside an hour 'on a pitch playing little worse than in the first innings', as Brearley was at pains to point out.

Australia now required fifty-five runs to win. Lillee and Bright added thirty-five in four overs, making it clear that, whatever the odds going, the bowlers were determined to beat Australia's batsmen.

Lillee cut Willis, now in his thirteenth over, his fourth since lunch. As Willis dropped the ball short, Lillee put it over slips, with an Alan Knott-type shot. He then cut him wider of Dilley at deep third man, put him away behind square-leg for three, and cut him for another four. Bright pulled two leg-side fours over mid-wicket off Old in what proved to be the Yorkshire workhorse's last over. His eight previous overs had cost just eleven runs, but this one went for ten. Lillee then cut Willis for two more fours in his fourteenth over.

Lillee and Bright had reduced the deficit to twenty when Willis opened his fifteenth over bowling to a fuller length. A straight ball to Lillee was enough to make him miscue the stroke off his legs and lift the shot slightly to mid-on. There Gatting, who had already offered an acute piece of tactical advice to his county captain Brearley – that Willis should keep the ball in line on a full length – gave England supporters another anxious moment before his dive allowed him to get his hands under the chance. Australia were now 9-110. Twenty runs still remained.

Brearley later noted that the memory of successive Lillee deliveries narrowly missing Willis's nose as he played forward during the 1974–75 tour meant the big fast bowler was all too aware that bouncing the Australian could turn him into a helpless target for retaliation when it came his own next turn to bat. Thus may powerful self-preservatory thoughts thwart a captain's instructions to his bowlers, and their intention to carry them out.

Botham came on for Old, whereupon Old at third slip twice missed Alderman in three balls. The first was straightforward as these catches go. Onlookers saw it go to hand, but it didn't remain there. The second was low and left-handed – technically a chance, but missed.

With the first delivery of his sixteenth over, Willis yorked Bright, knocking his middle stump out of the ground with 'the perfect, most emphatic ball' as Brearley saw it. England had, amid national rejoicing, committed what *The Cricketer* called 'daylight robbery'. At 2.20, Australia had required 169 minutes for an innings which should have won them a game, although a bewildered Hughes thought his side 'didn't do much wrong except lose'.

Willis's career best innings return was also the best Headingley innings analysis, beating Blythe's figures in 1907 when England beat South Africa in a struggle dominated by slow bowlers. His subsequent verbal attack on the media, made in the context of their perceived vendetta against Botham, stunned everyone almost as much as Willis's bowling had done.

A twenty-two-year-old Adelaide man recalled that Leeds was not the place to be for other reasons.

> I had driven up from London and was at the game for a couple of days, I wandered alone in the freezing cold and alien outer. Did Yorkshiremen really wear knotted kerchiefs on their heads? I checked out the betting tents and saw the extraordinary odds, but couldn't work out the system of placing bets and was too shy to ask.
>
> I left on the third evening (England one down and following on, an Aussie victory assured, but no one to share the delight). I went to dinner somewhere out of Leeds. Things were hairy in the city where riots were beginning, and it seemed like a civil war with Mrs Thatcher's ruthless economic policies in full swing.
>
> Being a typically broke young tourist, I decided to sleep cheap in the car away from the city but a policeman woke me with a blinding flashlight in the early hours. 'Get out of town,' he said, 'it's not safe.' I drove back to London and watched disconsolately as Willis and Botham destroyed Australia, but was even more despondent when I heard about Lillee's and Marsh's winnings. I could have done with the cash.

Such matters aside, this game was significant in a number of ways. It was England's first win in thirteen tests since its ten-wicket win at Bombay in the Golden Jubilee Test of February 1980, when Botham made 114 and took 13-106 – the first century and ten-wicket double in test history. It became the second instance of a side (both times England) overcoming the follow-on to win a test. The previous occasion had been the 1894 match discussed in the second chapter. It was the narrowest winning margin since 1928–29 at Adelaide, as discussed in the fourth chapter of this book. It was the second instance of a player scoring a century and taking five wickets in a test innings during an Ashes test. Australian Jack Gregory was the first to do so, but this was the fourth time in tests Botham had achieved this feat, twice more than any other player. Finally, it was Mike Brearley's record ninth victory over Australia; he was to extend his win–loss ratio to eleven–four by the end of the series.

Kim Hughes was able to say that he was proud the Australian team had been part of one of the greatest tests of all. He went on to say that he was disappointed not to win, but knew his team had given immense enjoyment – a statement containing a certain amount of unintended irony. His side was to give more immense enjoyment of the same kind to England supporters at Birmingham and Manchester in the matches ahead.

Upon his return to Australia, Hughes went on to say that: 'You don't become an overnight sensation in a very hard and competitive field. It took Mike Brearley ten to twelve years and he still makes blues.' While still on tour, Hughes reportedly said that, had he been spoken to in the street the way he was routinely addressed by journalists, he, like anyone with 'any go at all' about them, would have 'decked' such people.

Such instances of 'naked aggression' presumably contributed to Alan McGilvray's assessment of Hughes. He thought both Hughes's captaincy and his batting were flawed by this tendency. Had he been given the opportunities to become a more mature test batsman before he received the captaincy; had he enjoyed the time to become a less angry young man; had the either/or alternatives between total attack and desperate defence that the broadcaster saw in his character been offset by belonging to a stronger batting line-up, then Hughes the player might have batted better more often and Hughes the captain won more games for Australia.

As it was, Hughes thought in 1981 that he had a lot to give as captain of his country and that he related well to the players. He enjoyed the role and wanted to make a success of it, statements that in the light of what really happened at Headingley and thereafter under his leadership illuminate why he was forced to resign the national captaincy to Allan Border in the summer of 1984–85.

By then, Hughes had finally replaced Greg Chappell, but only because the latter had permanently retired at the end of the previous 1983–84 season. Previously Chappell had come back to lead Australia in Australia against West Indies and New Zealand (1981–82), England (1982–83) and Pakistan (1983–84). A decade later, Allan Border would leave the Australian captaincy after nine years of occupancy, partly because the Australian Cricket Board would no longer allow captains to pick and choose their overseas tours. Had such a decision been made earlier, always allowing for Greg Chappell's great contributions to the test side, Kim Hughes might have enjoyed a longer tenure as captain and Australian player.

•NOTTINGHAM 1993•

AN HONOURABLE DRAW

Some cricket followers query whether great cricket matches can be draws, and whether draws can be great matches. We are not among their number.

For England, the game is a 'might have been' opportunity when, for the first time in the series it puts Australia under pressure. Had England been able to make a breakthrough just before tea on the final day, the outcome of the series might have been different. As it was, the outcome enables England to become a little more competitive and eventually to 'triumph' in the sixth test of the series at The Oval.

The Nottingham match is more significant, however, because it epitomises some of the problems of the modern game. The selection of 'foreign' players seems, in Australian eyes, to reach absurd levels with the choice of Martin McCague for England while, to English ears, the Australians plumb new depths with boorish abuse of their opponents. Where individual onlookers stand on these issues often depends on where they generally sit, but the old questions of player loyalty and national pride, which were alive in 1877, are now accompanied by a new outcry, from Australia, about protecting its investment in player development. One hundred and sixteen years after the first test, Australians can allege that it is England fielding a 'combination' team.

ENGLAND v AUSTRALIA 1993 (3rd Test)

Played at Trent Bridge on 1, 2, 3, 5, 6 July.
Toss: England. Result: Match drawn.

ENGLAND

MN Lathwell	c Healy b Hughes	20	lbw b Warne	33
MA Atherton	c Boon b Warne	11	c Healy b Hughes	9
RA Smith	c and b Julian	86	c Healy b Warne	50
AJ Stewart†	c M Waugh b Warne	25	lbw b Hughes	6
GA Gooch*	c Border b Hughes	38	c Taylor b Warne	120
GP Thorpe	c S Waugh b Hughes	6	(7) not out	114
N Hussain	c Boon b Warne	71	(8) not out	47
AR Caddick	lbw b Hughes	15	(6) c Boon b Julian	12
MJ McCague	c M Waugh b Hughes	9		
MC Ilott	c Taylor b May	6		
PM Such	not out	0		
Extras	(B 5, LB 23, W 4, NB 2)	34	(B 11, LB 11, NB 9)	31
Total		**321**	(6 wickets dec)	**422**

AUSTRALIA

MJ Slater	lbw b Caddick	40	(2) c Atherton b Such	26
MA Taylor	c Stewart b McCague	28	(1) b Such	28
DC Boon	b McCague	101	c Stewart b Caddick	18
ME Waugh	c McCague b Such	70	b Caddick	1
SR Waugh	c Stewart b McCague	13	(6) not out	47
IA Healy†	c Thorpe b Ilott	9	(7) lbw b Ilott	5
BP Julian	c Stewart b Ilott	5	(8) not out	56
AR Border*	c Smith b Such	38	(5) c Thorpe b Caddick	2
MG Hughes	b Ilott	17		
SK Warne	not out	35		
TBA May	lbw b McCague	1		
Extras	(B 4, LB 8, W 4)	16	(B 5, LB 5, W 4, NB 4)	19
Total		**373**	(6 wickets)	**202**

AUSTRALIA	O	M	R	W	O	M	R	W
Hughes	31	7	92	5	22	8	41	2
Julian	24	3	84	1	33	10	110	1
Warne	40	17	74	3	50	21	108	3
May	14.4	7	31	1	38	6	112	0
S Waugh	8	4	12	0	1	0	3	0
M Waugh	1	1	0	0	6	3	15	0
Border					5	0	11	0
ENGLAND								
McCague	32.3	5	121	4	19	6	58	0
Ilott	34	8	108	3	18	5	44	1
Such	20	7	51	2	23	6	58	2
Caddick	22	5	81	1	16	6	32	3

FALL OF WICKETS

	E	A	E	A
Wkt	**1st**	**1st**	**2nd**	**2nd**
1st	28	55	11	46
2nd	63	74	100	74
3rd	153	197	109	75
4th	159	239	117	81
5th	174	250	159	93
6th	220	262	309	115
7th	290	284		
8th	304	311		
9th	321	356		
10th	321	373		

Umpires: BJ Meyer and R Palmer. Third umpire: B Dudleston.
Referee: CH Lloyd (West Indies).

Martin McCague

(Press Association Ltd)

The Times leader of 7 July 1993 gave some indication of the place that cricket retains in John Major's England. 'Another Historic Notch', it was headed, and sub-headed 'Cricketing statistics are annals of the English tribe'. It began:

> In the backward-looking eye of history, to manage to draw a test match against Australia is not the summit of English sporting achievement. Yesterday, however, it felt like it. For the first time for years, for a short time after lunch England looked like winning, and deserved to win. Having been abused throughout the land and the media as pig-headed incompetents, the chairman of the England cricket committee and his selectors are suddenly being hailed as prophets.

In a word, the Third Test of the 1993 series at Nottingham was seen to have provided 'respite' for a hard-pressed home side. In two words, the 277th test between the two countries gave England players and selectors alike some 'breathing space'. In more words, mere absence of defeat at Nottingham offered a chance to regroup. After England had fallen behind 2–0 in the six-match series following heavy defeats in the opening matches at Old Trafford and Lord's, this was perhaps more than its followers could demand as their team's duty.

One of the first questions to be solved for England was the composition of its team. South African-born Robin Smith posed a major dilemma. A dominating batsman for the past five years, with a test average of forty-seven from forty-two matches, he was faltering against leg-spinner Shane Warne – as he had against Pakistani Mushtaq Ahmed the previous home series – with scores of 4, 18, 22 and 5 from the first two games. But a thrashing innings of 191 for Hampshire against the Australians (without Warne) at Southampton in the lead-up to the test put him back in favour. Given the paucity of obvious test match talent, who else to choose?

David Gower reminded Ted Dexter and his fellow selectors that he could play the turning ball better than anyone else in the land by steering Hampshire to a draw in that game, but his unruffled elegance remained unrequired by a captain and selection panel with whom he was clearly out of favour. After 114 tests between 1978 and the conclusion of the Australian tour of 1990–91, his recall for three tests against Pakistan in the acrimonious summer of 1992 availed the left-hander nothing except 150 runs in three completed innings, and the England record test aggregate, 8231 runs at 44.25. Out of Dexter's sides he stayed.

Out of the side and the middle order went enigmatic Graeme Hick and former England captain Mike Gatting, despite their second-innings half-centuries at Lord's. All-rounder Chris Lewis, whose form with bat and ball had been disappointing, and fellow opening bowler Phil DeFreitas also disappeared, as did left-arm spinner Phillip Tufnell. Tufnell had looked England's only aggressive bowler in the Second Test, though off-spinner Peter Such was retained on the strength of his unrepeated eight-wicket haul in the Old Trafford test.

Their replacements included Somerset's Mark Lathwell and Surrey's Graham Thorpe, two batsmen making their test debuts. Essex's Nasser Hussain, after three tests against the West Indies in 1989, also returned to the middle order. The attack had a different look with left-hander Mark Ilott of Essex and fellow opening bowler Martin McCague, of Kent and Western Australia, joining Andrew Caddick, Somerset's New Zealand-born speedster. Should the two new bowlers prove as stubborn with the bat in the lower order as had Caddick – fifty-three runs in three completed innings – but as unsuccessful with the ball – after two tests, his figures were 73-12-233-1 – England's chances of a draw would be improved.

The side had a new look with eight players having played less than three tests. There were the usual grumbles about Home Counties bias – eight of the team played for Essex, Surrey and Kent – but particular ones about McCague, whose selection also aroused Australian indignation. Complaints came from the top, with the chief executive of the Australian Cricket Board, Graham Halbish, wanting stricter application of the International Cricket Council qualification rules. McCague, who was born in Northern Ireland, had been raised in Western Australia from the age of two. He played for that state between 1990 and 1992, and attended the Australian Cricket Academy in Adelaide. During this time he also played Australian Rules football at senior club level, all of which made McCague seem more Australian than English. His allegiance was reportedly decided by his omission from Western Australia's Sheffield Shield Final side in 1990–91.

Halbish pointed out that Australia invested time and money in a player like McCague to provide depth for Australian rather than English cricket. Doubtless he was also concerned about other players (final 1993 figures in brackets) such as Leicestershire fast left-armer Allan Mullaly (62 wickets at 24.29), another Western Australia state representative; Jason Gallian (702 runs at 43.87), the Oxford University captain; Yorkshire all-rounder Craig White (896 runs at 34.46), who made his England debut in the Nottingham test of the 1994 season; and Derbyshire opening batsman, the paradoxically-surnamed Peter Bowler (1123 runs at 43.19), who played for Tasmania from 1986 to 1988. All four were born in England, before growing up and being educated in Australia.

Australian captain Allan Border supported his administrator regarding McCague. He thought that the ICC rules should be tightened, though he did not otherwise want to be deflected from concentrating on the game. For his part, McCague played the straightest of bats when asked to comment on accusations he was a traitor. 'It was up to me,' he was reported as saying, 'who I wanted to play international cricket for and I chose England.' He said he was not bothered by what people thought.

McCague might as easily have added that, as a professional cricketer, he had the right to be more bothered by the side on which his bread was buttered. As Gideon Haigh reported a few days later in the *Australian*, cricket rewards could be much greater in England than in Australia, and a player such as McCague could earn a million dollars were he to become and remain a leading player with Kent for a decade.

According to Haigh, a top of the range county contract would earn such a player £22,000 a year, while a well-run benefit season could net a further £150,000. With the addition of endorsements and sponsorships, playing in England represented an attractive proposition. This helped explain why Australians in the touring party, Border (Essex 1986, 1988), Mark Waugh (Essex 1988–90) and Steve Waugh (Somerset 1987–88) had played county cricket, and why Craig McDermott had considered becoming Yorkshire's first overseas signing the previous season before injury ruled him out.

Of players omitted from the touring party, Terry Alderman and Tony Dodemaide had played for Kent and Sussex respectively, and

Alderman advertised for playing/coaching offers in England through the June 1993 *Cricketer*. Another omission in Tom Moody had played for Worcestershire and did so again in 1994, while Dean Jones, bizarrely left out of the touring party, was with Durham. Ironically, and not entirely coincidentally, Western Australian coach Daryl Foster also coached McCague at Kent.

One difference between the Australian and England teams, of course, lay in the crucial step beyond first-class status to test representation. Another difference arose in the place of origin: Caddick was born in Christchurch, New Zealand, Hussain in Madras, India. They joined South Africa-born Robin Smith and Allan Lamb, Zimbabwe-born Phil Edmonds, Graeme Hick, Paul Parker and Neal Radford, Nairobi-born Derek Pringle, West Indies-born Norman Cowans, Phil DeFreitas, Chris Lewis, Devon Malcolm, Gladstone Small and Neil Williams, and Hong Kong-born Dermot Reeve, as part of a foreign legion that in recent years variously had been, was, or might again become forever England.

Selection of players with overseas affiliations was nothing new in English eyes. It could be seen as simply part of a long-term pattern deriving from the days of an imperial power with world-wide commercial, diplomatic, and military outposts. Since chairman of selectors Dexter, a former England captain, had himself been born in Italy, while former captains Gubby Allen (Australia), Freddie Brown (Peru) and Colin Cowdrey (India) had also been born outside the United Kingdom, and Mike Denness (Scotland) and Tony Lewis (Wales) had been born outside England, a fair line-up of overseas-born amateurs had captained England at cricket since the second world war without Australian protest.

Overlooked in all this was a real possibility that McCague and White might never have appeared in tests for their country of adoption anyway, given Australia's post-war record in this respect. Of all the England-born migrants to reach Australia in the previous half-century, only Tony Dell has worn the baggy green at test level, with

England-born Ken MacLeay, of Western Australia and Somerset, having played one-day internationals for Australia.

By far the pithiest comment on the McCague case came from Mark Breslauer of Bushey, Hertfordshire. In the briefest of letters to *The Times*, he wrote, 'If you can't beat them, select them.' This was not the view of columnist John Woodcock, who was moved by the England reshuffle to describe the resulting combination as a Commonwealth eleven.

For its part Australia had few selection worries except the form of its young pace-bowling trio, Brendon Julian, Wayne Holdsworth and Paul Reiffel. It fielded an eleven unchanged from Lord's except for the departure of the ill McDermott, replaced by left-armer Julian, leaving the attack with two spinners, Warne and off-spinner Tim May, and the ferocious Merv Hughes as its leading lights. David Boon with 858 runs at 107.25 was top of the English first-class averages, followed by teammates Michael Slater and Damien Martyn, with Graham Gooch, the leading England player, next.

On the bowling side, Warne's 45 wickets at 17.57 put him third in the averages behind Kent's Alan Igglesden, omitted from the Old Trafford Test, and Pakistani Wasim Akram. In the first two tests Warne and Hughes had carried all before them for Australia, with sixteen and twelve wickets respectively, compared to England's premier performer Peter Such, with eight.

England's main hope lay in the pitch at Trent Bridge, where groundsman Ron Allsop admitted the state of the series had influenced his preparation. He was surprisingly candid in his remarks, revealing that he had been influenced by the team selection and thought he should be doing his bit to help England. Allan Border might have been surprised to learn that Allsop believed, 'It's okay, provided it's done in a sensible manner,' but Allsop would have been dismayed by Border's reaction. The Australian captain thought it looked a good batting strip with a little more help for the pace bowlers. He had no complaints.

DAY 1

The England reshuffle brought hope. When Graham Gooch won the toss, he batted. On this occasion, though, it was not Gooch who went in first with Michael Atherton to face Merv Hughes and Brendon Julian, but the newcomer Lathwell. The latter made a promising, if brief, start to his test career by bringing up three boundaries in his innings of just over half an hour. A streaky drive brought his first four but his other strokes were more authoritative, a cover-drive against Julian and a hook off Hughes, before the big Victorian had him caught behind off a ball moving away.

England were 1-28 when Robin Smith joined Atherton in an innings which would, in the short-term, resurrect his career. Smith was fortunate to survive the first over after Julian had a confident lbw appeal rejected, but he then launched into attack and had reached 30 when Atherton left after an almost motionless innings of 11 in seventy-six minutes.

Smith revealed his aggressive instincts either side of the lunch break, the features being his off- and cover-driving, and flicks through mid-wicket. Smith feasted on some leg-side deliveries by Julian and punished both Warne and May, so that England's position looked healthy at 2-153, when Alec Stewart popped a Warne long-hop off the end of his bat to cover, where he was caught by Mark Waugh.

Gooch came to the crease, but lost his rampant partner almost immediately. A century had beckoned for Smith, and a knee-high full-toss from Julian hardly seemed the ball to dismiss him. But in driving it hard Smith gave the bowler the opportunity to pull off a superb, instinctive left-hand catch. Smith's 86 in 135 minutes included fifteen fours, but England were now 4-159.

By far the best of the Australian bowlers on the opening day was the resourceful Hughes, who changed his pace subtly short of a length. He took the wicket of England's second debutant Thorpe with a short ball that looped to gully at 5-174, and completed England's misery by dispatching Gooch for a solid 38 with another rising ball that flew to the covers. Gooch's wicket fell shortly after tea at 220, and the English team must have felt an enormous opportunity had been wasted.

Fortunately, however, resolute defensive batting by Hussain and Caddick, who would again show more nuisance value with the bat, saw England through to stumps. At 6-276, with Hussain 50 and Caddick ten, honours were even in the series for the first time after the first day.

||| DAY 2

On the second day England's last four wickets fell for forty-five in an hour and a half. Hussain and Caddick took their partnership to seventy, with Caddick resisting for two hours for 15 before Hughes removed him lbw. McCague then struck a couple of belligerent blows before Hughes had him caught from a vicious ball that he gloved to second slip. England's innings closed at 321 when Hussain fell bat-pad to Warne after four-and-a-half hours at the crease, and Ilott was caught at slip off May.

The pick of the Australian bowlers was Hughes with 5-92 off thirty-one overs. His seventh five-wicket test bag moved him to 194 wickets in his forty-eighth test, thereby putting him in company with other pace bowlers possessing similar strike rates. These included his new-ball partner Craig McDermott (198 wickets in forty-nine tests), and legendary figures such as Wes Hall (192 wickets in forty-eight tests), John Snow (202 wickets in forty-nine tests), and Jeff Thomson (200 wickets in fifty-one tests).

Furthermore, although it almost sounded sacrilegious, Glen Camarlinghi of Innisfail, Queensland, had pointed out in the June edition of *Wisden Cricket Monthly* that 'Mac 'n Merv' had a better strike rate in tests in which they were paired than 'Lillee 'n Thomson'. To the start of the series, in twenty-five tests McDermott and Hughes had captured 219 wickets at 26.10 with a wicket every 53.06 balls, compared to Lillee and Thomson's 217 wickets at 27.21 with a wicket every 54.34 balls from twenty-six matches.

'Sumo' Hughes, as he was nicknamed in this series, had come a long way from being the 'big mug' he appeared to be when his Ashes career began with a hammering from Ian Botham at Brisbane in 1986–87. Since then, he had done his own fair share of hammering, as well as sledging, to make himself an indispensable if unlikely element of the Australian attack. With McDermott's operation for a twisted bowel meaning he would play no further part in the series, Hughes became the leader of the attack, a role he filled to the letter for all the damage it did to his own physique.

The Australian reply began shortly before lunch, with the Wagga Wagga and New South Wales openers Mark Taylor and Michael Slater beginning where they had left off at Old Trafford and Lord's. Their solid start of fifty-five was the smallest of their four consecutive half-century partnerships, following 128 and seventy-one in the First Test at Manchester and 260 in the only Australian innings at Lord's. Slater was dropped from a slash off Mark Ilott in the last over before lunch but otherwise the Australian pair proceeded safely until Taylor succumbed to the extra pace of McCague and was caught behind by Stewart playing a defensive stroke. Australia were 1-55.

McCague and left-armer Ilott provided only the sixth instance, other than the first test of all, of debutants opening the England attack. The by now relatively experienced Caddick, in his third test, followed the quickish off-spinner Peter Such, also in his third test, as second change. It was the equivalent of the Australian attack at Sydney in 1971 in terms of experience, but Gooch was no Ian Chappell and there was little to cheer about. After Slater fell lbw to Caddick at 2-74, the Australian batting continued to assert itself.

Boon and Mark Waugh hustled on 123 runs in ninety-six minutes with Waugh being the dominant partner. His 70 off sixty-eight balls with twelve fours was another exquisite innings. As at Lord's, and perhaps like Smith in this match, a century seemed to be there for the taking but impetuosity got the better of him as he launched an attack on Such, and McCague took a running catch at wide mid-on.

Boon and Steve Waugh then added forty-two in just better than even time before the second Waugh misjudged a quicker ball from McCague, touching it to the wicketkeeper for Australia to become 4-239. When Healy was out caught in the slips off Ilott, there had been a minor collapse to 5-250, but Boon, 88, and Julian, five, carried the side through to the end of the day without further loss.

DAY 3

Australia's first innings lead was not yet substantial when it started at 5-262 with Border still to bat. Then Julian, who had started the tour with all-rounder status, failed to live up to his promise with the bat and was out in the first over without addition to the score. Shortly after Boon had registered his sixteenth test century, he was out chopping a wide ball from McCague on his stumps. His 101 took 259 minutes, with seventeen fours, and the total read 7-284.

Border and Hughes took the total past 300 but had still not reached England's score when Hughes was bowled by Ilott for a breezy 17. Border, who scratched around for four minutes under three hours for 38, despite hitting seven fours, found a willing ally in Warne. The pair added forty-five for the ninth wicket before Border departed driving Such to mid-on. Warne hit out at the finish, to remain 35 not out. When May fell lbw to McCague, it was the fast bowler's fourth wicket in Australia's score of 373.

This was an impressive comeback by the Australians and they sustained it in the final half hour when their attack captured three wickets for seventeen runs. In between, England recovered from Atherton's early loss and, with Smith and Lathwell adding eighty-nine runs in seventy-nine minutes, looked to be stealing the game. Smith carried on his dashing form from the first innings against an inaccurate Julian and an unsteady May and Warne, and was receiving good support from Lathwell.

With Border off the field suffering from the hay fever that affected him several times in the series, England had a golden opportunity to strike a psychological blow if they could maintain the tempo for a few more minutes. But Warne and Hughes again produced the setbacks.

No sooner had Smith raised his half-century than he groped forward to a perfectly pitched Warne leg-break that caused his downfall as the ball took the outside edge of his bat. The total now read 2-100, but Stewart soon lost his wicket lbw, playing across a well-pitched-up ball from Hughes. Then Lathwell was out lbw to Warne without playing a stroke. Gooch, who had come in at the fall of Smith's wicket, was on 12 and Caddick, impeccable in defence, batted for seventeen minutes without opening his account. England were 4-122 at the close, a lead of seventy.

Only a heroic innings by Gooch seemed to stand in the way of Australia's victory, although one optimist was England manager Keith Fletcher, whose Essex loyalties allowed him to imagine that Peter Such might win the game if he had a sufficient target to bowl at. But Fletcher appeared to let those loyalties run away with him entirely when he claimed Such could turn the ball more than could Australian off-spinner Tim May, whose flight and prodigious spin throughout the series made him a serious attacking proposition and a perfect foil for Warne.

Had the dramas ended on the field on the third day, that would have been sufficient. But there were more to come off the field. ICC match referee Clive Lloyd warned the Australians for abusive language and 'constant and excessive appealing', and met with Australian coach Bob Simpson and acting captain Mark Taylor to discuss the matter. According to a Test and County Cricket Board official, umpires Barrie Meyer and Roy Palmer were concerned about appeals being continued after a batsman had been given not out. Warne had displayed some petulance when an lbw appeal against Lathwell was turned down, before dismissing the batsman a short time later in identical fashion.

||| DAY 4

The fourth day's play was unquestionably England's best of the series so far. First it dug itself out of a very large hole, and then opened up the possibility of actually winning. Only two wickets fell while 240 runs were scored. As so often for England, though less frequently against Australia prior to this series, Gooch was the centrepiece in keeping England's hopes alive, commanding the crease for all but seventy minutes of the day. He received strong support from the obstinate Caddick, who hung around for the same period of time in the morning session. Other young players in Thorpe and Hussain also played their part in an encouraging feature of the recovery.

Gooch's century was his first down the order for England. It brought a wry reminder of how, eighteen years before, he had begun his test career against Australia with a pair of spectacles batting number five at Edgbaston. Simply, the mature Gooch has been a revelation. Whereas he struggled twenty-one tests for his first century, and always against Australia, Essex Man was now able to overcome both bogeys. In his 103rd test he became the third Englishman after Gower and Boycott to pass 8000 test runs. His nineteenth century, his fourth against Australia, was his twelfth in twenty-nine tests since taking over the England captaincy in 1990.

Gooch and Caddick saw off the dual Victorian menace of Hughes and Warne, and Gooch welcomed Julian's presence by cover-driving his first ball of the day to the boundary. It was Julian, however, who removed Caddick when he pushed a short ball to Boon at short-leg. The partnership had yielded forty-two runs in twenty-four overs.

England's score was 5-159 when Graeme Thorpe made his way out to join his captain, and there were plenty of question marks

Graham Thorpe and Nasser Hussain gave England a winning chance.
Wisden Cricket Monthly *rejoiced.*

beside his name. First, although he had the merit (against Warne) of being a left-hander, a lot of people considered him a poor man's Gower. Second, his batting average for Surrey during the season stood at only twenty-five, and plenty of batsmen could press stronger statistical claims. Gatting and Hick, who had made way for him, for instance, both underlined their potential for possible recall by each making scores of 173 while the test was in progress, in county matches at Cardiff and Kidderminster respectively. Third, there was the manner of his dismissal in the first innings, a loose shot outside the off stump. Would he be another one-test wonder?

Gooch was 35 when Thorpe joined him, and he no doubt gave the young batsman confidence by his rough treatment of Julian and May. Thirteen runs came off Julian's fifth over of the day and Gooch raised his fifty with his tenth four when he lofted May to the long-on boundary. By lunch the partnership was still intact. In the afternoon session Gooch was strangely subdued, scoring from only eight of the eighty-nine balls he faced. Only fifty-four runs were added and Julian's 14-7-26-0 spell was his best in terms of control. It was at this time that Thorpe began to grow in authority. England were still not out of danger, but more importantly no wicket was lost. A blow to Australia was the loss of strike bowler Hughes for half the day with a strained groin.

After tea, Gooch and Thorpe opened out against May but Warne bowled tightly, and it was he who made the breakthrough. Gooch raised his century in five hours with a leg-glance from Julian and moved swiftly to 120 before a big-spinning leg-break from Warne caught the edge of his bat to give Taylor a catch at slip. Gooch's innings had included eighteen fours and lasted 325 minutes. With the total at 5-309 the partnership that had gone most of the way towards saving England had added 150 runs in 224 minutes. Thorpe's share was 55.

In just over the last hour Thorpe and Hussain added a further fifty-three runs with Thorpe now doing the bulk of the scoring. At stumps England's score read 6-362, with Thorpe 88 and Hussain 16, a lead of 310. It could be argued that if Gooch was serious about winning the match he would have declared earlier. No doubt seven test defeats in succession were enough for any man, let alone for an England captain with a hitherto ineffectual attack at his disposal.

DAY 5

Thorpe and Hussain pushed the score along quickly on the final morning. The former had done the hard work the day before but he took only eight balls to add the twelve runs to bring up his century, reaching his target in five hours by hooking Julian to the fine-leg boundary. In so doing he also joined the august company of WG Grace and Ranjitsinhji among those who achieved a century on debut against Australia in England. When Gooch closed the innings at 6-422, Thorpe had batted for 337 minutes for his undefeated 114 with eleven fours. Hussain had lent him good support with 47, helping to add sixty runs in forty minutes.

Now came the Australian reply and, while saving the game looked relatively straightforward, unquestionably they were under some pressure for the first time in the series. A victory target of 371 off seventy-seven overs was always going to be beyond reach.

Taylor and Slater opened with forty-six, but Taylor was scratchy and Slater streaky. Needing to negotiate sixteen overs until lunch, both sides made an initial effort. McCague bowled with good pace to worry Taylor, but it was Slater who departed ten minutes short, charging Such and being bowled between bat and pad. Such gained a second wicket when he spun a ball sharply from the rough, for Taylor to edge it to the gully. Would Fletcher's man bring England home after all? Australia were 2-74 and fifty-five overs remained.

England now began to play like it had a chance of winning. Caddick at last started to bowl for England like he did for Somerset, and in three overs got rid of both Mark Waugh and Border. The last ball of his first over took the inside edge of Waugh's bat and deflected on to his leg stump. Then Border was caught half-back, half-forward, steering Caddick to slip. The third wicket, that of Waugh, fell at 75, and when Border left it was 4-81. Australia's score became 5-93 when Caddick enticed Boon to cut and had him caught behind. Half the side was out, there was no chance left for Australia to win, two-and-a-half hours remained. Caddick the impassive, whose action closely resembled Richard Hadlee in taking two wickets for 314 runs in the series, now became a man of positive emotive passion with three quick wickets as he began to swing the ball disconcertingly.

Caddick might have won the game for England as Steve Waugh stumbled over a superb early yorker and was all but bowled. When Ilott trapped Healy in the last over before tea at 6-115, the Australian position seemed precarious. England certainly must have favoured its chances. Waugh had rarely to this point in his career shown fighting qualities in tight situations, and new bat Julian's previous highest score in eleven innings on the tour was 28.

Steve Waugh saved Australia, however, with a brave innings of 47 in 198 minutes. After tea he was once scoreless for an hour. Julian defended at first but then found his confidence. His undefeated 56 in just over two hours included seven boundaries. At the finish, England were left to rue the fact they had chosen the 'straight spinner' Such instead of Tufnell who, two days earlier, spun the ball sharply in taking career-best innings figures of 8-29 in Middlesex's turnabout win over Glamorgan.

The batting highlights of the Trent Bridge match were undoubtedly the efforts of Gooch, Thorpe, Smith and Hussain for England, and Boon's dogged first-innings century for Australia. With the ball, McCague bowled with spirit for England and Caddick came alive for the first time. As almost always on this tour, Hughes gave a grand display in his five-wicket first-innings haul, taking seven wickets for the match. Warne bowled ninety-one accurate and penetrating overs for six wickets.

In raising Thorpe as a new English hero, and linking him with Ranji, the journalist John Woodcock was also able to make the neat point that Ranji's selection in 1896 had been, in its day, even more controversial – and certainly more adventurous – than McCague's. For a national cricket team searching for its cultural roots and identity, Thorpe's Farnham pedigree was ideal, since Farnham had defeated the great Hambledon side in the cradle days of the game.

The significance of the match is difficult to assess in the short and medium term. As in 1989, the score after three tests saw Australia 2–0 up and, as in that earlier series, Australia continued to dominate. This time it followed up with wins at Leeds and Birmingham before falling at The Oval to an England attack which had, by that time, been further recast. McCague, Ilott and Caddick had given way to a major strike bowler in the often-injured Angus Fraser, the extra pace of Devon Malcolm, and Steve Watkin, who gained recognition at last for his consistent Glamorgan performances. Peter Such was the only member of the attack to play as many as five tests, but then missed selection for the spring West Indies tour.

More significantly, Michael Atherton had by then taken over as captain, and Ted Dexter had announced his resignation as chairman of selectors. He was replaced by Ray Illingworth. Though Robin Smith had temporarily lost his place in the middle order, he returned for the West Indies tour, and Gooch, after missing that tour, announced his availability for at least two more seasons, including the Australian tour of 1994–95.

Though Atherton's 1994 touring team to the West Indies was beaten 2–1, Thorpe and Caddick built on their Nottingham experience to play substantial roles in England's courageous Fourth Test victory in Bridgetown, though thereafter they followed that by fielding to Brian Lara's new world-record test score of 375 at Antigua's tiny St John's ground.

For the Australians, Nottingham was just another bridge to cross, one more test to pass. Amid various kinds of controversy, they went on to defeat New Zealand and draw a six-test double series against South Africa in 1993–94.

For Allan Border, the prospect of the tour of Pakistan that preceded England's arrival in Australia in October 1994 proved a bridge too far. After intense speculation and ninety-three tests as captain, the South African series in March proved to be his swansong as an Australian player.

The fight for the Ashes then continued with two new captains. Mark Taylor was asked to take an Australian side to Pakistan comprising a mixture of experienced players and newcomers. Atherton's side rebuilt although Illingworth initially followed traditional English practice and recalled experienced players from Border's vintage such as the forty-one-year-old Gooch and thirty-seven-year-old Gatting to the 1994–95 Ashes touring party. For each, it proved one tour too many. The only batting successes were Thorpe and Atherton who alone topped 400 runs, and Gough and Fraser with the ball. The trouble with Gough and Fraser was that each played only three Tests – the first through injury breakdown and the second due to being a late draftee into the tour party.

In 1993 Australia faced a future in which its experienced pace bowling reserves looked thin. Injuries to Hughes and McDermott meant that new men like Glenn McGrath, Damien Fleming and Jo Angel would have to progress rapidly to fill their places. Australia's spin bowling looked healthy while Warne and May remained in partnership although May often experienced lean patches and had a history of injury.

Australia's top order batting looked much more solid, though remaindering Dean Jones at thirty-three was premature and David Boon's knees were showing signs of wearing out through hours spent at the crease. Certainly, if he, Taylor, Slater or the Waughs faltered, a line-up of prolific scoring batsmen such as Matthew Hayden, Justin Langer, Michael Bevan, Damien Martyn, Ricky Ponting, Greg Blewett, Darren Lehmann and Stuart Law was ready to take over.

The 1994–95 series saw Australia maintain its dominance in Ashes clashes with a comfortable 3–1 win. The regular batsmen scored heavily with eight centuries to England's two and Blewett, who vaulted into the side over several rivals, made a perfect start with hundreds in his two matches. The bowling picture was less clear. McDermott powered back with 32 wickets and Warne took 27 but the supports were a long way behind and May gathered just one wicket in three games.

McDermott broke down on the 1995 West Indies tour where McGrath emerged and his combination with Warne ever since has been a major factor, along with the batting riches mentioned above, in Australia's dominance of world cricket since. Ashes struggles continued to come and go but generally it was England doing the struggling.

In 1995 a furore broke out in the English game over the David Frith–Robert Henderson–*Wisden Cricket Monthly* muddle regarding racism and national identity following a Henderson article, 'Is it in the Blood?', which purported to suggest that 'foreign-born' players lacked commitment to England. According to Mike Marqusee in *Anyone But England*, the article 'seemed a veritable catalogue of exhausted racist casuistries, bristling with resentment, stuffed with the pseudo-sociological paranoia of the bigot at sea in the modern cosmopolis, and replete with the venerable fascist mantra about the "liberal elite" betraying the national heritage'.

The so-called debate about the effects of race, heritage, and place of origin on English team spirit surrounded players in two camps: those described as 'mercenaries' as well as the black and Asian cricketers either born in, raised and qualified for England. It put a slur on both. Cricketers such as Allan Lamb and Robin Smith, who had both given honourable service, and newcomers such as Andrew Caddick, Martin McCague, Graeme Hick and Craig White were in the first category; and Philip de Freitas, Devon Malcolm, Chris Lewis, Nasser Hussain and Mark Ramprakash were in the second.

In many ways this diversion – an ugly diversion – was nevertheless just that. There were systemic weaknesses in the English game, the most serious being the long-time problem of putting county ahead of country. The introduction of two divisions in the County Championship in 2000, the adoption of a National Academy (following the Australian model) and the appointment of Rod Marsh as Academy coach in 2002, and as an England selector in 2003, all helped. But a brilliant Australian side continued to win, and win well until a competitive England presented itself in 2005.

Glenn McGrath was injured before the Edgbaston Test began

•EDGBASTON 2005•

LIVING THE DREAM

Australia has held the Ashes since 1989 but England is now competitive. Except that after Australia wins the first test at Lord's easily it seems like business as usual. Then Glenn McGrath treads on a cricket ball playing touch rugby and tears ankle ligaments an hour before play. Then Ricky Ponting, without his key strike bowler, wins the toss and puts England in to bat. England make Australia pay. Crash, bash, thump with Kevin Pietersen and Andrew Flintoff in full flight. Then it's Flintoff with ball, bat, ball as England lead, crumble, revive, set Australia a tough target and break through a second time. It might sound like a one-man game but Shane Warne has taken ten wickets and is still at the crease. On the fourth morning, England lead by 107 with two wickets to fall but Warne and Brett Lee reduce it to 62, and Lee and Michael Kasprowicz keep reducing it, and reducing it, until Stephen Harmison produces the ball of his career. England wins when the thought of losing would have been too horrible to contemplate.

ENGLAND v AUSTRALIA 2005 (2nd Test)

Played at Edgbaston, Birmingham on 4,5,6,7 August.
Toss: Australia. Result: ENGLAND won by 2 runs.

ENGLAND

Batsman	1st innings		2nd innings	
M.E. Trescothick	c Gilchrist b Kasprowicz	90	c Gilchrist b Lee	21
A.J. Strauss	b Warne	48	b Warne	6
M.P. Vaughan*	c Lee b Gillespie	24	(4) b Lee	1
I.R. Bell	c Gilchrist b Kasprowicz	6	(5) c Gilchrist b Warne	21
K.P. Pietersen	c Katich b Lee	71	(6) c Gilchrist b Warne	20
A. Flintoff	c Gilchrist b Gillespie	68	(7) b Warne	73
G.O. Jones†	c Gilchrist b Kasprowicz	1	(8) c Ponting b Lee	9
A.F. Giles	lbw b Warne	23	(9) c Hayden b Warne	8
M.J. Hoggard	lbw b Warne	16	(3) c Hayden b Lee	1
S.J. Harmison	b Warne	17	c Ponting b Warne	0
S.P. Jones	not out	19	not out	12
Extras	(LB 9, W 1, NB 14)	24	(LB 1, NB 9)	10
Total		**407**		**182**

AUSTRALIA

Batsman	1st innings		2nd innings	
J.L. Langer	lbw b S. Jones	82	b Flintoff	28
M.L. Hayden	c Strauss b Hoggard	0	c Trescothick b S. Jones	31
R.T. Ponting*	c Vaughan b Giles	61	c G. Jones b Flintoff	0
D.R. Martyn	run out	20	c Bell b Hoggard	28
M.J. Clarke	c G. Jones b Giles	40	b Harmison	30
S.M. Katich	c G. Jones b Flintoff	4	c Trescothick b Giles	16
A.C. Gilchrist†	not out	49	c Flintoff b Giles	1
S.K. Warne	b Giles	8	hit wicket b Flintoff	42
B. Lee	c Flintoff b S. Jones	6	not out	43
J.N. Gillespie	lbw b Flintoff	7	lbw b Flintoff	0
M.S. Kasprowicz	lbw b Flintoff	0	c G. Jones b Harmison	20
Extras	(B 13, LB 7, W 1, NB 10)	31	(B 13, LB 8, W 1, NB 18)	40
Total		**308**		**279**

AUSTRALIA	**O**	**M**	**R**	**W**	**O**	**M**	**R**	**W**
Lee	17	1	111	1	18	1	82	4
Gillespie	22	3	91	2	8	0	24	0
Kasprowicz	15	3	80	3	3	0	29	0
Warne	25.2	4	116	4	23.1	7	46	6
ENGLAND								
Harmison	11	1	48	0	17.3	3	62	2
Hoggard	8	0	41	1	5	0	26	1
S. Jones	16	2	69	2	5	1	23	1
Flintoff	15	1	52	3	22	3	79	4
Giles	26	2	78	3	15	3	68	2

FALL OF WICKETS

	E	A	E	A
Wkt	1st	1st	2nd	2nd
1st	112	0	25	47
2nd	164	88	27	48
3rd	170	118	29	82
4th	187	194	32	107
5th	290	208	72	134
6th	293	262	75	136
7th	342	273	101	137
8th	348	282	131	175
9th	375	308	131	220
10th	407	308	182	279

Umpires: B.F. Bowden (NZ) and R.E. Koertzen (SA)
TV Umpire: J.W. Lloyds
Match Referee: R.S. Madugalle (SL)

Kasprowicz is given out caught Jones bowled Harmison and English fans breathe again

Could England make an Ashes contest for the first time in two decades? Home supporters were cautious remembering the drubbings they had suffered since Mike Gatting's tour of Australia in 1986–87. Their side looked good on paper: a new powerful opener in Andrew Strauss, who had peeled three centuries off the South Africans in a series and five test hundreds in his first twelve months; potentially heavy run-scorers in fellow opener Marcus Trescothick and captain Michael Vaughan, the latter having taken over 600 runs from the Australian attack in 2002–03; dependable middle-order batsman Graham Thorpe, who had always done well in Ashes matches when available; good looking young batsmen in Ian Bell and Kevin Pietersen; the man emerging as the best all-rounder in the game in the Botham mould, Andrew Flintoff; new wicket-keeper batsman Geraint Jones, who already had a test century to his name; plus a penetrative pace attack consisting of Steve Harmison, whose steepling bounce made him a leading strike bowler in the manner of the famous West Indian quicks, Matthew Hoggard, who could swing the new ball, and Simon Jones, who moved the old ball at speeds of up to ninety miles an hour. The one weakness seemed to be the lack of a class spinner even though Ashley Giles had gathered a lot of wickets in the past two years. In the last year England had won 11, lost one and drawn two of their 14 test matches against New Zealand and the West Indies at home, South Africa abroad, and Bangladesh at home at the start of the summer. The Australians were an old side with maybe their best years behind them. Maybe.

The Australians might have been old, with only Simon Katich and Michael Clarke of their regular players under thirty, but they were good'uns. Four of the batsmen, in captain Ricky Ponting, opener Matthew Hayden, Damien Martyn and the best wicket-keeper batsman in test cricket history, Adam Gilchrist, boasted batting averages over fifty, Justin Langer was in the high forties, and Katich and Clarke in the low forties. Of the bowling attack at the start of the series Glenn McGrath and Jason Gillespie, Australia's most successful new ball pair, had 499 and 248 wickets apiece; Michael Kasprowicz, who had enjoyed a great last eighteen months, 102; and leg-spin wizard Shane Warne held the world record of 583 wickets. For good measure express bowler Brett Lee, whom Kasprowicz had displaced, had 139 test scalps; and Stuart MacGill, a world-class leggie, 160 victims. In the previous twelve months Australia had also played 14 test matches for a slightly inferior 10 wins, one loss and three draws against Sri Lanka at home, India abroad, New Zealand and Pakistan at home, and New Zealand abroad. They were not to be messed with.

And they weren't. After all, the series began at Lord's where Australia lost only once in the twentieth century and had started well in the new millennium. There were no surprises in the Australian team with Lee forcing his way into the side after some impressive one-day form and Kasprowicz the unlucky man to miss out. For England, the replacement of Thorpe with debutant Pietersen probably caused some murmurs but the latter's thrilling displays in the limited-over arena saw him get the selectors' nod. A difficult position for England was that thrashing wins in two tests over Bangladesh in May and June had given their bats time in the middle and polished their bowling averages but the question mark was whether it represented quality time. One thing appeared certain and that was that Ian Bell would not maintain a test average of 297 for long.

England had their opportunities on a lively pitch at cricket's traditional headquarters but after Harmison (chiefly) had smashed through Australia before tea for 190 on the first day, the metronomic McGrath replied with what one critic described as 80 mph off-breaks to skedaddle England for 155. Sloppy fielding contributed strongly to Australia's second innings of 384 and thereafter McGrath and Warne mopped up the English innings after an opening stand of 80 by Trescothick and Strauss gave hope of stronger resistance. Aggressive newcomer Pietersen was England's shining light with the bat with his twin half-centuries but otherwise the home team's only solace was that its bowlers dismissed Australia twice. Against that, double failures by captain Vaughan (3 and 4), Bell (6 and 8) and Flintoff (0 and 3) in a 239-run defeat brought the deepest gloom and fears that for the Australians the series would fall into a pattern of business as usual.

Edgbaston has been kinder to England in the past than Lord's and former captain, Nasser Hussain, had stated he loved the passionate and parochial football-style support the crowd gave his team. In eleven previous games at the ground England had won four, Australia three and there had been four draws. In the previous four series the sides had won two matches each – England by an innings and 118 runs in 1985 and Australia by an identical margin in 2001, and Australia by eight wickets and England by nine wickets in between.

The only close match which had brought a result was England's win by 29 runs in 1981.

Before the test the Australians drew a three-day game against Worcestershire at New Road after gaining valuable batting practice. Reserve wicket-keeper Brad Haddin top-scored with 94 and half-centuries were made by Langer, Hayden, Gillespie, Clarke and Ponting. Pace-man Kasprowicz also ran into form with 5-67 in Worcestershire's only innings and Gillespie bowled a spell of twelve overs for 2-45 and found better rhythm, although perhaps the most notable feature of the game was Warne and McGrath acting as drinks waiters on the final day! As for Warne, whose sexual philandering had caused the break-up of his marriage only weeks before, he was also in the news following an interview with *GQ* magazine in which he said he would prefer to bowl the leg break that bowled Mike Gatting in 1993 to spending a night with a beautiful woman. Warne added, 'When you are thrust into the limelight at 22, it can be hard to deal with. The problem is there's still a kid inside me who likes to have fun.' The comment was a reminder of Eric Midwinter's description of W.G. Grace as an 'eternal boy' and the same could be said for a wide range of sportsmen.

One spinner who hadn't been having fun was Ashley Giles. After the Lord's test, Australian coach John Buchanan had said that he was a player they were targeting. 'We understand his role so if we can erode that, it's pretty important in the context of the whole series.' Buchanan went on: 'He's a key part of [England's] strategy for containing and also resting their impact bowlers. Therefore if he's not allowed to do the containment it's unlikely he can stay at the crease.' For his part, Giles' baring his soul in his column in the *Guardian* in response to criticism from Derbyshire coach, David Houghton, that by selecting him England were taking only ten men on the field seemed like poor preparation. And sticking it up his critics brought both criticism and support. Former Australian paceman Geoff Lawson said that players should do their talking on the pitch and former England quick bowler (and *Independent* reporter) Angus Fraser concluded that Giles was 'paranoid and insecure'. Offering support was Nasser Hussain, who said Giles was 'one of the mentally strongest cricketers he'd played with'.

Putting psychology aside, and whether Giles might also have to bear the brunt of Australian sledging, the pre-match discussion of tactics to be used was fascinating. First of all, what sort of pitch would be prepared? Heavy rain around Birmingham in the previous few days, including a tornado which had passed only a half a mile from the ground, hampered the efforts of groundsman, Steve Rouse, who felt his wicket was about four days behind and would play slowly. According to Angus Fraser, the English batsmen had two options. They should either bat as they did at Lord's and hope that McGrath and Warne did not bowl as well, or attempt to unsettle the bowlers although he did not say how. For the bowlers his prediction was that a damp, slow, seaming wicket could suit McGrath but also the English pace-men provided they pitched the ball up.

A surprise late addition to the England team was Durham all-rounder Paul Collingwood if only because he was a bits-and-pieces player and his selection represented a loss of nerve despite the player's big scores in county matches. A fright for the home team came the day before the game when captain Vaughan was struck on the right elbow by Chris Tremlett in the nets causing severe bruising. While Vaughan had failed in the first test, he had come back to form with a century for Yorkshire against Kent in a National League Division Two limited-over match at Headingley on the previous Sunday.

How would the test shape up? England fast bowler Darren Gough criticised the poor planning associated with England's Ashes campaign. Among his complaints were that the Australians had been given seven weeks to acclimatise; that it had been a mistake not to schedule Headingley for a test; and that Graham Thorpe should have been bolstering the middle-order batting. Steve Waugh predicted that Australia would improve and that England had missed a golden opportunity at Lord's by failing to take the initiative after dismissing Australia cheaply. Australia, he thought, had 'more scope to prosper'. Of all the views expressed before the game, that of former English spinner Phil Tufnell that England should try to score at four runs an over seemed most fanciful.

DAY 1

The day began badly for the Australians when McGrath was forced out of the team after tearing ligaments in his right ankle. The thirty-five-year-old trod on a cricket ball while playing touch rugby in a dumb sporting accident which reminded English supporters of all-rounder Chris Lewis shaving his head during a tour of the West Indies in 1994 and then suffering sunstroke.

McGrath's loss was acute on a pitch expected to suit him but also for his overall value to the side. Of the 110 tests in which he played, Australia had won two-thirds as against less than half in the 26 games when he had been absent. Although McGrath and Warne had been the lynchpins of the Australian attack for twelve years, Warne's winning percentage did not match the fast bowler and in his absence Australia still won 56 per cent of games.

A further shock for the Australians came when Ponting went ahead with a pre-game plan on winning the toss and put England into bat. Dumb and dumber. The underprepared pitch might have given some weight to the decision as Australia had been bowled out on the same wicket, in similar conditions, in 1997 in less than half a day for 118. But what might have made sense with McGrath as psychological pressure, following his 8-92 in the previous match, was now either foolhardy or arrogant without him. Kasprowicz came into the side.

According to *The Mail on Sunday*, Ponting's action in giving England first use of the wicket led to a stand-up row with Shane

Warne requiring the intercession of vice-captain Adam Gilchrist. Although this was subsequently denied as a 'fabrication' and a 'blatant lie', the effect of a McGrath-less attack was slaughter. Trescothick and Strauss got away at a hell of a lick against Lee and Gillespie although the latter, who had been battling for form all tour, was unlucky to have Strauss dropped with just a single to his name. Strauss scored the first of England's boundaries when he nicked Gillespie through slips but Trescothick was more convincing. In Lee's second over he smashed three drives through cover. Trescothick had some luck when he was caught by Hayden off a no-ball from Kasprowicz and then made two or three streaky shots through gaps in the slips but the openers brought up the first fifty in just 10.4 overs. As the pace-men continued to bowl loosely, Ponting was forced to bring Warne into the attack.

Prior to the series Warne had targeted Strauss as his bunny but the batsman was quick to respond. To the spinner's fourth delivery he advanced down the pitch and lofted the ball over the bowler's head for four. With Trescothick adopting similar methods, one blow which landed on the covers at the City End and rolled into the gutters was returned sodden to the bowler. England raised 100 in 22.4 overs but when the total had reached 112, Warne ripped a savage leg-break through Strauss's half-cock defence to send him on his way for 48. Without doubt it was the ball of the morning. This brought Vaughan to the crease with just seven minutes before lunch but if it was expected that England would play safely, such thoughts were put aside. Trescothick cranked up the momentum again by smashing Lee for a six over third man and three boundaries in the last over before the break. At the long adjournment England had reached 1-132 with Trescothick on 77 and Vaughan on 1.

Trescothick is a curious batsman. Powerful and aggressive, he is also often a bit leaden-footed like Matthew Hayden at his worst. At the end of the previous test, television commentator Dean Jones stated he would drop him, and certainly his average of 29 from 11 tests against Australia suggested plenty of opportunities but little fulfilment. One does not know whether he was apprised of Jones' criticism but his powerful driving off the front foot was like Hayden at his best and he now had a great chance to launch a big innings. Vaughan was certainly in need of a big innings after Lord's and his performances with the bat (as captain) were modest compared with his outstanding success in Australia two-and-a-half-years before.

The batting onslaught continued immediately after lunch with 30 runs added in four overs and Trescothick and Vaughan raising their 50 partnership in just 35 balls. However, just when the Australian attack was on the ropes, Gillespie tightened his line and this slight curb on the scoring brought a wicket at the other end. Trescothick held his bat out weakly against Kasprowicz when he had reached 90 and succeeded only in edging the ball to Gilchrist, a tame end to an innings in which he faced just 102 balls and struck fifteen fours and two sixes. At 2-164, Trescothick and Vaughan had produced some blazing batting but bigger things were demanded.

Local Warwickshire lad Bell came in to a huge reception and in need of runs. Something of a boy wonder, he was drafted into an England squad in New Zealand in 2001–02 while still a teenager, then slipped back for a couple of seasons until making his test debut against the West Indies at The Oval with an assured 70 in 2004. He then returned at the start of the summer with unbeaten innings of 65 and 162 not out at Lord's and Chester-le-Street against Bangladesh. Bell got off to a perky start with two off his first ball and a cut for four but then received a superb ball from Kasprowicz which pitched perfectly on off stump and moved away, drawing a fine touch to Gilchrist. Two wickets in an over to the burly Queenslander was a welcome return to the test arena for a player who at the start of the day imagined he would again be fulfilling twelfth man duties. 3-170.

The run rate of more than five per over was impressive but the commentators were beginning to remark on England's wasted opportunity. Suddenly the game was back on an even keel and

England would have to look to a composed Vaughan and Pietersen, England's only batting hero from Lord's, to regain the initiative.

The newcomer did not want to be restrained and he clipped his first delivery for four. Vaughan needed to play a captain's innings but he failed to do so. Although Vaughan moved effortlessly along to 24, he then swung wildly at a bouncer from Gillespie and succeeded only in skying it to fine leg where Lee took a good catch low down to his left to give the lanky South Australian pace-man his first wicket for the series. At 4-187 Australia was back on top on a pitch which began to look full of runs.

Now came a moment of truth for England. As Flintoff joined Pietersen the home side had its two most punishing strokemakers at the crease but was it the time for fireworks? Flintoff had a huge reputation to uphold. He had disappointed with the bat at Lord's where his bowling in the second innings had been ragged. Would he now be able to raise his game against the Australians? Would the two power hitters transform the game? Not quite, but they provided plenty of fireworks in reaching an unbeaten century stand before tea.

At first Flintoff was tentative against Warne but a mighty six into the grandstands settled his nerves and he repeated the stroke twice more from the slow bowler. As Flintoff unveiled his prodigious power, Pietersen seemed happy to turn over the strike although, as Angus Fraser noted, 'one awesome stroke, a top-spin forehand drive through mid-on brought back memories of Viv Richards in his pomp'. Pietersen and Flintoff were certainly cavalier in their assault on the Australians so that the 200 was raised in 40.4 overs, the 250 in 48.3 overs and Flintoff's fifty in just 48 balls. In a scintillating afternoon session, 157 runs were added so that at tea the score was 4-289 with Pietersen on 40 and Flintoff on 68, including six fours and five sixes. England's position was now healthy but although the helter-skelter tactics were thrilling, they also needed to occupy the crease. Perhaps there was something all too 'fairytale' about the batting because even if the two swordsmen were not knights, they were certainly bold. The tea break brought a halt to the destruction and an immediate fight-back by the Australians when play resumed.

Gillespie made the breakthrough just three balls into the new session when Flintoff gloved an attempted hook to Gilchrist to make the score 5-290 in 54.3 overs. Flintoff's departure brought Kent wicket-keeper Geraint Jones to the crease. Jones had gained the keeper's position from Chris Read because of his superior batting but an appalling display with the gloves in the previous match threatened his tenure so he was another batsman in search of a score. Instead, he lasted 14 balls for a solitary run before becoming Gilchrist's fourth catch of the innings and Kasprowicz's third dismissal. 6-293.

The breakthrough put Australia back in the game and once again there was a feeling that England had ruined its great building blocks. The sober assessment was that smashing boundaries was all very well, but 500 runs were there for the asking and England might struggle to make 350.

Fortunately for the home side, Giles showed that he possessed more mettle than his early-week admissions indicated as he came together in another furious alliance with Pietersen of 49 runs in 34 minutes until Warne trapped him lbw for 23 at 7-342. Still England were rolling along at more than five runs per over and the novice Pietersen was playing an innings of great maturity. Oddly, therefore, it was a lack of maturity that overtook him in the end. Having pulled Lee for six, he seemed to go for broke for fear of running out of partners when he might have trusted them more. Pietersen was caught by Katich on the mid-wicket boundary off Lee for 71 in just over two-and-a-half hours with ten fours and a six, leaving just Harmison and Simon Jones to support an obdurate Hoggard.

As it turned out Hoggard dug in like a traditional Yorkshireman while his partners waved the willow with abandon. Harmison took 17 off 11 balls with two boundaries and a six before being bowled by Warne at 9-375, and Jones made merry for 19 off 24 balls in a breezy last wicket partnership before Hoggard was trapped lbw by Warne.

The leg-spinner was perhaps flattered by his four wickets whereas Kasprowicz and Gillespie had worked hard for less reward, while Lee had been profligate in giving away 111 runs in seventeen overs. England's 407 came in the amazing time of 357 minutes off 79.2 overs and left Australia twenty minutes to negotiate before stumps.

Openers Hayden and Langer would not have been unhappy when light rain fell and prevented the innings from starting.

||| DAY 2

England held the honours at the end of the day when the much-derided left-arm spinner Giles bowled a long, tight spell to finish with 3-78 from 26 overs. Not only did he rein in the scoring, but he gathered wickets at critical times.

Australia got off to a horror start when Hayden was out with a weak chip to cover off Hoggard from his first ball of the day and without a run on the board. However, Ponting was so quickly into stride, with Langer giving grafting support, that the visitors' fifty came up in even less time than England's – off just 8.4 overs. Ponting was in imperious form, particularly his driving down the ground, and appeared to be wanting to make personal amends for his decision to put England in to bat. Harmison gave away 35 runs from his opening seven-over spell and Hoggard's opening four overs cost 26 runs. Simon Jones started with two maiden overs but when Ponting spanked him for three boundaries in his third, Vaughan was forced to bring Giles into the attack.

The decision brought an early reward. Although Ponting took boundaries in each of Giles' first two overs, a misjudged paddle sweep in his third saw a catch lobbed to Vaughan at short fine-leg. Ponting's 61 was a brilliant miniature, coming in just 76 balls, and when he left the score was 2-88.

Martyn now joined his Western Australian team-mate and looked a little streaky against a hostile Flintoff who was hitting the pitch hard from the City End. Although he made a couple of pretty strokes past point, what he imagined would be an easy single brought about his downfall for 20 as Vaughan at mid-on swept on to the ball, picked up and, turning through 200 degrees, threw down the wicket at the bowler's end in the last over before lunch. A brilliant session ended in England's favour at 3-118 with Langer on 27.

Clarke was now the new man at the crease and carried some of his form from his second-innings 91 at Lord's into this knock by getting into double figures from the first half-dozen balls he faced. The middle-order batsman had cracked seven boundaries and added 76 with Langer in 85 minutes when he was beaten by a quicker ball from Giles and smartly caught behind by Geraint Jones for 40 at 4-194, a decisive end to what was mounting as a major rescue operation.

Langer grafted on. The little opener had adopted that role from his test baptism of fire against the West Indies at Adelaide Oval in 1993 and continued in his years down the list. In the past four years, however, and particularly during his dominant opening associations with Hayden, he had scored as rapidly as many of the game's dashers. Now he played in the old mode and it would be up to Katich and Gilchrist to help him boost Australia's total towards England's tally.

It was not to be. Katich troubled the scorers with just one boundary from 18 balls before touching Flintoff to the keeper at 5-208. The second session was entertaining with 101 runs and two wickets as Australia took tea at 5-219 with Langer on 72 and Gilchrist on 5.

The Western Australian left-handers began to fashion a valuable partnership in the fifth hour but once again England broke through at a crucial time. Getting his reverse swing going, Simon Jones trapped Langer lbw with a full-length delivery for 82 in 276 minutes out of 262. Although the batsman appeared unhappy, the ball would clearly have taken the leg stump.

Gilchrist was now left with the tail and in a position from which Australia's superhero has launched a number of blazing centuries. Of course he would need the support of the lower order and this time it was not forthcoming. Warne has always been a capable batsman but prone to some soft dismissals. On this occasion, he hit two boundaries from 14 balls before an agricultural slog against Giles saw the ball wreck his stumps and bring a soft shake of the head from Gilchrist. Quickly 7-273 became 8-282 as Lee's snick to second slip off Simon Jones was taken by Flintoff. Only Gillespie offered resistance for 37 balls as the 300 was passed. Finally, Flintoff captured the wickets of Gillespie and Kasprowicz lbw with successive balls at 308 with Gilchrist one run short of his fifty.

England led by 99 runs but how had they gained the advantage? According to Peter Roebuck:

> Michael Vaughan's plan was admirably simple and revealed both an appreciation of the strengths and weaknesses of his side, and of the psychology of his opponents. Nor is the theory quite as hard to put into words as Kierkegaard's version of existentialism. Thump 'em around with the bat. Dry 'em with the ball. It worked.

It worked but there was still work to be done. England had to negotiate seven overs of play for the night and they would want to do so without the loss of a wicket. They almost got there. At least, they got through six overs of McGrath, Gillespie and Kasprowicz before Warne bowled, as he often does, the last over of the day. And as he often does, he made something happen. With his second ball he produced an amazing sharp, spinning leg-break to bowl Strauss for 6 behind his legs. Night-watchman Hoggard kept the last four balls out as England ended the day at 1-25 with Trescothick on 19 and a lead of 124.

When it came to facing a press conference after play, an unexpected figure facing the microphones was Giles. Following a topsy-turvy week he admitted that it was a great comfort to perform in front of his home crowd: 'I'm just happy that, having done my preparation, I've come out and done well today,' he told the press.

||| DAY 3

Australia looked for a long time for second Bradmans: Jack Badcock among his contemporaries, and then Ian Craig, Norm O'Neill and Doug Walters. Craig and Walters bore some physical resemblance. Then, fortunately, they gave up trying. England have long sought a second Botham: Derek Pringle and Chris Lewis were the main contenders but then there were the players who were neither good enough with bat or ball: Ian Greig (Tony's brother), David Capel, Mark Ealham, Dermot Reeve, Ronnie Irani and Adam Hollioake. The tragic Ben Hollioake necessarily remains an enigmatic figure. Of this whole group, Lewis could bat and bowl but he was no Botham. Then came the theory of choosing wicket-keeper batsmen and making them all-rounders. Alec Stewart was clearly the best but his average as a batsman was nearly twenty runs higher than when he played as a keeper, when his figures were scarcely different from those of the man he replaced, Jack Russell. Then came Flintoff.

Seventeen wickets fell while 332 runs were scored in one of the most amazing days in all test cricket history. Part One was the Australian comeback and it was Lee who made the early breakthroughs in a fiery first spell, which was a marked contrast to his wild bowling of the first innings.

Trescothick was the first to depart, again waving a wand at a wide ball without moving his feet and edging to Gilchrist at 2-27. Then Vaughan was caught in two minds and bowled through the gate by a ball which kept low with just two runs added to the score. When Hoggard jabbed Lee to Hayden in the gully to make the total 4-31 in the fourteenth over, the pendulum had probably swung back in Australia's favour. Lee's opening spell was his best for the series as he stood up to lead the pace attack in McGrath's absence. England's newcomers Bell and Pietersen were left to do the repair work.

After three single-figure innings, Bell worked hard but Hampshire team-mates Pietersen and Warne seemed set for a battle of the titans. Pietersen hoisted Warne for two sixes over mid-wicket but the spin maestro then ripped a leg break past his adversary's probing bat and appeared to strike his elbow, although the batsman was given out caught behind for 20. The total was 5-72 and three runs later Bell left for 21 courtesy of a faint edge to Gilchrist from another ball which turned appreciably out of the rough. Flintoff and Geraint Jones were now at the crease and English supporters groaned as Flintoff appeared to strain his left shoulder after striking a ball towards point with a flourishing follow-through. At lunch England were 6-95 after 33 overs and the first session had clearly been won by Australia who captured five wickets for 70 runs. England's lead was now 194 with four wickets in hand.

Australia continued to up the ante in the first over of the afternoon session when a hostile, short delivery from Lee saw Jones fend the ball to Ponting in the slips at 7-101. New batsman Giles stuck around for three-quarters of an hour and helped Flintoff add 30 but when Warne removed him and Harmison with consecutive deliveries, Australia appeared to be well on top. For the second time in the match, however, Flintoff would turn the tide of play.

In a crash/slash/smash next half-hour, the odds swung back towards England. Receiving able support from last-man Simon Jones, Flintoff took two towering sixes off Kasprowicz's third over which went for 20 runs and then cracked 6,4,6 off successive balls from Lee with the first six careering straight to the top of a grandstand. The last pair added 51 in just 7.3 overs before Warne bowled Flintoff for 73, with six fours and four sixes, right on tea. Warne ended with innings figures of 23.1-7-46-6 and ten wickets for the match, causing former England captain Mike Brearley to write in the *Observer*:

> He has done more to shift the game from a relentless cycle of fast-medium bowling to a theatre of subtlety, variation and psychological and technical intensity. There is a case for thinking of cricket, even at its best, as a Theatre of the Absurd; with Warne it is also a Theatre of Cruelty and Delight, but never of the Banal.

The English lead was a highly competitive 282 runs and for its part, Australia would commit to a fight. Hayden and Langer made an impressive start by adding 47 at nearly four runs an over before Flintoff became the fourth bowler called into the attack. On a hat-trick, after ending the first innings with two wickets in two balls, Langer, on 28, avoided calamity from his first ball but was cleaned up by the second which he edged onto his stumps. Flintoff had made an important breakthrough and four balls later he enticed Ponting to drive and succeed only in nicking a slight away-swinger to the wicket-keeper. 2-48.

England was back in the game but surely Martyn, who had peeled off 1353 runs at 56.37 with six centuries in the 2004 calendar year, and who, in 2001, joined Bradman (and Bill Johnston) as only the third Australian to average 100 on an English tour, would have some answers. Some, but not enough. Hayden and Martyn added 34 in ten overs and the Queensland left-hander looked to be running into form when he hammered Simon Jones for two boundaries to reach 31, only to be undone in the same over by reverse swing and an edge to Trescothick at first slip. At 3-82 Clarke joined Martyn and again the Australians must have hoped that at least one of their champion batsmen could make more than a modest contribution.

It was not to be. As Peter English remarked on the Cricinfo website, 'Waiting for a saviour, the rescuers kept failing their auditions. Plenty of starts looked smooth, but England's pace quartet, backed up by Ashley Giles, allowed no substance.' When Vaughan brought Hoggard back for his second spell he immediately claimed Martyn, who drove weakly to mid-wicket to depart for 28 with the score 4-107, and before the rot truly set in at the 130s. Giles did what he had to do when he removed both Katich and Gilchrist in successive overs. Katich attempted to drive an arm ball which pitched in the rough and was caught at slip and Gilchrist flicked a simple catch to mid-on. And when Flintoff stormed in to trap Gillespie lbw for nought, the scorecard revealed a sorry progression: 5-134, 6-136, 7-137.

The youngster Clarke was left surveying the damage from the other end until he finally found an ally in Warne until the last over of the day. Warne stated in his column in the *Times* that, when he had joined 'Pup' with 145 to win, he had said: 'Let's have some fun and enjoy it.' The pair did so, adding 38 in nine overs, with Warne delighting in two pulls shots for six off Giles on his way to 20. Clarke, by then, had moved calmly on to 30 when he was deceived by a slow leg-cutter from Harmison which shattered his wicket with just two balls of the day remaining. All Australian hopes of winning seemed to have evaporated as the day ended at 8-175. With 107 runs to get and just two wickets in hand it was – as the cliché has it – a big ask.

DAY 4

What should have been a formality for Michael Vaughan and his team ended 99 gut-gnawing minutes later with an English win by just two runs, the smallest victory margin in Ashes test history.

At the outset it seemed strange that Vaughan ceded an advantage to Australia when Warne and Lee resumed. Instead of having more close catchers in position, the English captain had three catchers near the bat and four guarding the boundaries, leaving plenty of singles available – singles the Australians were happy to take.

Warne struck the first boundary of the day in Harmison's third over during which the lanky fast bowler gave away 13 runs. Indeed, both he and Flintoff pitched the ball too short as the 200 was raised. More importantly for the visitors, the margin was reduced by 25 at nearly a run a ball. Vaughan now brought Giles back into the attack but unlike the first innings, he neither took wickets nor reduced the scoring rate. Two overs from the orthodox spinner yielded 16 runs. Thanks very much.

Warne used unorthodox enterprise and created room for some powerful leg-side blows but was moving so far across to his off-side that it seemed only a matter of time before a yorker from Flintoff or Harmison might see him undone. This is what happened but not in the manner imagined. When the target had fallen to 62, Flintoff pitched a ball behind his legs and most observers thought he had been bowled. Instead, in avoiding the swinging delivery, Warne went back and across but lost his balance and knocked his stumps down with his back heel, the first hit-wicket dismissal of his career. Warne's 42 with four fours and two sixes was an innings of great character but his departure at 9-220 caused the ground to erupt as the England players, and most of the partisan supporters in the crowd, thought Super Freddie had brought them home. Not yet.

Michael Kasprowicz is a very proud cricketer. Early in his career as an Australian player he spoke at an Australian Cricket Society meeting in Adelaide and, when asked by one of the members whether he hoped to be the 'second Glenn McGrath' his reply was: 'No! I'm the first Michael Kasprowicz.' Kasper has had an in-and-out career in the Australian side since 1996 and his place as third pace-man had been lost at times to the swing of Damien Fleming, the firepower of Lee, and exchanged with big-hearted Queensland team-mate Andy Bichel. For the previous eighteen months, however, he had kept Lee out of the team while enjoying a late renaissance and passing 100 test wickets. Now he would join him in the middle.

Kasprowicz had a test batting average of 10.52 from 33 matches and a top score of only 25 but he was far from a no-hoper. He had over 4000 runs to his name in first-class cricket at an average of 17, including eleven half-centuries and a top score of 92. Kasprowicz took a four off Flintoff and he and Lee made merry with 13 off an over by Giles. The best way for Australia to win was to continue attacking. When drinks were taken after an hour, 77 runs had come in 13.2 overs. For England the margin had now been reduced to a worrying 30.

It was about this time that comparisons began to be raised with the Melbourne test of 1982. On that occasion Allan Border and Jeff

Thomson added 70 for the last wicket and fell an agonising three runs short of victory when Thomson was caught off a relayed catch from Chris Tavare to Geoff Miller off the bowling of Ian Botham, giving Botham his 100th Ashes wicket. There were big differences also. Border and Thomson worked their side back into the game using defence. Their partnership lasted 129 minutes and an irony of their defeat was that they had declined to run 29 easy singles during their stand.

The irony for England had they lost this game would have been the 40 extras they gave away during the final innings, including 13 byes and 18 no-balls. Harmison replaced Flintoff who was then immediately reinstated in the attack. Flintoff maintained his aggression and struck Lee on the left hand with 20 runs needed. With 14 runs left, Flintoff pitched short and Kasprowicz lifted the ball to third man but the normally reliable outfielder Simon Jones moved late and grassed the catch. Had England blown their last winning chance? When Flintoff fired his next ball, a no-ball, down the leg side it went for four byes and the margin was nine. Heads sank.

The Australians may not have determined to get the runs in singles but now that the prize was theirs for the taking perhaps it was understandable that nerves should play a huge part for both teams. Six singles were added and the heretical thought may have passed Australian minds that it was just as well in this situation that Kasper was playing instead of McGrath. The Australians needed just three runs to win when Harmison charged in and delivered the ball of his career. It was a wicked, in-dipping bouncer which jammed into Kasprowicz's ribs and he succeeded only in gloving down the leg side to be out for a valiant 20. The irony for England was that Geraint Jones, who had kept wickets so clumsily in the series that he would have struggled to hold the gloves in a club side, now took a great catch low to his left. England were home.

Counterfactual history is a bit of a parlour game. The 'what ifs' can certainly be more fun than 'what is' or 'what actually happened'.

But if Australia had won the game, the series would have been what is termed down under as 'cactus' or, to use an older phrase, 'dead as a doornail'. In the words of Andrew Miller on Cricinfo: 'One game apiece would leave everything to play for, but 2–0 down and the floating voters would drift away and the finest England team of a generation would have been exposed as just another herd of nearly-men. It was a fate too horrific to contemplate.'

English skipper Vaughan acknowledged as much in a post-match interview when he said: 'If we had gone two down in the series, I think the Ashes would have gone. I don't think we could have recovered from that against this Australian side.' Naturally Vaughan didn't imagine the result would be so close and was elated with the win. But his further remark that 'even when it was getting tight I felt we were going to create opportunities and I just kept telling everyone that to force one mistake was all that was needed' was both the belated reflection of a lucky man, yet one who had kept his head in a crisis. Ponting admitted he had made a mistake in putting England in to bat but thought that his side's effort in almost grabbing an astonishing victory brought a lot of positives for his team.

The 'what is' was Flintoff – and his man-of-the-match performance was delightful both to witness and to contemplate. Flintoff's 141 runs and seven wickets outgunned Warne's ten wickets and game forty. Flintoff was the new Botham but as Richard Hobson pointed out in a fine analytical article in the *Times*, the trajectories of their careers were different. Botham burst out of the blocks as a bowler who could bat and his first 20 tests saw him score 997 runs at 39.88 and take 100 wickets at 19.36; Flintoff, by contrast, began as a batsman – an under-achieving batsman – but he has made late leaps as a bowler. Botham, after 51 tests – the exact half-way point of his career – had made 2833 runs at 38.80 and taken 231 wickets at 23.06, which was a long way ahead of Flintoff's figures for his 49 tests of 2383 runs at 32.64 and 130 wickets at 32.84. However, the new man was improving. In his last 20 tests (as Hobson showed),

Flintoff had averaged 45 with the bat and taken 78 wickets at 24.37 with the ball.

So much for the statistics. The adjectives praising the hero flowed thick and fast but perhaps James Lawton in the *Independent* put it best: 'Flintoff was untameable, an untrammelled spirit, a force of nature, a whirlwind ... As a batsman he was herculean. As a bowler he was awash with adrenalin.' In the modern commercial sporting world, one of the most important considerations is what a star is worth and two of the most appealing (as well as marketable) elements in the game are the ability to hit long and hard, and bowl fast. Flintoff's playing contract with England earns him around £350,000 a year but the vigour of his play, including hitting nine sixes off the best team in the world, make him a sponsors' dream worth millions of pounds.

If the game was a boon for Flintoff, it was naturally a boon for English cricket. With the series now locked at one game apiece, the caravan would roll to Old Trafford for the next match four days away.

Michael Vaughan

•TRENT BRIDGE 2005•

THINKING THE UNTHINKABLE

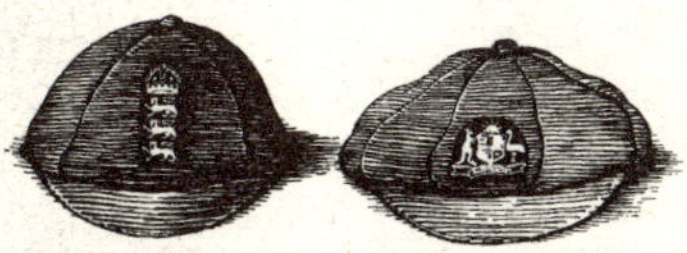

The series is tied 1–1 after England is denied and Australia fights back at Old Trafford. England looks to stamp its authority and begins to do so with a commanding 477 in the first innings. Australia whimpers out for 218, courtesy of Simon Jones' reverse swing, and is forced to follow on for the first time since early in Allan Border's captaincy. An ankle injury to Jones hobbles England's attack and Australia digs in hard the second time around, leaving England 129 runs to win. Shane Warne and Brett Lee give lion-hearted displays as England makes a manic start, wobbles, calms, and then wobbles again. Where two or three thirties are needed from top bats, Marcus Trescothick, Andrew Strauss, Kevin Pietersen and Andrew Flintoff oblige with twenties. At 7-116 the Australians can win the match and retain the Ashes but England finds heroes in plain men as Ashley Giles and Matthew Hoggard see them through.

ENGLAND v AUSTRALIA 2005 (4th Test)

Played at Trent Bridge, Nottingham on 25,26,27,28 August.
Toss: England. Result: ENGLAND won by 3 wickets.

ENGLAND

M.E. Trescothick	b Tait	65	c Ponting b Warne	27
A.J. Strauss	c Hayden b Warne	35	c Clarke b Warne	23
M.P. Vaughan*	c Gilchrist b Ponting	58	c Hayden b Warne	0
I.R. Bell	c Gilchrist b Tait	3	c Kasprowicz b Lee	3
M.J. Clarke	c G. Jones b Giles	40	b Harmison	30
K.P. Pietersen	c Gilchrist b Lee	45	c Gilchrist b Lee	23
A. Flintoff	lbw b Tait	102	b Lee	26
G.O. Jones†	c & b Kasprowicz	85	c Kasprowicz b Warne	3
A.F. Giles	lbw b Warne	15	not out	7
M.J. Hoggard	c Gilchrist b Warne	10	not out	8
S.J. Harmison	st Gilchrist b Warne	2		
S.P. Jones	not out	15		
Extras (B 1, LB 15, W 1, NB 25)		42	(LB 4, NB 5)	9
Total		**477**	**(7 wickets)**	**129**

AUSTRALIA

J.L. Langer	c Bell b Hoggard	27	c Bell b Giles	61
M.L. Hayden	lbw b Hoggard	7	c Giles b Flintoff	26
R.T. Ponting*	lbw b S. Jones	1	run out	48
D.R. Martyn	lbw b Hoggard	1	c G. Jones b Flintoff	13
M.J. Clarke	lbw b Harmison	36	c G. Jones b Hoggard	56
S.M. Katich	c Strauss b S. Jones	45	lbw b Harmison	59
A.C. Gilchrist†	c Strauss b Flintoff	27	lbw b Hoggard	11
S.K. Warne	c Bell b S. Jones	0	st G. Jones b Giles	45
B. Lee	c Bell b S. Jones	47	not out	26
M.S. Kasprowicz	b S. Jones	5	c G. Jones b Harmison	19
S.W. Tait	not out	3	b Harmison	4
Extras (LB 2, W 1, NB 16)		19	(B 1, LB 4, NB 14)	19
Total		**218**		**387**

AUSTRALIA	**O**	**M**	**R**	**W**	**O**	**M**	**R**	**W**
Lee	32	2	131	1	12	0	51	3
Kasprowicz	32	3	122	1	2	0	19	0
Tait	24	4	97	3	4	0	24	0
Warne	29.1	4	102	4	13.5	2	31	4
Ponting	6	2	9	1				
ENGLAND								
Harmison	9	1	48	1	30	5	93	3
Hoggard	15	3	70	3	27	7	72	2
S. Jones	14.1	4	44	5	4	0	15	0
Flintoff	11	1	54	1	29	4	83	2
Giles					28	3	107	2
Bell					6	2	12	0

FALL OF WICKETS

	E	A	E	A
Wkt	1st	1st	2nd	2nd
1st	105	20	50	32
2nd	137	21	129	36
3rd	146	22	155	57
4th	213	58	161	57
5th	241	99	261	103
6th	418	157	277	111
7th	450	157	314	116
8th	450	163	342	
9th	454	175	373	
10th	477	218	387	

Umpires: Aleem Dar (Pak) and S.A. Bucknor (WI)
TV Umpire: M.R. Benson
Match Referee: R.S. Madugalle (SL)

Simon Jones was in fine form

A lot happened in the seventeen days between the second and fourth tests. Most notably, the greatest draw in test cricket history at Old Trafford. It was a game where Australia were dogged by selection problems. Where it was thought leg-spinner Stuart MacGill might join Shane Warne on a spin-friendly pitch; where Glenn McGrath was still hobbling around on crutches on the Sunday before the game and given little chance of taking part in play; where just two days before the match, Brett Lee was admitted to a Birmingham hospital, placed on an intravenous drip and given a 50-50 chance of playing; where former Australian test captain Ian Chappell and fast bowler Geoff Lawson were both critical of Matthew Hayden and felt he should temper his bullying tactics and start to play more balls on their merits; and where Ian Botham urged England to doctor the wicket to nullify Warne by producing 'a rock-hard surface with an even covering of grass, pace and bounce'.

As it turned out Old Trafford groundsman Peter Marron gave England the sort of pitch they wanted, McGrath arose Lazarus-like, Lee recovered, MacGill was not considered, and Jason Gillespie was retained for one test longer than he should have been. In the game itself Shane Warne took his 600th wicket when he got rid of Marcus Trescothick but Australia's fielding was the pits on the first day as Michael Vaughan benefited to crack a classical hundred. England then went on to a solid total of 444 on the second day before Ashley Giles' spin and Simon Jones' reverse swing wrecked the Australian innings with the visitors scrambling to avoid the follow-on. Rain ruined England's prospects on the third day when the Australians were able to regroup psychologically, and Warne and Gillespie batted Australia into a more secure position on the fourth morning for 302, although Jones finished the innings off in style with his best test figures of 6-53. In England's second innings Strauss's century was full of character and their declaration at 6-280 left Australia with 423 runs to win and 115 overs in which to get them, provided they could survive. On the last day England took wickets regularly at one end. At the other Ricky Ponting played one of the great rearguard and captain's innings of all time for 156 out of 9-371, but when he got out with 25 balls left there was just one wicket to fall. Lee and McGrath saw Australia to safety.

Although he sounded upbeat at the end of the game, and suggested his side had played better than at Edgbaston, England captain Vaughan must have been disappointed. England could certainly take more positives out of the game than Australia and, if bad weather had not robbed them of most of the crucial third day, a win would have been a virtual certainty. A weakness for England on the final day was the bowling of Giles who had performed well in the first innings. His figures of 26-4-93-0 on a fifth-day pitch, including an inability to bowl round the wicket, revealed his limitations. If Daniel Vettori, say, had been in the English side, Australia would have struggled to make

200. The Australians, and particularly Ponting, produced their own heroics and fought the game out to the finish and the series remained locked at 1–1.

The next test at Trent Bridge was ten days away and the only tour games scheduled for the Australians were a one-day fixture against Scotland in Edinburgh and a two-day 12-a-side second-class match against Northamptonshire. They polished up their golf form at Gleneagles but the one-day game at the quaint little Citylets Grange (formerly Grange Cricket Club) ground was washed out. At Northampton in a drawn game there were some curiosities. Australia made 6-374 declared from 96 overs, dismissed Northampton in fifty overs for 169, and then got extra batting practice to reach 2-226 in its second innings. Hayden and Michael Clarke made hundreds in the first innings and Simon Katich and Justin Langer half-centuries in the second but what was curious was the bowling. McGrath, Lee, Michael Kasprowicz and Shaun Tait all got solid workouts but MacGill, who had been named in the twelve, did not bowl. The only spin delivered in the Northampton innings was three overs of gentle off-spin by Brad Hodge. A notable omission from the line-up in the game was Gillespie. After 70 tests and 251 wickets his card had been marked.

For Tait his chance at Northampton was a rare opportunity to impress and he did so with figures of 2-52 from 14 overs. The fourth bowler used, he took two wickets in his first spell, the first that of former test batsman Usman Afzaal from a poor pull shot, and the second with a yorker which removed the leg stump of former England A batsman David Sales. He also forced opening batsman Tim Roberts to retire hurt from a ball which burst through the grille of his helmet and left him with a gash above his eye requiring five stitches.

The position of third pace-man would come down to a choice between Tait and Kasprowicz with the conservative view favouring Kasprowicz on account of his accuracy. Tait's selection, on the other hand, was supported by former test greats Dennis Lillee and Jeff Thomson (with whom his slinging action was perhaps unwisely compared), as well as by his South Australian captain Darren Lehmann, and Queensland opening batsman Jimmy Maher, who said he'd never faced a more awkward bowler in a decade of state, county and international cricket. As if to emphasise his potential danger, Tait worked over Justin Langer at the Tuesday net session, bowling the opener with a fast inswinger and then dropping him to his knees with a fast, short ball which struck him in the midriff.

The blow saw Australian coach John Buchanan sprint across the outfield to check on Langer, one of the toughest competitors in the game, but he left training with further worries as McGrath felt soreness in his bowling elbow and was sent for scans to determine the extent of the injury. Suddenly, for the third test in a row, McGrath's fitness was dominating Australia's preparation.

England maintained an unchanged team and it must be admitted one player had a good escape from the spotlight with Andrew Flintoff getting away to France the previous week. England's strength was their attack, which had taken 59 Australian wickets in three tests and was worth recognising: Steve Harmison with speed, bounce, seam movement and a slower ball; Flintoff with speed, bounce, in-swing, and reverse swing from both over and round the wicket; Matthew Hoggard with outswing and straighter deliveries; Simon Jones with speed, outswing and reverse swing; and Ashley Giles with orthodox spin and an arm ball.

Heavy rain fell the day before the game but when groundsman Steve Birks lifted the covers in mid-afternoon it revealed a straw-covered pitch with a smattering of dry grass. It was predicted that such a strip might give slight assistance to bowlers early but would later become a good batting wicket. The main prediction was that England were better equipped for the conditions with Hoggard and Jones likely to play an increased role in the game with conventional swing. The ground had tended to favour swing more since the redevelopment of the ground at the Radcliffe Road End and overcast conditions were tipped for the start of play.

||| DAY 1

Before the game began McGrath dropped out of the side allowing Kasprowicz to retain his place, and then spectators were treated to a spot of farce as two impostors in umpiring attire walked to the centre of the ground and opened beer cans. The men, who had attempted a similar stunt in the previous test, entered the ground from the Bridgford Road side, removed the bails and while one made a signal calling for a TV replay another signalled a wide. They were arrested and charged with aggravated trespass and missed the cricket before being released from the Bridewell police station at 8pm.

England and Australia were even at the end of the opening day but when England really had the opportunity to turn the screws on a sloppy Australian fielding side and ill-disciplined attack, they merely gave them a tweak. The Australians dropped easy catches, bungled a run-out chance, and in the first session bowled the ludicrous total of eighteen no-balls.

Trescothick and Strauss got away to an unruffled start against Lee and Kasprowicz with Tait stationed at mid-on and offering support to his fellow quicks as they walked back to their marks. Trescothick, in particular, started to strike the ball powerfully into the gaps and after ten overs the score had moved to 35. In the eleventh Ponting called Tait on and although Strauss pulled him for two off a ball which clocked 93mph, it was not a convincing stroke. Tait's second over was even less convincing, however, as Trescothick hammered him for two boundaries and he gave away 11 runs.

England's fifty came inside the hour as Trescothick threatened to bully the newcomer. Ponting brought Warne on in the 17th over but, with the ball turning slowly, Trescothick launched a straight drive for six in his second over as he moved to his own half-century. The batsmen brought up their second 100 partnership of the series one minute later but when the total had reached 105 Strauss was out in freakish circumstances. In Warne's third over Strauss attempted a paddle sweep and bottom-edged the ball on to his foot and an easy catch went to Hayden at first slip. The Australians appealed but umpire Steve Bucknor was uncertain. In the past he would have consulted his colleague Aleem Dar but a recent innovation allowing the third umpire to adjudicate on bump-ball decisions saw Mark Benson view the television replay and give Strauss out.

If Strauss was aggrieved, Trescothick was fortunate. Lee, who came back to replace Tait after his five overs went for 26 runs, caused Trescothick to chop a ball on to his stumps, only to discover he had overstepped the crease. With Vaughan now at the wicket and looking at ease, England went to lunch well on top at 1-129 with Trescothick 62 and Vaughan 14.

Rain stopped play and the batting flow. A shower held up the game for an hour, then it resumed for 3.1 overs in which the score was taken to 1-134, then there was a longer rain break from 2.23 until 3.55 during which tea was taken. When the players came back in the final session, batting was tougher.

In fact, it was only four balls old when Tait claimed his first wicket from a full-length delivery which swung past Trescothick's attempted drive and knocked back his off stump. Trescothick's 65 included eight fours and a six but despite a promising start and a let-off, he had still not been able to reach three figures against Australia.

England were now 2-137 and soon 3-146 when Bell edged a Tait outswinger to give Gilchrist his 300th test dismissal and the debutant a second wicket in the space of eleven balls. Pietersen joined Vaughan and the batsmen unveiled some fine strokes, including a special cover drive by Vaughan off Lee which split the field and sped to the boundary at such a rate that the fielders scarcely moved. In between, though, there were some bad misses, especially a caught-and-bowled chance which Pietersen offered to Kasprowicz when on 14. Hayden also made two errors, dropping Vaughan on 30 from Kasprowicz at backward point, and failing to run out Pietersen on 23. England appeared to be coasting in the 46th over when Ponting brought himself into the attack in what might have seemed a desperate move but proved a successful one. In his fifth over Ponting induced Vaughan to give a thin edge to Gilchrist to take his fifth test wicket and first since 1999. Vaughan's dismissal for 58 at 4-213 left the batsman stunned and came when England looked like seizing control. When more rain ended play five overs later the score had advanced to 4-229 with Pietersen 33 and Flintoff 8.

One of the interesting post-mortems on the day's play was that Ponting's decision to bowl himself was an acknowledgement of Australia's need for an all-rounder. It seemed to be a very English reflection when Gilchrist had effectively been Australia's all-rounder for the past six years. Given his fantastic run-scoring at number seven, a number six batsman often seemed a luxury. Of course, it could also be argued that in Australia's years as top dog since 1995 with McGrath, Warne, Gillespie, MacGill, Lee and other bowlers in full flight there was scarcely any need for more than a four-man attack. Now came suggestions that Australia had erred by not selecting Shane Watson or Andrew Symonds as all-rounders. They were fine batsmen but was their bowling up to test standard?

In the 1950s and 1960s Australia had a succession of brilliant all-rounders in Keith Miller, Ron Archer (briefly), Richie Benaud and Alan Davidson but in the last forty years just two who might have filled that role: the explosive Gary Gilmour, often seen as a second Davidson in his 15 tests, and Greg Matthews, a gritty batsman with a test average over forty and an able second spinner. Steve Waugh had originally been selected for Australia as an all-rounder when his medium-pace bowling was penetrative but it was his batting which maintained his team place. Michael Bevan might also have played more for Australia if he had developed his spin bowling. Batsmen in the current side such as Katich and Clarke can certainly bowl a bit as Warne and Lee are bowlers who can bat. The question in settling a side is balance. And quality.

The morning session the following day would be crucial for both sides. If Pietersen and Flintoff could survive until lunch,

England would build a winning platform. A total of 400 seemed a suitable figure. John Buchanan quoted former Australian captain Bill Lawry about adding two wickets to the score and seeing how it looked but that would mean early breakthroughs would be necessary.

||| DAY 2

That man Flintoff, with more than a little help from his colleagues Geraint Jones and Matthew Hoggard, enabled England to stamp their authority on the match and begin to break the series apart.

The day didn't start out that way as Warne, operating from the Pavilion End, gave the ball a lot of air in attempting to entice Flintoff into a miscued drive. The batsman, however, was in a state of early denial and when locked on the back foot he was lucky to escape an lbw appeal which had a lot of Australian lounge lizards kicking their television sets in. Flintoff had not added to his overnight score and the let-off was a wake-up call. Thereafter his foot placement was precise as he read and responded to Warne with aplomb.

The previous evening's script of Pietersen–Flintoff heroics did not eventuate. Pietersen had cracked a couple of Lee deliveries to the boundary but to the first ball of the fifth over he was caught behind for 45, edging a full-length ball. Trescothick, Vaughan and Pietersen had all received reprieves but none had truly cashed in. Buchanan might have smiled but it was difficult to know what Ponting was thinking. Flintoff was in passive mode, Geraint Jones was new to the crease and yet Ponting kept four men patrolling the boundaries. Where was the pressure?

Without any pressure Flintoff took charge. A four off Warne through the covers, before going down on one knee to hoist the leg-spinner into the Fox Road stand for a huge six, got the scoreboard rolling, and he found an ally in Jones who batted stylishly after easing a cover drive from a Lee half-volley to the boundary. Old England might have collapsed from 5-241 to 290 all out. New

England would not and there was little sign of either the pace-men or Warne making any impact.

The 300 came up off 77.4 overs and Ponting took the new ball at 11.52pm as soon as it was available, hoping for a couple of wickets. Instead, it served merely as an opportunity to punish different bowlers. One of the strokes of the day was Geraint Jones' cracking cover drive off a fast full-length outswinger from Tait which raced to the boundary. When England took lunch at 5-344 with Flintoff 73 and Jones 34 the pair had raised their 100 partnership, the session had delivered 115 runs to England, and just one wicket had been taken by the Australians.

Jones opened up after lunch and outscored Flintoff who reached his century with a quiet push to square leg off Warne for a single. England's hero celebrated in the calmest manner, removing his helmet and raised both arms to all sections of the crowd which gave him a standing ovation. Flintoff's manner epitomised his play which had been cool and composed and he seemed intent on another 50 runs at least, pushing England past 500.

It was a shock then when he swung across the line of a full-length Tait inswinger and was given out lbw for 102 made in 201 minutes from 132 balls with fourteen fours and a six. Flintoff looked disappointed as he left the field, possibly because Tait's delivery might have missed the leg stump. However, his magnificent partnership of 177 with Jones from 39.1 overs was the highest of the series and had put England in a strong position.

Still, the home side would not relent and Jones maintained the impetus in partnership with Giles. He must have even been eyeing a century himself when, having added 51 in 70 balls in the afternoon session to reach 85, he inside-edged a ball on to his pad to give the persistent Kasprowicz a return catch, and his only reward for the innings. The score was then 7-450 and although Warne ran through the tail, there was some purposeful resistance by Hoggard, and useful blows by Simon Jones, before the innings ended for 477 and tea was taken. Warne again led the attack to finish with four wickets, Tait impressed with his three scalps but Kasprowicz bowled without luck. Thirty-four overs remained.

Matthew Hoggard had thus far been a bit-player in the series. For a man who had taken 26 wickets at 25.50 in the series against South Africa at the beginning of the year, including match figures of 12-205 in the Fourth test at New Wanderers Stadium in Johannesburg, he had been used lightly by Vaughan. In picking up 7 wickets at 33.42 from 56 overs in the first three matches, however, he had dismissed Hayden twice, Langer, Ponting, Martyn, Clarke and Gillespie, and only Clarke's 91 at Lord's had been a substantial score. Now he took centre stage.

From his first over Hoggard's late outswinger – a sharp indipper to the left-handers – had the batsmen all at sea so that Vaughan kept him going for eleven overs straight. Langer and Hayden made a watchful start but it wasn't until the tenth over that Hoggard accounted for Hayden with a late inswinger. The batsman had got an inside edge to the previous delivery but Aleem Dar made no hesitation in giving him out when the very next ball struck his right pad. 1-20.

Next came two more lbw decisions where the visitors could feel they received rough justice. In the next over from Simon Jones umpire Bucknor raised his finger to send an incredulous Australian captain on his way. According to televised replays the ball hit the inside edge of Ponting's bat before striking his pad at 2-21. Next over Aleem Dar gave Martyn out to Hoggard the same way. Cricketing *Ground Hog Day*? No – a different batsman! Batsmen are supposed to take the good with the bad. One good lbw: two bad. 3-22 and Australia's innings was rocked to its foundations.

Clarke joined Langer and Australia's position was retrieved. Fractionally. At 58 Hoggard gained his third victim when Langer edged on to his thigh and Bell took a simple catch at short leg. Eight runs later Hoggard gave way to Flintoff who was typically fast and furious, especially against Katich. Clarke was both elegant and skilful, and struck five boundaries in his 36 before Harmison speared the third ball of his fifth over sharply into his pads to gain a fourth lbw decision with what turned out to be the last delivery of the day. Australia were 5-99 with Katich on 20 and a mammoth task was required of him and Gilchrist the next day with the prospect of a follow-on staring them in the face.

That situation had been avoided on the third day at Old Trafford but here with 179 runs still needed it seemed far more likely. The previous time Australia had been in that position was early in Allan Border's captaincy in September 1988. Or to put it another way, given the presence of John Howard and John Major at the Lord's test, it had occurred during Bob Hawke's prime ministership. The occasion was the First test at the National Stadium in Karachi and, in reply to Pakistan's 9-469 declared, Australia were out for 165 and 116. Bad times!

It was perhaps surprising given Gilchrist's task as the next man in that he was also a player spokesman at the end of play. In part he commented:

> England are doing to us what we have done to other sides for a number of years. They have shown the rest of the world that they are a very dangerous team at the top of their game. In my time I do not think I have come across a bowling attack that has worked so well hunting as a pack.

Was Gilchrist's admission likely to draw the I-told-you-so response from critics who argued that Ponting's side (and maybe Waugh's and Taylor's teams as well) were overrated? They would be harsh critics if they did so but few would claim that England's attack hunted quite as well as a pack as the great West Indies fast men. Furthermore, was Gilchrist's admission part of the Australians' genuine (if new-found) respect for their opponents? Probably, but maybe it could also be seen as a shrewd psychological manoeuvre. After previous attempts to undermine the confidence of the English players, perhaps they would now try to lull them into a false sense of security. If so, one who wouldn't be sucked in would be Flintoff. 'We are in a great position with all those runs on the board,' he said. 'But we are not daft and we know Australia has some fine players, so we have to be disciplined – that is imperative. We cannot get ahead of ourselves and we must stay with the moment!' It was wise to be wary.

||| DAY 3

Honours were about even on the day with the Australian resistance going bang-whimper-bang to see out the first innings. The second Australian innings offered cricket of a more solid variety. While England held an overall advantage, Australia made a respectable 341 runs for the loss of nine wickets.

Katich and Gilchrist started off with some audacious batting. After two quiet overs Hoggard quickly became yesterday's hero as both batsmen grabbed the attack by the scruff of the neck. Hoggard's next two overs cost 32 and, with Flintoff's over in between going for nine, England started to lose the plot. Gilchrist, in full flight, was the one man England feared and, when he pulled Hoggard for four and struck him straight for six, hearts were pumping and jumping. Gilchrist also inspired Katich who unleashed two cover drives for four. Hoggard's last over cost 22, an Ashes record, and a reminder of what Australia's stars could do if the bowling strayed.

Simon Jones came on for the ninth over and made an immediate double breakthrough. With his second ball Katich, on 45, searched for another stroke through the covers but succeeded only in slicing to the squarer of two gullies to be caught by Strauss. Next ball Warne was caught from a leading edge to Bell in the covers.

The whimpering began with 6-157, 7-157 and continued at 8-163 and 9-175. Gilchrist saw the demise of Katich and Warne but then had to deal with Flintoff who had proved his nemesis during the summer. Flintoff gave him little room and Gilchrist, having reached

27, attempted a cut too close to his body. The ball flew high and wide to the left of Strauss at second slip but the fielder took a spectacular catch. Lee and Kasprowicz were now together but the circumstances were unlike their stand at Edgbaston. England remained on fire as Jones smashed through his Glamorgan team-mate's stumps. Tait joined Lee and a first-class average of 10.96 from 27 matches meant that while he was not the worst number 11 in the world, he could not be expected to hold up a rampant attack for long. Lee, however, was not ready for a limp surrender. Having been struck on the shoulder by a short ball from Flintoff he simply went berserk, striking Harmison out of the ground twice and a third six over the ropes.

The strokes were as big as any yet mustered in the series, including those by Pietersen and Flintoff. Lee commandeered the strike so that the last wicket stand with Tait added 43 of which Tait contributed three runs from nine balls. Lee's firebrand 47 came at better than a run a ball, and gave his team heart, until he skyed Jones to Bell at third man giving the Welshman 5-44 from 14.1 overs, his second five-wicket haul in successive matches and four wickets from 31 balls in his morning's spell. As Simon Wilde observed in the *Sunday Times*:

> If there's been a secret weapon in this series, it hasn't been Shane Warne's slider, or Stephen Harmison's slower ball, but Jones: Jones in all his forms – his fast arm, his newly discovered outswinger, his command of reverse swing and his unswerving belief that this is his time.

Australia's final total of 218 was better than it might have been and the 119 runs added off 18.4 overs was exhilarating stuff. Still, the total was 259 short of England and the bowlers were fresh. Vaughan enforced the follow-on with Australia facing awkward overs before lunch. The English skipper kept faith with Hoggard's swing by throwing him the new ball first and in a wily move kept Jones going. The Australians reached 0-14 at the interval with Langer 9 and Hayden 5.

The visitors brought their fifty up in 12.5 overs but immediately Flintoff had Hayden caught in the gully for 26 by Giles off a thick-edged drive. Again Hayden failed to build an innings and his dismissal revealed how much he (like Gilchrist) was outpsyched by Vaughan's placement of a sweeper on either side of the wicket. Shortly afterwards Simon Jones left the ground with a sore right ankle, a heavy blow to the fielding side. Ponting and Langer now came together in a productive stand although Langer was fortunate to survive a slips chance to Strauss off Flintoff on 37. At tea the Australian batting looked more secure at 1-115 with Langer 54 and Ponting 28.

The first hour of the final session saw the match tip England's way. Langer added just seven runs when he became Giles' first victim at 2-129 in the bowler's fourth over, from a catch off pad and glove to Bell at short-leg. It is a worrying sign when batsmen fail to learn from previous errors as this was the third time in the series that Langer had been snared by the Giles–Bell combination.

England kept the game tight after Langer was out, with Hoggard's three consecutive maiden overs maintaining pressure and this contributed in part to Ponting's controversial run-out. Ponting had reached 48 and the total 155 when Martyn stroked a ball into the covers and took off for a single, only for substitute fielder Gary Pratt to collect the ball and throw down the stumps at the wicket-keeper's end from about fifteen yards. The 23-year-old Pratt was recognised as a fielding specialist, although the Australians could hardly have known that as he was not even playing first-class cricket with Durham in the current season. But that was only part of the problem.

Ponting delayed his departure, appeared to speak angrily to umpire Aleem Dar, exchanged words with some English players, and then television images showed him cursing as he went off. He also gave a spray to English coach Duncan Fletcher on the pavilion balcony, his actions undoubtedly offending against the 'spirit of

Ponting loses out to Gary Pratt's excellent throw

cricket' clause in the Australian Player's Code of Conduct. Ponting's dismissal, however, came at an important time in the game and the Australians were annoyed at what they believed was England's abuse of regulations governing the use of twelfth men. While players are supposed to be injured or ill in order to leave the field, there were accusations that England's bowlers had been freshening up with massages between spells.

Pratt was on the field in place of Simon Jones who had a legitimate injury and Law 2.2 states that: 'The opposing captain shall have no right of objection to any player acting as a substitute, nor as to where the substitute shall field.' Perhaps the law was in need of an overhaul. England used four twelfth men in this game: Nottinghamshire's Graeme Swann and Samit Patel, Pratt and their fielding coach, Warwickshire's Trevor Penney. That might have been bad enough but thirteen players had taken the field as substitutes during the series. The others were Somerset's John Francis and John Hildreth at Lord's; Swann and Pratt at Edgbaston, along with Warwickshire's Jim Troughton and Jonathon Trott; and Lancashire's Paul Horton and Oliver Newby, and Worcestershire's Daryl Mitchell and Stephen Peters at Old Trafford. It seemed a bit glib of Fletcher to say, 'If someone wants to try and take a single into the covers and gets run out, whose fault is that?' Batting is all about risk assessment and balancing probabilities. Test cricketers playing against each other work out individual's weaknesses and capabilities. When running, a batsman backs his judgement against a fielder he knows. Too many substitutes is too many wild cards in a pack.

Martyn left shortly after, dabbing at a Flintoff delivery which straightened and giving a fine touch to Geraint Jones at 4-161. The position might have been worse when a stumping chance from Clarke off Giles went begging. Had it been taken Flintoff would undoubtedly have been let loose at Gilchrist. Instead Australia avoided further losses. When bad light ended play at 6.10pm, the visitors had taken their total to 4-222 with Clarke 39 and Katich 24.

With Australia trailing by 37, much would depend on the batsmen in occupation and on Simon Jones whose ankle injury would be assessed before play. Jones bowled only four overs before leaving the field, having a hospital check-up which proved inconclusive, and being fitted with a surgical boot as a precautionary measure. England coped in his absence but if Australia could dig in and pass 400, a run chase of 150 might yet produce another exciting climax.

||| DAY 4

The fourth morning was old-fashioned test cricket. Pure grit. Clarke was occasionally edgy against Giles but he and Katich put their heads down and were generally in little difficulty against the old ball. At times like these Vaughan had been able to chuck the ball to Jones to get his reverse swing going but now he was an onlooker from the players' balcony. The batting pace was funereal. When Vaughan took the second new ball after just over an hour's play at 4-248 a mere 26 runs had been added in 16.2 overs. It got even slower. The next twelve overs brought 13 runs but just ten minutes before lunch Clarke snicked a Hoggard outswinger to be caught behind for 56. Clarke's innings lasted 209 minutes and he faced 170 balls with six fours and his partnership with Katich was exactly 100 when they were separated. But Australia were finally in credit. Gilchrist came in and gathered two boundaries as the break came at 5-270 with Katich 41 and Gilchrist 9. Forty-eight runs were gathered from 29 overs. Australia led by 11 with five wickets standing.

Gilchrist again had the platform for a Sir Galahad innings: something perfect, something chivalric. Then again he was as game as Ned Kelly. Time and again he has turned test matches. Time and again in this series he failed. Eleven runs in eleven balls was an insufficient offering as he was caught on his crease by a perfect Hoggard inswinger in the third over of the session. 6-277.

Simon Katich has a bit of mongrel about him, according to Steve Waugh. His innings of 59 in 262 minutes from 183 balls with four boundaries had a fair bit of mongrel in it, and he got a bit of a mongrel of a decision when Aleem Dar gave him out lbw to a Harmison delivery which appeared to have pitched outside the leg stump.

Warne's arrival at the wicket saw the Australians finally up their tempo and when Katich left at 7-314 Warne had already run along to 21. The danger for England was if the strong contributions from the Australian tailenders continued. Already in the series the last three wickets had added more than 100 runs four times: in the second innings at Lord's and Edgbaston where their 142 was more than half the team's score of 279; and in each innings at Old Trafford. Warne was in the best batting form of his career and Lee had made spirited forties at Edgbaston and in the first innings here.

Both Warne and Lee attacked but not together. Warne added 24 to Lee's 4 in five overs and got stuck into Giles, twice swinging him over the leg-side boundaries for six before being stumped off the same bowler for 45. At 8-342 Australia's lead was a very manageable 83 but Vaughan's lack of a fielder near square leg enabled Lee and Kasprowicz to work Giles away for singles whenever he pitched on leg stump. The pair who had gone so close at Edgbaston added 31 runs. Great nuisance value as England appeared to let the game drift. Finally Vaughan brought Harmison back and he made a swift end to the Australian innings for 387 at 3.22pm. While Australia's lead of 129 was small, it gave their bowlers a smaller chance. With tea being delayed there were 41 scheduled overs left for play.

When chasing a small total, two or three batsman only have to chip in with thirty apiece and you are home. The way Trescothick started it was plain he wanted to win quickly and most of the capacity crowd believed he would. In 22 balls he had run to 27 with four boundaries from drives and cuts against the new ball, Kasprowicz had gone for 19 in two overs, and England's tally was 0-32, 97 remaining. Then came Warne.

With the lead fast diminishing, Ponting called on Warne for the sixth over. Warne has throughout his career had the uncanny ability to make dramatic things happen. With his first ball he did. It spun sharply out of the footmarks outside the left-hander's off stump, caught Trescothick's pad and bat, and was snapped up by Ponting at silly point. Would English bats wobble as they had since the Gatting ball? Vaughan came in and played out a maiden. Strauss took a boundary off Lee to move to 5 so he was finally moving. Warne to Vaughan next over and the first ball again pitched in the rough, spat sharply and the captain got an outside edge to Hayden at slip. 2-36 and shades of Benaud bowling May for nought at Old Trafford in 1961. The unthinkable becomes ... thinkable.

Bell has come to the wicket to join Strauss. They hang together with Strauss doing most of the run-scoring. The fifty comes up in 11 overs and 51 minutes as if that is relevant. The crowd is cheering every run and home fans are starting to feel a little easier when the target slips under eighty. Then there's a double-strike to the Australians.

Strauss had moved to 23 when he flicked Warne to leg slip and Clarke took the catch. Unsure whether the ball carried, Strauss waited for the third umpire to confirm it. For the second time in the match Strauss is given out by television replays. He must love technology. 3-57 becomes 4-57 as Bell top-edged Lee to be caught by Kasprowicz at fine leg. A schoolboy shot by a batsman not long ago a schoolboy. Panic stations. The 72 runs required are starting to look a long way away. In situations like this you can't keep relying on the same players. Pietersen had played well with his half-centuries at Lord's and Edgbaston; Flintoff had been brilliant at Edgbaston and in the first innings here when his partnership with Geraint Jones had been claimed by many as a match-winner. Now was time for those thirties.

Lee took an enforced rest after a spell of 8-0-35-1 but Warne would continue for the remainder of the innings. Ponting gave Tait his chance and the youngster bowled commendably straight. Pietersen digs out a couple of yorkers which might have wrecked his stumps. Pietersen and Flintoff rebuild England's innings in their free aggressive manner with Flintoff looking the calmer of the two. Tait gives away three boundaries in his four overs. Ponting cannot afford the luxury. The 100 has been raised, 26 runs are needed, both batsmen are in their twenties, six wickets are required.

Ponting threw the ball to Lee for a last roll of the dice. The field is spread all over the place. There are no slips. A couple of nicks to the boundary and the game will be over. With his first ball Lee pitches it up, Pietersen drives and nicks, and Gilchrist takes a great diving catch to his right. 5-103.

Geraint Jones joins Flintoff and the first innings saviours have work to do. However, Flintoff looks calm, his technique against Warne impeccable. Lee is tearing in at his absolute fastest and with the fourth ball of his next over he bowls as good a ball as he has delivered in his career. It beats Flintoff for pace and knocks back his off stump. Lee erupts, roaring excitement from the pit of his stomach. England are 6-111, 18 runs to get, all the recognised bats are gone, four wickets in hand. Nerves start jangling.

Jones had already played brilliantly in this game, Giles had a cool head, English fans had been cheering every single, every extra for a while now. Five runs are added the difference is down to 13 when Jones elects to break free.

When it works you're a hero. When it fails you can be history. A flighted Warne leg-break appears to be there for the hitting except it isn't, or Jones isn't, and a lofted drive for six is taken by Kasprowicz at deep mid-off. Australia might not only steal the match – they might steal the Ashes in one fell swoop. It was Australia's last hurrah. Giles and Hoggard carried their side home. Lee threw everything at Hoggard – short and full – but the Yorkshireman was equal to the task and, when he short-arm-powered a Lee full toss through cover for four, it left four to get. Hoggard then took two more down to fine leg, leaving Giles to clip Warne through mid-wicket for two in the next over to win the game, and leave 15,000 fans screaming their heads off with delight.

It would be hard in the shock of the moment to think of English heroes in the second innings but Giles and Hoggard make two. In the after-the-match interviews Hoggard talked about how nervous the atmosphere had become in the dressing room but when he went out to bat he was confident. 'Everything seemed to be in slow motion. I didn't play the first ball too well, but after that I just thought, "Here we go."' Giles added that all sorts of things had been racing through his head when the seventh wicket went down but that when Hoggard had come out he had a nervous smile on his face and said, 'Come on then, let's get on with it. Let's do it.' Warne and Lee were magnificent for the Australians, the leg-spinner bowling unchanged for figures of 13.5-2-31-4 and Lee finishing with 12-0-51-3 in his two spells.

Bloody excruciating agony and final welcome relief must have been the emotions experienced by England and a bloody near thing for the Australians, whose fightback showed that the Ashes might yet be retained. It was difficult to know how to read the outcome. A lot of Australian supporters probably reckoned that England had been exposed as the nervous nellies they always were and that they would be smashed in the final test at The Oval. Others thought that England had won so many sessions in the second, third and fourth Tests that they already deserved to have won the Ashes, and that if they batted first they could play Australia out of the game. Nervous English supporters prayed in advance for rain. More nervous English supporters began to talk about moral victories which was a way of hedging bets if Australia did win at The Oval. Strong, believing English supporters wanted a home win at The Oval but would settle for a draw.

The main point was that with Australia trailing 1–2, they had to win. They had to make positive selections, which meant choosing a side capable of taking 20 wickets, and they had to execute positive team plans when they got on to the field.

• AFTERWORD •

In batting order Australia's team for the last test in 2005 should have been: Langer, Katich, Ponting, Martyn, Clarke, Gilchrist, Warne, Lee, Tait, MacGill and McGrath. Sure, with three number elevens in the side there might be some room for manoeuvre but the top eight would be right. Would this have been too daring a choice? Hayden was out of form and should finally have been omitted. Was sentiment at work? It was at The Oval in 2001 where Hayden and Langer first joined up and what a partnership they had formed. But less sympathy was shown to Michael Slater then than to Hayden now. Katich hadn't opened for Australia before but he probably should have got the nod in the same match four years ago, and he had batted at number three on Australia's tour of India less than a year ago. Should Gilchrist be pushed up to six when he hadn't been getting runs in this series? Yes, although he wasn't getting them at seven the extra responsibility might bring out the best in him.

On the bowling side McGrath was coming back but a question mark hung over him given his injury ins and outs. Imagine the attack if he broke down – just Lee, Tait and Warne. So what about MacGill as that extra insurance, especially on a pitch where Saqlain Mushtaq and Ian Salisbury had had success for Surrey? He was a wicket-taking bowler who had been forced to while away his time on the sidelines. As he said in an interview with Sydney's *Sun-Herald* newspaper when he got home, he received no word of explanation from the selectors for the whole series.

There was obviously some conservative thinking there and some nerves in the decision-making. I can understand it to a point, particularly when you consider that my forte isn't keeping the runs down, but thinking like that isn't how you win Test matches.

Precisely. Critics who argued that MacGill blew his chance in the final second-class warm-up game against Essex at Chelmsford by taking 0-128 off 24 overs were missing the point. With Essex making 4-502 declared, the other Australian bowling figures weren't too flash either: Lee 0-69 from 13 overs, Gillespie 0-80 from 22, Tait 2-72 from 15, Kasprowicz 2-85 from 19, and Hodge 0-59 from 12. And those who wanted to retain Hayden on the basis of his 150 retired in Australia's reply were also missing the point. Hayden had also made a hundred at Northampton in a similar fixture and failed at Trent Bridge. This test would be for keeps. Brad Hodge made 166 but nobody was choosing him. The difficult thing for good sides is changing a winning formula but as Andrew Longmore put it in the *Sunday Times* during the previous test, 'Winning induces complacency and psychological rigidity.' Hayden stayed. MacGill stayed out.

England was forced to replace Simon Jones and thus missed the opportunity to become the first side to go through a five-test series unchanged since 1884–85. His ankle hadn't come good. They called up Lancashire fast-medium James Anderson and Durham all-rounder Paul Collingwood. Collingwood had made six centuries in county cricket during the season and Anderson had taken fifty wickets. Anderson, who'd made an impressive debut for England two years ago, represented the attacking option. Collingwood was the safe move. Collingwood was picked.

England batted first to reach 7-319 on the first day of The Oval test but the Australians had a sense of urgency about their fielding with Ponting exceptional in the covers. Finally, they had awoken from their slumber. Strauss made a grand century and Flintoff a mature 72 while Warne led the attack with five wickets. The second day saw England extend their score to 373 to which Australia replied with 0-112, with Langer far more fluent than Hayden. The surprise was that the

Australians took the offer of bad light when the players came back after the tea break. England wouldn't argue as it was Australia who had to win the game. The weather gods smiled on England over the next two days in which time both Langer and Hayden raised their hundreds. Hayden might have built an innings again, although as the Australian sports satirist Rampaging Roy Slaven remarked: 'It took him weeks.' On the fourth day when Australia resumed at 2-277, the ideal intention for Australia would have been to build towards 600 and then have a day and a bit to bowl England out. These plans went awry when the Australians were forced to attack in bad light against ferocious bowling by Flintoff. The result was that they lost their last eight wickets for 86 runs to trail by six runs. When bad light continued to intervene England were happy to leave play at 1-34. Australia now had roughly half a day to bowl England out but with Warne in their side anything was possible.

England looked smooth enough for forty minutes on the final morning with Vaughan playing a captain's innings. Then he was out fanning at McGrath, Bell left next ball and Pietersen was within inches of being a hat-trick victim. Hearts were in mouths. If Warne had taken a sitter from Pietersen at slip when he was 15 ... If. The irony was that the man who had done most to win the Ashes for Australia lost them. Not necessarily. Warne spun out Trescothick and Flintoff leaving England 5-127 at lunch and plenty of time for Australia to win. He went on to take a fabulous 12-246 in the game. Lee bowled fast and faster at Pietersen before lunch, and at Giles before tea, but after putting the frighteners on them with short-pitched deliveries, failed to deliver the knock-out. Pietersen hooked the short ball boldly after lunch and drove brilliantly. His 158 was an innings for the ages: Lee's match figures were 1-182. Collingwood chipped in for 10, one of the most important tens in cricket history as it consumed 72 minutes when the crease needed occupying. Finally Giles revealed himself the staunch yeoman to go with Pietersen's gallant heroics. England, after sixteen years, was home.

When number two beats number one it doesn't necessarily mean a changing of the guard but it does mean a time for assessment. Australia has twelve tests and England ten in the next thirteen months before the next Ashes tour. Australia's one-off test against an ICC World XI in October may be little more than an exhibition game, and series against a divided West Indies in the early part of the Australian summer, and Bangladesh in April, will not prove a major examination. However, six matches against South Africa at home and away in between will be tougher. England will tour Pakistan in November probably too soon after recent celebrations for its liking, and will then host Sri Lanka and Pakistan at home next summer.

The teams for those tests would suggest that more changes might be made by the Australians than England if only because Australia has more players over the age of thirty. Anglo–Australian test cricket is back at the zenith of the game, the first time for thirty years, and it has been revived as a contest. When it began, the British Empire was at its high noon. Many countries that now play test cricket were then colonies but are now independent, some outside the commonwealth that replaced the empire. Member nations of the European Economic Community also play cricket and, as noted earlier, some of their nationals play first-class cricket in England. The game has also moved into more countries in Asia and Africa and become stronger in North America.

Australia in 1877 was said to be searching for an identity, and cricket has been one element of a nationalist push that has not yet ended. Though much change and development has taken place, Australia in 2005 is still seeking an identity. Australia's first cricket victory over England mattered a great deal to both sides. To the colonials it was a win against the world's greatest nation, as well as its own spiritual home. For the colonisers, the loss challenged the certainties with which the country, little suspecting it was about to enter a long economic decline, fortified itself and justified its imperial pretensions. Both England and Australia have shed many of their old attitudes and priorities, but there is no mistaking the fact that, to increasing numbers of people on both sides of the globe, Ashes wins and losses still matter.

•SELECT BIBLIOGRAPHY•

Altham, HS and Swanton, EW, *A History of Cricket* Volumes I and II, George Allen & Unwin, London, 1962

Bailey, P, Thorn, P, and Wynne-Thomas, P, *Who's Who of Cricketers*, Guild Publishing, London, 1984

Barker, R, *Ten Great Bowlers*, Chatto & Windus, London, 1964, 1967

Barker, R and Rosewater, I, *Test Cricket England v Australia*, BT Batsford, London, 1969

Benaud, R, *On Reflection*, William Collins, London, 1984

Benaud, R, *Willow Patterns*, Hodder & Stoughton, London, 1969

Bradman, DG, *Farewell to Cricket*, Hodder & Stoughton, London, 1950

Brearley, JM, *The Art of Captaincy*, Hodder & Stoughton, London, 1985

Brearley, JM, *Phoenix from the Ashes*, Hodder & Stoughton, London, 1982

Brodribb, G, *Maurice Tate: A Biography*, London Magazines Edition, London, 1976

Brown, LH, *Victor Trumper & the 1902 Australians*, Secker & Warburg, London, 1981

Buchanan, H (ed), *Great Cricket Matches*, Eyre & Spottiswoode, London, 1962

Chester, F, *How's That*, Hutchinson, London, 1956

Dalby, K, *Headingley Test Cricket 1899–1975*, Olicana Books, Otley, 1976

Davidson, AK, *Fifteen Paces*, Souvenir Press, London, 1963

Douglas, C, *Douglas Jardine: Spartan Cricketer*, George Allen & Unwin, London, 1984

Dundas, R and Pollard, J, *Highest, Most and Best: Australian Cricket 1850–1990*, Angus & Robertson, Sydney, 1991

Dunstan, K, *The Paddock That Grew*, Hutchinson Australia, Sydney, 1988

Fender, PGH, *Turn of the Wheel*, Faber, London, 1929

Fingleton, JHW, *Batting from Memory*, William Collins & Son, London, 1981

Fingleton, JHW, *Masters of Cricket From Trumper to May*, Heinemann, London, 1958

Fortune, C, *The Australians in England 1961*, Robert Hale, London, 1961

Frindall, W, *The Wisden Books of Test Cricket I: 1876–7 to 1977–8* and *II: 1977–1989*, Queen Anne Press, London, 1979 and 1990

Frindall, W, *The Wisden Book of Cricket Records*, Queen Anne Press, London, 1986

Frith, D, *Archie Jackson: The Keats of Cricket*, Pavilion Books, London, 1987

Gibb, J, *Test Cricket Records from 1877*, William Collins, London, 1979

Haigh, G, *The Cricket War*, Text Publishing Co., Melbourne, 1993

Harte, C, with Whimpress, B, *A History of Australian Cricket*, Andre Deutsch, London, 2003

Harvey, RN, *My World of Cricket*, Hodder & Stoughton, London, 1963

Hutton, L, *Cricket is My Life*, Hutchinson, London, 1949

Illingworth, R, *Captaincy*, Pelham Books, London, 1980

Illingworth, R, *Spin Bowling*, Pelham Books, London, 1979

Kilburn, JM, *The History of Yorkshire County Cricket 1923–1949*, Yorkshire CCC, Leeds, 1950

Knott, A, *Stumper's View*, Sportsman Book Club, Newton Abbott, 1974

Laker, JC, *Spinning Round the World*, Sportsmans Book Club, London, 1959

Laker, JC, *The Australian Tour of 1961*, Frederick Muller, London, 1961

Lawry, WM & Tresidder, P, *Run Digger*, Souvenir Press, London, 1966

Mackay, KD, *Slasher Opens Up*, Pelham Books, London, 1964

McGilvray, A, *Captains of The Game*, ABC Books, Sydney, 1992

McGilvray, A, *The Game is Not the Same*, ABC Books, Sydney, 1985

McHarg, J, *Bill O'Reilly: A Cricketing Life*, Millenium Books, Sydney, 1990

Mallett, AA, *Clarrie Grimmett: The Bradman of Spin*, University of Queensland Press, St Lucia, 1993

Marshall, J, *Headingley*, Sportsmans Book Club, Newton Abbot, 1972
Marshall, J, *Old Trafford*, Sportsmans Book Club, Newton Abbot 1973
Marqusee, M, *Anyone But England*, Aurum, London 2005
Martin-Jenkins, CDM, *The Complete Who's Who of Test Cricketers*, Rigby, Adelaide, 1980
Moyes, AG, *Bradman*, Angus and Robertson, Sydney, 1948
Murphy, P, *Fifty Incredible Test Matches*, Stanley Paul, London, 1987
Pollard, J, *Australian Cricket – The Game and The Players*, Hodder & Stoughton, Sydney, 1982
Pollard, J, *The Formative Years of Australian Cricket 1803–93*, Angus & Robertson, Sydney, 1990
Pollard, J, *The Turbulent Years of Australian Cricket 1893–1917*, Angus & Robertson, Sydney, 1990
Pullin, AW, *Alfred Shaw Cricketer: His Career and Reminiscences*, Cassell and Co Ltd, London, 1902
Randall, DW, *The Sun Has Got His Hat On*, Collins Willow, London, 1984
Robinson, R, *On Top Down Under: Australia's Cricket Captains*, Cassell, North Ryde, 1981
Robinson, R, *The Wildest Tests*, Vikas Publishing House, Delhi, 1974
Ross, A, *Australia 55: A Journal of the MCC Tour*, Michael Joseph, London, 1955
Rowan, LP, *The Umpire's Story*, Jack Pollard PL, Sydney, 1973
Sharpham, P, *Victor Trumper: The Definitive Biography*, Hodder & Stoughton, London, 1985
Sheppard, DS, *Parson's Pitch*, Hodder & Stoughton, London, 1964
Snow, JA, *Cricket Rebel*, Hamlyn Publishing Group, London, 1976
Synge, A, *Sins of Omission: The Story of the Test Selectors 1899–1990*, Pelham Books, London, 1990
Thomas, P, *Yorkshire Cricketers 1839–1939*, Derek Hodgson Publisher, Manchester, 1973
Thomson, AA, *Hirst & Rhodes*, The Epworth Press, 1959
Thomson, AA, *Hutton & Washbrook*, The Epworth Press, 1963
Tyson, FS, *A Typhoon called Tyson*, Heinemann, London, 1961
Wakley, BJ, *Bradman the Great*, Nicholas Kaye, London, 1959
Wakley, BJ, *Classic Centuries in the Test Matches between England and Australia*, Nicholas Kaye, London, 1964
Webster, R, *First-Class Cricket in Australia* Vol I 1850–51 to 1941–42, Melbourne, 1992
West, GD, *Six More Days of Grace*, Darf Publishers, London, 1992
Whimpress, BJ and Hart, N, *Adelaide Oval Test Cricket 1884–1984*, Wakefield Press, Adelaide, 1984
White, C & Webber, R, *England Keep the Ashes: The Record of the England & MCC Tour of Australia 1954–55*, News Chronicle, London, 1955
Whitington, RS, *Time of the Tiger: The Bill O'Reilly Story*, Hutchison Australia, Melbourne, 1970
Willis, RGD & Murphy, P, *The Cricket Revolution: Test Cricket in the 1970s*, Sidgwick & Jackson, London, 1981

Newspapers, Journals, Websites

Advertiser (Adelaide)
Age (Melbourne)
Argus (Melbourne)
Association of Cricket Statisticians
Australasian
Australian
Australian Cricket
Bulletin
Cricketer (Australia)
Cricketer (Australia)
The Cricketer
Cricket Lore
Daily Telegraph (Sydney)
The Independent (London)
News (Adelaide)
The Observer (London)
Sydney Morning Herald
Sporting Traditions
The Sunday Times (London)
Sun Herald (Sydney)
The Times (London)
Wisden
Wisden Australia
Wisden Cricket Monthly
The Yorkshire Post

www.cricinfo.com